Los Yarderos

LATINOS IN CHICAGO AND THE MIDWEST

Series Editors
Omar Valerio-Jiménez, University of Texas at San Antonio
Sujey Vega, Arizona State University

Founding Editor
Frances R. Aparicio

For a list of books in the series, please see our website at www.press.uillinois.edu.

Los Yarderos

Mexican Yard Workers in Transborder Chicago

SERGIO LEMUS

UNIVERSITY OF ILLINOIS PRESS
Urbana, Chicago, and Springfield

Publication of this book was supported in part by the University of Illinois Press Fund for Anthropology.

1 2 3 4 5 C P 5 4 3 2 1
∞ This book is printed on acid-free paper.

Cataloging data available from the Library of Congress

ISBN 9780252046551 (hardcover)
ISBN 9780252088667 (paperback)
ISBN 9780252047862 (ebook)

Para mi esposa Teresa
y para Emma, Matthew, y Sarah

Contents

PREFACE

Inspecting Borders

> On a hot, humid, and exhausting June afternoon (Chicago, IL). Drops of sweat slowly slide down my brown face as I mow lawns—*yardas*—for residential clients while the heat approaches unbearable temperatures in the triple digits. I have thick, dark eyebrows; sometimes, the sweat settles there until I wipe my hand across my brow. My green, button-down shirt is wet from the saline elements the body expels. Sticky grass clippings and dirt texture my pants. We are in the middle of June, and as we approach the Fourth of July celebration, we are putting in extra hours, so the lawns of our clients will look pretty for that day. I am wearing brown work boots, and my left foot has started to hurt from eight hours of walking and mowing with only noticeably short breaks. Just like any other landscaper in Chicago, we usually work for ten hours during the summer. On the way home, I regularly see lawn-care workers or maintenance workers—*yarderos*—still mowing grass around seven or eight into the late evening.
>
> —Author's Field Note, June 28, 2013

THE PHRASE *el Norte* is a Spanish noun that denotes a cardinal direction on the Earth's surface; however, as a linguistic metaphor within migration, it exerts deep, emotional intensity on those who travel to the United States and those who are left behind. First, from the perspective of Mexicans in Mexico, el Norte is a fluctuating space in the United States where many Mexican migrants travel to find work. In the context of working-class *Mexicanos* who travel to the United States, el Norte often carries a class, spatial, and cultural transformation for those who arrive at or depart from it. The stories I write about in this book are explored within what I call el Norte's *long dure*—that is, the deeper historical forces that have contributed to a powerful attraction that draws populations seeking opportunities toward regions of the United States for a better life. *Los Yarderos* is an exploration of the long and recent trajectory of Mexican migrants who, traveling north and crossing borders, have made the US Midwest their home.

First Crossing, First Inspection

In anthropology and the social sciences in general, there has been tension in recent decades about engaging and using personal narratives to discover the interrelation between the ethnographer and the political implications of carrying out research. Thus, I refuse to delink my work from my political life as a migrant as well. My ethnographic account is a serious attempt to understand better my collaborators' lives and my place as a translator of their experiences as I attempt to transcribe their lives to a minority—that is, us academics. However, the hope is that this text reaches many more and will transform the ways they think about Mexican migrants in the United States.

I realize we must get to know ourselves first to understand others. This task is especially true in moments that ground you. For example, I still recall their *caras de enfadados,* or "the awkward looks of the immigration officers," when my father took my mom and his eight children (five sons and three daughters) to request our social security numbers in Laredo, Texas, after getting our permanent resident visas, or as Mexicans and other Spanish speaking migrants call them, *los papeles* (the papers). I was eleven years old then. The trip from Laredo, Texas, to Chicago seems fuzzy now. I remember waking up in the gray Ford conversion van my family was traveling in, looking out the window while the rain fell on the highway, and hearing my older brother telling us that we were in *Tejas* (Texas). I instantly thought about the roof of my home in the state of Jalisco, Mexico. It was my only material and linguistic reference to this new distant land.

Many hours passed before we reached the state of Illinois; then my older brother, Anselmo, told us we were crossing *el rio misisipi* (the Mississippi River). As soon as we entered the state of Illinois, a police officer pulled my father over for driving ten miles above the speed limit. Now that I think about that moment, I am aware of other inspectors along our track north. Indeed, as Gloria Anzaldúa and anthropologist Alejandro Lugo remind us, the US-Mexico border does not stop as soon as one crosses it; its power matrix follows you into those northern cities such as Chicago.[1] To be more specific, borders follow us all, and we incorporate them into our bodies. As I argue in this book, directly and metaphorically at times, once the US-Mexico border is crossed, additional layers of meaning are produced and transformed, accounting for the new experiences of the US racial order operating across different geographic locations, and fall on us crossers. A few weeks after we arrived in Chicago, my father had to go to the local court in Cairo, Illinois—about 370 miles away—for a court date, or else get his license suspended.

After twenty-two hours of driving since crossing *pal Norte* (to the north), I recollect asking how far we were from Chicago. My father said that we were about two hours away, but we would stop for gas and grab something to eat at a gas station in "*Champain,*" as I heard it in Spanish; of course, in English, it is Champaign, Illinois. Two decades later, while completing my graduate training at the University of Illinois at Urbana-Champaign, I always took the Market Street exit on Illinois Interstate I-57. One can interpret it as a symbolic gesture, a reminder of my past. We arrived in Chicago close to midnight in mid-July 1995, which I later learned was one of the hottest summers on record in the city. Indeed, it was. We could not believe how hot it was when we arrived. *Mi Ama y mi Apa,* brothers, and sisters; we had all finally arrived. We slept in my father's two-bedroom apartment on Baltimore Avenue in South Chicago. I recall hearing my father saying, "*Ya llegamos a la casa!*" (We have arrived at the house!). It was another place, far away from the one I grew up in, Mexico. We felt safe now. We had crossed. We had been inspected. We were *en el Norte*!

Living in South Chicago

I went to public schools in the second half of the 1990s. It was a time when you could walk *de la casa* (from home) *a la escuela* (to the school). I had counselors advising me not to go to college but to complete a practical, job-oriented education. If I had listened, you would not be reading this book. Thus, my personal history and narrative give form and texture to this book, focusing on working-class Mexicans working as yarderos (gardeners) in Chicago. As such, throughout the chapters of the book, I attempt to answer the question of why we all have migrated north in search of a phantomlike thing we call the American Dream or, as I heard it back in 1995 as I saw many folks deciding to travel north, "*a buscarle al Norte*" (to find a living in the north). To this day, many yarderos are still searching for that dream.

Of you, reader, I ask a favor: Please suspend shocking accounts of what the media and politics tell us about immigration when you read and learn about these people and their labor. Like many migrants over the past century, they come to the United States embracing it, loving it, hating it, caring for it, and sometimes refusing to accept it as their own. In this process of becoming a Mexican migrant and, later, adopting Latino identifications, a sense of home emerges. It takes time; just like a lawn, it needs to be cared for.

Class, color, and labor are the inequalities of power that I emphasize in this story, but they are not the only power differentials. My hope is that someone else will pick up what they see good from this ethnography and produce a better and thicker description of Mexican migrants' sacrifice. I hope they will continue pushing for a better society that is kind to immigrants in the United States and the Mexico *que dejaron* (that they left behind). I hope this story becomes your story and, to a small degree, changes your understanding of Mexican yardero lives. I hope this story also allows you to see the humanity of those who migrate to seek a better life for their families.

As I finished writing this sentence, a shooting massacre just occurred in Uvalde, Texas, in an elementary school in a heavily Latino small city. This should not happen, especially for a community already experiencing tremendous economic, political, and social inequality and a history of state abandonment at the US-Mexico borderlands and beyond. Let us hope this does not happen again—ever.

Acknowledgments

My decision to write about a complex, challenging, and national issue—Mexican migration—emerges because of the injustices observed against *la clase trabajadora* (working class folks) as they continually search for an American Dream despite being a fractured, and often unreachable moving horizon. In this book, I intend to bear witness to the challenges Mexican migrants experience in the United States. Thus, I have ethnographically documented, since the early 2010s, the border-making and ordering processes that Mexicans encounter as they "travel north to those northern cities," to use a phrase by Gloria Anzaldúa, and as I write about Mexican migrants, I hope to represent them accurately and respectfully.

The first person I would like to thank is *mi mama*, Martha Sevilla Salazar, for enduring all those years without my father's company and caring for us all. The silence that many women experience as they see their husbands come to the United States continues to be ignored. They often suffer the most and have a stronger will than the men that migrate. To *mi papa*, Luis Lemus Murillo, thank you. Your decision to migrate *pal norte* in the late 1970s as a migrant worker to provide us with a better life is a gift I carry dearly. Thank you for the support throughout these years to our family. I cannot thank enough the other family that my wife brought into my life. I am incredibly grateful to Dona Ramona Garcia Rubio and Don Salvador Vitela Iglesias. Both departed to a better life all too early; we miss you. The wisdom I learned while in your company is with my children as they grow older and remember their *abuelito* Chava and *abuelita* Mona.

Institutionally and beyond, first, I would like to thank my mentor, friend, and now colleague Alejandro Lugo. Thank you for your guidance throughout these past two decades and for your rigor as an anthropologist, Latino, and Chicano scholar. You taught me to be patient and fight the small academic battles to win the big ones. Next, the arduous questioning and intellectual acumen of Gilberto Rosas has constantly reminded me that there is much more we can do to critique power, racism, and neoliberalism. Jonathan X. Inda has always been there to look at my work, suggest changes, and help me see the gaps in the literature. Since the project began as an idea, your support has been there all along. Queer theorist and scholar Martin Manalansan, thank you for your poignant, illuminating comments on my ethnographic material. Your ethnographic vision has allowed me to see that we all can do more in the ethnographic representation of the people we study. At the University of Illinois, many other colleagues have directly or indirectly helped me find a space to think and exchange ideas as they formed during my graduate training. I am especially thankful to Ellen Moodie, Andrew Orta, Nancy Abelmann, Karen Kelsky, Junaid Rana, and others who impacted this research in the late 2000s and early 2010s. My fellow graduate colleagues Jason Romero, Aide Acosta, and Anthony Jerry, my sincere thanks for the hours of conversation about anthropology and Latino Studies.

The time spent at the University of California at Riverside early in my graduate training left a deep intellectual mark on how I think about anthropology. Thank you, Michael Kearney, for having your door always open to talk with students; I know you are in a better place now. I would also like to especially thank Dr. Thomas C. Patterson; sometimes you only need a few moments to make an impact on others. Your classes and interactions taught me that we are better off as analysts if we do not leave capitalism behind. Marx was right about capitalism, despite our need to refuse it in our writings; we need to grapple with it in our everyday lives and in the lives of our interlocutors.

As I entered the professional life as a professor, my colleagues in the Latino Studies Program at Indiana University at Bloomington always showed care, support, and encouragement to continue working on this book. I would like to thank Sylvia Martinez and Alberto Varon for supporting my candidacy as a visiting assistant professor and for offering me the opportunity to teach at Indiana University. My family made good memories while living in Bloomington, Indiana. The fall of leaves during the autumn season was beautiful to witness. The not-so-harsh winters in this part of Indiana made it a breeze compared to the hard cold winters up north in Chicago. While the summers were muggy, they were not comparable with the not-so-wonderful Texas heat during *la canícula* (dog days). Historian John Nieto-Phillips, thank you for supporting our scholars of color at Indiana University and for your work on diversity at the Bloomington campus for future generations.

In August 2019, as this book was taking its final shape, I moved to a new position at Texas A&M University (TAMU) in the Department of Anthropology. Many thanks for the department's trust and support in my projects. Especially, I would like to thank the following folks for their warm welcome to my new academic home: Cynthia Werner, Carlos Bolanos, Robin Means Coleman, Darryl De Ruiter, Jeffrey Winking, Ted Goebel, Kelly Graft, Allison Hopkins, Michael Waters, Michael Alvarad, Sharon Gursky, Kevin Crisman, Benjamin Kofi Nutor, Monya Anderson, Naomi Rodriquez, and Rebekah Luza. At Texas A&M, Robin Means Coleman produced changes in diversity and inclusion that will leave a mark in decades to come through all the subsequent ACES (Accountability, Climate, Equity, and Scholarship) fellows. I wish you the best in your efforts at your new academic home at the University of Virginia. I am sure this is a place where rich scholarly engagements will develop for decades to come. This book was revised while holding the ACES Fellowship with the funding support of TAMU's Office for Diversity and the Department of Anthropology. This period allowed me to think and make this manuscript better. To all the graduate students who have heard me talk about yardero lives and other stories about Chicago, thank you for listening and responding to my questions. Warm regards to Kevin Johnson, Emma Newman, Damesh Satova, Viviane Clement, Megan Crutcher, and many others. Slowly we are building the study of borders and borderlands at Texas A&M University through your curiosity about border theory as I have come to visualize it within cultural anthropology and beyond.

The faculty associated with Latino/a and Mexican American Studies has also allowed me to visualize the kind of scholarship produced here. Thank you to the following *colegas* for their friendship: Felipe Hinojosa, Omar Rivera, Sonia Hernandez, and Nancy Plankey-Videla.

Being an anthropologist allows me to connect with colleagues across the United States through my engagement with the Association of Latina and Latino Anthropologists and the Latinx Studies Association. Thus, thank you, *colegas,* for your support. A special mention to Nicholas De Genova, Almita Miranda, Xóchitl C. Chávez, Gina Pérez, Alex E. Chávez, and Hilario Lomeli. Some of the chapters for this book have received feedback at these venues, and for that I am grateful.

From the first email conversation with Dawn Durante at the University of Illinois Press, as I proposed the project, I came to believe that other people care about our Latino community and that there is a space for us writers of color and other historically marginalized scholars to tell the world about our communities. Thank you for your work on this project and for being available when I needed you the most. As I transitioned to work on the final stage of the manuscript, Dominique Moore supported my work cheerfully and has worked to see that this book comes to life. A very special thank you to the outside reviewers who kindly took time out of their busy lives to read about Mexican yarderos/as in Chicago and suggest how to improve the stories I am telling here. Of course, I am also extremely thankful to the Latinos in Chicago and the Midwest series editors, Sujey Vega and Omar Valerio-Jiménez. Their support is what has kept me moving forward despite the long road to publication. A special recognition to Frances Aparicio for reading earlier versions of the manuscript and offering excellent suggestions on how to make it better.

I also want to thank all my interlocutors who kindly took the time to talk to me about their everyday lives. I especially would like to mention the core group: Don Antonio, Cesar, Andres, Don Raul, Enrique, Rodrigo, Julia, Feliciano, Guillermo, Martina, Ernesto, Guillermo, Julio, and Arturo. Thank you to everyone who directly or indirectly helped me think about the problems facing the Mexican working class in transborder Chicago.

Finally, and most importantly, I want to thank *mi esposa* (my wife) and partner in life, Teresa Vitela-Lemus. You have believed in this project all along, and I thank you for all the support, patience, and love. You are an extraordinary person—better than me. I cannot thank you for all the incommensurable hours you spent focusing on home while I was busy in the halls of anthropology departments. I wish you the best in your new career as an elementary teacher. I think your challenges are even greater than mine given the recent changes in the educational landscape. Emma Fernanda and Matthew Esteban, I hope that I am a father you can be proud of and that you will remember your youth as happy as I have tried to make it for the two of you. Sarah Isabelle, the world is up to you to grab as well; always reach for the stars. To the three of you: Dream; dream big. Never let anyone tell you that you cannot do it. All of you are present on every page of this book.

To end, let me remind you that all errors of misrepresentation (if any), analysis, and prose are mine. All of those mentioned here have helped make this story better, and for that I am thankful.

Los Yarderos

Introduction

The Northern Borderlands of Mexican Migration

> Those who make it past the checking points of the Border Patrol find themselves in the midst of 150 years of racism in Chicano barrios in the Southwest and in big northern cities. Living in a no-man's land, caught between being treated as criminals and being able to eat, between resistance and deportation, the illegal refugees are some of the poorest and the most exploited of any people in the U.S.
>
> —Gloria Anzaldúa, *Borderlands, La Frontera*

> The last two decades have seen a dramatic rise in the number of informal day labor sites throughout the continental United States, to the point that they have become a ubiquitous presence in most of the country's urban areas.
>
> —Juan Ordóñez, *Jornaleros*

If you drive through the South Chicago neighborhood on Commercial Avenue between 83rd and 92nd Streets, you will encounter a range of businesses mostly belonging to African Americans and ethnic Mexicans. For example, you will see Panadería Marzeya (Marzeya Bakery); Mexican restaurants such as Restaurante Cocula (from Cocula, Jalisco) and Gomez Tacos; gift shops selling typical Mexican products; and—let us not forget—places like the famous El Guero (The Blonde), a fruit market with a taquería (taco place) in the back. If you are in love, Samantha's Flowers, owned by a hardworking Latina named Samantha, will make you the best arrangement of red roses for your *novia* (girlfriend), *esposa* (wife), or nonnormative gender partner. Like many other neighborhoods in the city of Chicago, South Chicago is unique in many respects. As a city, Chicago is rich in history as a destination for Mexican migration at the turn of the twentieth century, and it continues to be a magnet for contemporary migrants of many other Latin American origin populations through the present day.[1] The neighborhood of South Chicago retains vestiges from an era when eastern Europeans were the majority population in this part of the city and dominated the landscape. One church in South Chicago is dedicated to the Lady of Guadalupe under the name of the National Shrine of St. Jude. Its founding dates to the earliest arrival of Mexican migrants to this neighborhood in the early 1900s. The other Catholic church, Immaculate Conception, still holds a mass on Sunday in the Polish language.

This book is about the lives of Mexican working-class people in South Chicago. The ethnic Mexican migrant community sits at a crossroads, where the dividing lines of class, color hierarchies, gender, and belonging define their everyday lives. From the outset, I hope you understand the sacrifices many people make and the struggles they face to find a better life *en el Norte* (in the North) by the end of the book. More specifically, I hope to paint a more complete picture of the yarderos, that is, the Mexican migrants who make their way of life working to care for the lawns of Chicago—*en las yardas* (in the yards), as they would say.[2] The book title speaks to a central preoccupation; that is, it attempts to explain the lives of Mexican yard workers and their cultural transformation as they make Chicago their home.

Throughout the book, I narrate how they experience their lives as yarderos, exploring the historical, economic, cultural, and political ramifications of acquiring this working-class identity. Tense political discourse on immigration is constant within mainstream media; however, this book chooses not to engage with much of the anti-immigrant rhetoric of late. In some ways, I write this book to ground the discussion farther down below, metaphorically and as praxis at the grass level, where Mexican yarderos are making and remaking their lives amid the increasing nativist politics and policies in the United States. But most importantly, the story I present requests that you, the reader, cultivate an "inclination to care." If you care about what happens here in the United States and what lies ahead, you must care about the lives of Mexican migrants and all immigrants. In particular, I follow historian Vicki Ruiz's suggestion that Latino history is American history, and we ought to revise the place that Latinos hold in our historical imagination of who we are as a nation that privileges a racialized white subjectivity and refuses to accept Brownness or Blackness as part of the imaginary American nation-state.[3] Ultimately, it is forcefully suggested in this book that the United States is a nation of immigrants and will continue to be so, despite a resurgence of American nationalist rhetoric that seeks to reposition, in a Gramscian sense, an idealized and racialized white, sovereign subject at its center.[4]

Ethnographically, the book focuses on first- and second-generation Mexican migrants who came and settled from the states of Zacatecas, Guanajuato, Jalisco, and Michoacán to the US Midwest region—and Chicago in particular. In this major metropolitan city, they work as landscapers and gardeners in middle- and upper-class neighborhoods. I discuss their struggles, the arduous task of finding and securing a job, and the lives they establish in the American Midwest. Borders and borderlands are central themes in these stories. This book aims to foreground a call for a closer examination of the effects of the US-Mexico border on big northern cities such as Chicago.[5] I write about Mexican yarderos who now live in a shifting terrain marked by geopolitical, cultural, and economic borders. I envision the current period, especially after 2010, not as a transnational but as a fundamentally transborder cultural moment. Indeed, I argue that yarderos now find themselves at the crossings and inspections of multiple borders, sometimes not of their own making.[6]

Mexican Migration

I am not the first to write about Mexican migration; thus, I situate the book in an ongoing conversation among scholars examining the lives of Mexicans in the United States from interdisciplinary and discipline-specific approaches. For example, Nicholas De Genova's 2005 book *Working the Boundaries* details how race, space, and racialization shape the experience of Mexican migration to Chicago. Published seventeen years ago, his work still captures the inner contours of the Mexican communities of Pilsen in Chicago and other areas. Michael Innis-Jiménez's *Steel Barrio* (2013) brilliantly details the formation of an early Mexican colony in South Chicago in 1910. Another work informing my understanding of Mexican and Puerto Rican relations in Chicago is Lilia Fernandez's exemplary ethnic history in her book, *Brown in the Windy City* (2012). This work documents the migration of these Latino populations amid the massive decline in industrial employment and urban improvement projects. Religion has also been a focus of scholars of Mexican migration to Chicago. For example, Deborah Kanter's *Chicago Catolico* (2020) tells the story of a neighborhood change and rebirth in Chicago's Mexican American communites amid major urban changes in the city. Further, Christine Walley's *Exit Zero:*

Family and Class in Postindustrial Chicago (2013) documents the lives of folks living in southeast Chicago. This monograph tells the stories of local families to trace the social impact of deindustrialization and explores how the closing of the steel mills affected the community. In all the works mentioned above, the different and varied theoretical and methodological approaches to studying Chicago's Mexican and Mexican American population suggest that this community is neither complete nor finite. Their local histories are diverse and complex. Thus, each author has uncovered some of the layers of community formation that allow for a rich understanding of the historical and cultural trajectories of the Mexican presence in the Midwest region, the city of Chicago, and its localized Mexican border zones.

Furthermore, others have focused on Mexican forms of illegality in Chicago as well: Ruth Gomberg-Muñoz's *An Ethnography of a Mexican Immigrant Network* (2019) offers an overview of how undocumented migrants who work as busboys produced social networks through kinship and nonkin relations at a Chicago-area restaurant. Focusing on the post-1970s socioeconomic and political conditions in the United States and Mexico, Gomberg-Muñoz's work allows us to examine the strategies that nurture emotional wellbeing and promote dignity among workers.

Recently, some studies beyond traditional destinations in the Midwest have offered a glimpse of how Latino migrant communities have made accommodations to live alongside folks living in the Heartland. For example, Sujey Vega's *Latino Heartland: Of Border and Belonging in the Midwest* (2015) offers a view of how Latino and non-Latino residents of a small Indiana town challenge stereotypical portrayals of migrants and immigration. More importantly, she articulates how communities form, how they express acts of ethnic belonging, and how folks claim the right to belong. This pathbreaking ethnography moves the theorization of borders to the inside of the United States and offers us a way in which communities embrace complexity and belonging within and beyond citizenship practices.[7]

Without a doubt, the Mexican Midwest is yielding important scholarship on Latino lives. For example, Theresa Delgadillo's *Latina Lives in Milwaukee* (2015), is an important intervention in documenting the vibrant Mexican and Mexican American community of the 1920s, incorporating additional layers of Latin American migrants. Specifically, Delgadillo looks at stories of women who saw entrepreneurial skills, pursued education, and other range of occupations were able to develop coalitions to fight for a better future despite their precarious conditions in the city.

This book is also in conversation with other scholars documenting the lives of Mexican immigrants beyond the city of Chicago and the Midwest. For example, Christian Zlolniski's *Janitors, Street Vendors, and Activists in Silicon Valley* (2006) is a model ethnography examining how capitalist economies employ undocumented immigrants through subcontract labor practices in the informal sector. His work contributes to how Mexicans explore unionizing to fight social injustice under precarious labor conditions in San Jose, California. Next, Patricia Zavella's *I'm Neither Here nor There: Mexicans' Quotidian Struggles with Migration and Poverty* (2011) offers a clear view of how Chicanos/as, Mexican Americans, and Mexican migrants struggle to find agency in California's Central Coast region.

Further, two other important scholarly interventions have influenced, directly and indirectly, my eventual understanding of yarderos in Chicago. First, Juan Thomas Ordóñez, in his ethnography *Jornalero: Being a Day Laborer in the USA* (2015), carries out participant observation on street corners in Berkeley, California, attempting to understand how day laborers, who are mostly men, experience the informal labor market. As the epigraph at the start of this introduction demonstrates, the informal market, which is a central pillar in my study of Mexican yarderos in Chicago, has been dramatically on the rise since the 1980s. This has been a consequence of the neoliberal turn in the United States, the increasing militarization of the US-Mexico border, and the contours of citizenship.[8] The second distant ethnography that has provided us with important conversations about how the bodies of migrants, both documented and undocumented, are put on the line in daily life in the United States is Seth M. Holmes's *Fresh Fruit, Broken Bodies: Migrant Farmworkers in the United States* (2013). Holmes's work is a detailed ethnographic study describing the irreparable bodily damage done to undocumented and documented migrants who cross the US-Mexico border; it is a powerful take on the issues that matter for migrant communities and their families. While farmwork is structurally positioned in different spaces than lawncare service workers—that is, in a rural, rather than urban setting—this ethnographic examination of yadero labor is also of importance for scholars who study labor in nonurban settings.

Indeed, Los Yarderos benefits from the wealth of scholarship on Mexican migration to the United States. However, this book adds a nuanced story as experienced by lawncare service workers in Chicago. This study also illuminates the intimate relationship between gender and power and how capitalism and migrant cultures interact in a moment labeled as postracial, coming out of the 2008 presidential election of Barack Obama. Further, this book offers a new ethnographic vision of an understudied neighborhood yarderos called their home, South Chicago.

The existence of this book is only possible because I emigrated from Mexico to Chicago in 1995. Indeed, my migration path began after the North American Free Trade Agreement started to take an economic toll on the small towns of western Mexico that had previously based their economy on maize cultivation. A few years before I migrated to the United States, the tequila industry had slowly begun to buy up land from *rancheros* (small-scale landowners) who relied on subsistence agriculture and local-level economic exchanges connected to an ongoing migration of men to the United States. By the early 2000s tequila production intensified around the state of Jalisco and the surrounding regions. Agave plants took the place of maize, and the tequila economy seeped into every corner of my small town of Jesús María, Jalisco. While some families benefited by renting their plots of land to tequila entrepreneurs, entering this practice meant they would often work as wage laborers for the same individuals they rented their lands to for agave plantations. For many, the only path to make a living and a life was to migrate.[9] But let us return to South Chicago.

The Making of Mexican Chicago

Mexican and indigenous origin populations have been in border spaces between Mexico and the United States for a long time, even before the current geopolitical border that separates the two nation-states was drawn. Often, Mexican populations and other groups have been "bumping" against one another, as Carlos G. Vélez-Ibáñez commented in the late 1990s.[10] For example, scholarship on Chicanx and Mexican American communities has historically and ethnographically documented the presence of Mexicans in what would later become the American Southwest.[11] Indeed, after 1848 the social, political, economic, and cultural formation of the current US-Mexico border became a critical power grid placed on the populations that lived in these territories and on those who would eventually come into contact with this uneven distribution of raw power by the American state. While the international border, in the 1890s, was "just one more property line in a vast landscape of extractive industries in which some Americans owned land on both sides of the line," it was not until the eve of the 1910 Mexican Revolution that additional enforcement to the US-Mexico border quelled increasing anti-Mexican violence, especially in South Texas.[12] However, Mexicans in much of the American Southwest were already treated as second-class citizens. This treatment was particularly virulent in the state of Texas.[13] By the early twentieth century, it became evident that the United States was becoming an economic engine driving trade in Mexico and beyond. Thus, after 1910 Mexican migrants began arriving in large numbers, and the transborder circulation of goods, people, and services grew exponentially with each passing decade.

Described as one of the great immigrant waves in US history, Mexican migration has received significant attention from scholars interested in this topic as a social, political, economic, and cultural phenomenon.[14] Since the early 1900s, distinct periods of increased emigration from Mexico had created the present-day Mexican and Mexican American populations in the United States, as well as those present before the United States took over what would later become the American Southwest, or for border theorist Carlos Vélez-Ibáñez, the northern part of the Southwest North American Region (SWNAR).[15] Other scholars have accurately highlighted the fact that communities along the Rio Grande, who at times formed into small villages and communities, had a whole range of identities that emerged in the borderland region such as in the Lower Rio Grande. For instance, Omar S. Valerio-Jiménez portrays this region as one with enduring legacies of race and class, where Spain, Mexico, and the United States competed for the control of the lower Rio Grande region and in the process shaped the political identities of its inhabitants.[16] For example, the state formation process analyzed by Valerio-Jiménez chronicles a history of violence of multiple conquests and argues that the transition from a colonial subject to a national one is not straightforward. These identities are embedded with regionalism and transcultural and kinship ties that challenge forms of state centralization and its respective border-making and border-ordering processes in this part of the United States.

Later, in 1910, the Mexican Revolution brought approximately one hundred thousand Mexican nationals to the United States. According to census data, the Mexico-born population of the United States grew from 103,000 to 1,400,000 between 1900 and 1930.[17] Historian Zaragosa Vargas further estimates that in the 1920s, about twenty thousand or more Mexican workers passed through San Antonio each year on their way *para el Norte* (to the North).[18] Keep in mind that these numbers do not account for the population of Mexican ethnic background that settled in the area before the 1800s when the territories of the US Southwest were part of the Spanish empire. But today, for instance, after crossing through the Nuevo Laredo/Laredo, Texas, entry post, San Antonio, Texas, is only a two-and-a-half-hour car ride away; Dallas is a six-hour trip. Today these cities and Austin maintain the strongest Mexican and Mexican American presence within their culture, politics, and economy of the state of Texas.

The influence of Mexican migration stretches north from Texas to states such as Kansas, Missouri, Indiana, Wisconsin, Michigan, Iowa, and Illinois. Many immigrants in this Midwest region are a family connection away from Texas. The scholarship of José Limón reminds us of the longstanding and intimate ties between Texas and the Midwest region.[19] Further, later work by Omar Valerio-Jiménez has described the experience of Mexican immigrants in North Central Iowa as one in which settlement took place there, in many ways, because of the lower intensity of racial tensions and their easier adaptation as a nonwhite category of the region.[20]

Mexican migration to the American Midwest has varied geographically; Mexican settlements have developed in rural as well as urban centers since the turn of the twentieth century.[21] Discussing the urbanization of Mexicans in this region, Midwestern historian Juan Garcia notes that by the 1920s, 70 percent of Midwestern Mexicans lived in urban centers.[22] Many of the major metropolitan areas in the Midwest maintained a sizable Mexican population. This list includes cities such as Detroit, Michigan, Minneapolis, Minnesota, South Bend, Indiana, Grand Rapids, Michigan, Louisville, Kentucky, and St. Louis, Missouri. The Mexican presence is also slowly growing in the rural Midwest and powering the local economies of places such as Lorraine, Illinois.[23]

While teaching at Indiana University in 2017, I often drove from Bloomington, Indiana, to Louisville, Kentucky, to do some shopping over the weekend. The opening scene from the 1986 film *Hoosiers* neatly captures the landscape I encountered on my drives through southern Indiana. Cornfields stretch out on both sides of the two-lane highway, and rustic housing would pop up from time to time. Along the way, restaurants and businesses emblazoned with Spanish surnames appear in places one would never imagine that Latinxs would settle in this part of the country. Sujey Vega, in her work on Latinxs in West Lafayette demonstrates that the demography of Indiana reminds us that Latinx Hoosiers often prefer the heartland precisely because its rural or *rancho* (ranch) lifestyle is similar to the style of living that many Mexican migrants come from—especially those from parts of central Mexico.[24] This cultural practice is also documented by anthropologist Alex E. Chávez in his study of *huapangueros* (hupango style musical performers) moving from San Luis Potosí to Texas and the Midwest.[25]

Historically, in the case of the Chicagoland area, the influx of Mexicans in the early twentieth century and today was triggered by labor demands in the United States. So significant was the need for workers in the Midwest region that, in 1916, railroad companies brought hundreds of Mexicans to the Near West Side of Chicago, South Chicago, and South Bend, Indiana.[26] All these Mexican colonies had several features in common: First, Mexican colonies appeared in direct response to the employment necessities of the Mexican worker and the US capitalist alike.[27] Second, most Mexican migrants came from the central states of

Mexico. And third, there was a greater gender homogeneity in the Midwestern colonies than in the barrios of the Southwest. Historian Zaragosa Vargas also notes that by the time Mexicanos and Chicanos arrived in the Midwest, they had already put Texas on the map agriculturally.[28] For example, in Texas, in the earlier decades of the 1900s, Mexicanos and Chicanos laboriously cleared cactus, dense chaparral, and mesquite trees from hundreds of acres of land. The arduous task of clearing mesquites was called grubbing, and as has been noted, marks this activity as a "Mexican job." The root system of mesquites sometimes go down fifty feet into the ground; the men either cut the roots or pulled them out by hand and then burned the cactus and chaparral.[29]

Zaragosa Vargas' incisive documentation of the recruitment of Mexican and Chicano workers to Detroit, Michigan, illustrates that the kinds of jobs Mexicans were hired for often signaled a change in employment patterns. Indeed, as I argue in this book, these work patterns can also indicate changes in the structural hierarchies of class, labor, and color. For instance, in examining local Mexican and Anglo relations in the South Texas town of La Feria, Jennifer Najera accurately portrays the shifting educational system changes, especially after the 1920s. In her understanding of the tensions in South Texas, education served as a vehicle to keep the Mexican population in this area out of higher-paying jobs and integral to the agricultural economy at the lower end of the pay scale. Indeed, after clearing land in Texas, Mexicans were also recruited to harvest it.[30]

For example, the cotton industry first attracted Mexican immigrants to Texas, but "the repressive conditions and low wages characteristic of this industry eventually motivated tens of thousands to seek alternative work in the Midwest."[31] One might assume that given the transportation available then, in the early 1920s, places like Illinois and Indiana were too difficult to reach from Texas. This is true, but with the aid of an expansive railroad system, and later with vehicle transportation, the Midwest became an attractive and accessible destination. Geographically, the city on the farthest northeast tip of Texas is Texarkana. Between this city and Memphis, Tennessee, there is only the state of Arkansas in between. Memphis is about three hundred miles from Texas, and today you could make the trip between the northeastern tip of Texas and what is considered the lower Midwest by car in less than four hours.

News of employment travels within families. In the case of Mexican migration to the Midwest and the lawncare service workers I interviewed, this remains true through the present day. For example, after the 1920s, lured by the promise of more significant job opportunities and fueled by the desire to seek a better life, many Mexicans bypassed work in Texas and found work in rural and urban areas of the Midwest. By avoiding the state of Texas, Mexican workers could seek better labor opportunities, especially after the 1920–21 Depression, when Midwest steel, manufacturing, and agriculture necessitated an ever-increasing labor force. Dionicio Nodín Valdés notes that after World War I, a massive wave of immigration "permitted Chicago, already the second most populous city in the nation, to gain distinction for the largest concentration of Mexicans beyond the border states."[32] Valdés further explains that, by 1927, Mexican officials reported that more than 45,000 Mexicans resided in the zone extending from the northern to western suburbs of Chicago and into northwest Indiana. An additional 25,000 were reported in Lower Michigan, and Ohio; 3,000 in Upper Michigan, Wisconsin, and Minnesota; about 12,000 in Missouri, Iowa, and Western Illinois; and at least 25,000 more Mexicans resided in Kansas and Nebraska at the time, for a total of about 110,000 in the Great Plains and Great Lakes region.

Labor demands overwhelmingly drove Mexican migration to the Midwest; as soon as Mexicanos and Tejanos from the US Southwest settled in the Midwestern colonies (both rural and urban), these vibrant communities became magnets for further migration from the US Southwest and Mexico. By 1925 "over half of the 8,000 to 10,000 Mexican steelworkers in the Midwest held jobs in Chicago mills, and they constituted 14 percent of the total local workforce in steel."[33] Many steel plants are abandoned today, as overseas market opportunities drive companies to seek cheaper labor resources elsewhere. Several steel plants remain along the Indiana harbor area in the city of East Chicago, Indiana.

Mexicans have occupied the South Chicago landscape since as early as 1916. Still, in 1919, with the social, economic, and political processes taking place in Mexico and the United States, Mexicans arrived in large numbers in this steel-producing region of the Midwest. As documented in his historical analysis of South Chicago, Michael Innis-Jiménez tells us that according to the United States census, early in the twentieth century, "Mexicans comprised 1,141 of the 808,558 foreign-born residents in the entire city of Chicago . . . the official 1930 Mexican and Mexican-American population of Chicago had grown to 19,632. By the 1940s, however, the post-Great Depression Mexican community had shrunk to around 16,000." Although the first Mexicans that came to Chicago worked as *traqueros* (railroad workers), much of the early Mexican migrants to South Chicago found work in the steel mills that started operating in the last decade of the 1880s.[34]

By the 1940s World War II had brought an increasing demand for labor in the United States and the city of Chicago. To fix the labor shortage before and during the war, the US government produced binational agreements that brought Mexican workers to farms and other production sites in the United

States. For example, in 1943, under Public Law 45 (PL-45), "Mexican workers were contracted in their homeland." [Although] "national in scope, local, federal, and state officials tailored the federal farm labor system to meet the regional labor market demands." This law gave birth to the Bracero Program.[35] Indeed, this labor reserve was centrally important in the 1940s. Further, anthropologist Ruth Gomberg-Muñoz mentions that US businesses sent recruiters deep into Mexico where "they recruited Mexicans to come work in agriculture, construction, and manufacturing in the United States. This system came to be known as *el enganche* (the hook) in Mexico."[36]

After the war, the demand for Mexican labor decreased, forcing Mexicans to find alternative forms of work. Focusing on the critical period from World War II through the middle of the 1960s, Mae M. Ngai examines immigration policy restrictions after World War II and their dramatic increase through 1965.[37] In the case of the Midwest's political and economic restructuring—meaning the shift from manufacturing work, especially in urban centers—the agro-food labor market changed the availability of jobs and, thus, migration patterns. However, these changes to the labor market and the incoming Mexican and Central American immigrant populations up to and during the 1950s "resulted in weakened unions, relocation to nonmetropolitan counties in the Great Plains, lower-wage structures, further deskilling of the labor force, more limited career paths, and production line speeds more than tripled."[38] Mexicans arriving in the Midwest, specifically Chicago, found these shifting migration patterns slowly creating a space for them within the city where work was available.[39] Ethnic studies scholar Lilia Fernandez notes that by 1970, "Chicago reported nearly a quarter of a million 'Spanish speaking' or 'Spanish-surname' people, as they were referred to collectively during these years. . . . By 1980, over 42,000 Hispanic or 'Spanish-origin' people called Chicago home, constituting a remarkable 14 percent of all Chicagoans."[40] Regarding the Mexican population specifically, by 1970 "Chicago had the fourth-largest urban Mexican population in the United States with 106,000 people (about the seating capacity of the Los Angeles Memorial Coliseum). This figure increased to 255,770, or 60.6% of the Latino population in Chicago in 1980 and 325,560, or 64.6%, in 1990."[41]

These previous structural forces prompted the migration of Mexicans to Chicago to accelerate significantly after the 1970s. From a local perspective, the shifting economic activities within the city laid the groundwork that channeled Mexicans toward low-skilled, service-sector jobs. Moreover, within Chicago, other economic sectors slowly replaced manufacturing jobs. As further argued by others, the corporate sector (banking, research, real estate, marketing, trade) "brought along a highly polarized labor market with a large group of highly skilled, highly paid positions at one pole and the vast number of low paying, support occupations at the other."[42] The restructuring of the labor force occurred with the slow but constant movement away from the old liberalism of the postwar period toward new forms of labor management and control, or in many cases, such as the *jornaleros*[43] investigated by Juan Thomas Ordóñez, they were structurally abandoned by the biopolitical machinery of cities in northern California.[44]

A broad overview of the industrial distribution statistics of Latinxs in the Chicago metropolitan area tells of some changes that occurred through the 1970s and 1980s. For example, in manufacturing Latinos accounted for 61.6 percent of the workforce in the 1970s, while by the 1980s that number declined to about 48.3 percent. The jobs that registered an increase in these decades were service jobs. For example, in the 1970s Latinas/os performed clerical or administrative work as 11.7 percent of the workforce, but by 1980 that percentage increased to 17.2 percent. In that same period, service work that in 1970 had an 8.1 percent Latina/o workforce grew in 1980 to about a 14 percent Latina/o workforce.[45] John J. Betancur and Teresa Cordova make a critical observation regarding the overall changes and restructuring of the workforce and incorporation of Latinas/os into Chicago's economy. While manufacturing work declined in the decades of the 1970s and 1980s, "many Latinos" were "absorbed into low-paying jobs as busboys and dishwashers in restaurants, as maids and cleaners in hotels, as security guards, messengers, maintenance workers, *gardeners*, and similar low-end jobs in the service industry" (emphasis mine).[46] Perhaps it is time that we hear the voices of the people who have migrated to the United States within the past three decades, those who fill vital economic roles and carry—silently, *sin respingar* (without complaining)—the city of Chicago on their shoulders.

South Chicago

For much of the twentieth century, settlement patterns of Mexicans in Chicago remained concentrated in specific areas of the city: South Chicago, East Side, Little Village on 26th Street, Pilsen, and Back of the Yards. By 2018 Chicago was home to 2.8 million inhabitants: 49 percent identified as white, 30.5 percent as Black or African American, 29 percent as Hispanic or Latino, and 6.2 percent as Asian.[47] Just as in the early twentieth century, the South Chicago neighborhood remains one of the city's three major areas. A substantial percentage of its population comprises people of Mexican origin. In this book, I aim to bring to life a few of these individuals and their dreams for a better future in el Norte, despite the limitations working-class immigrants often face.

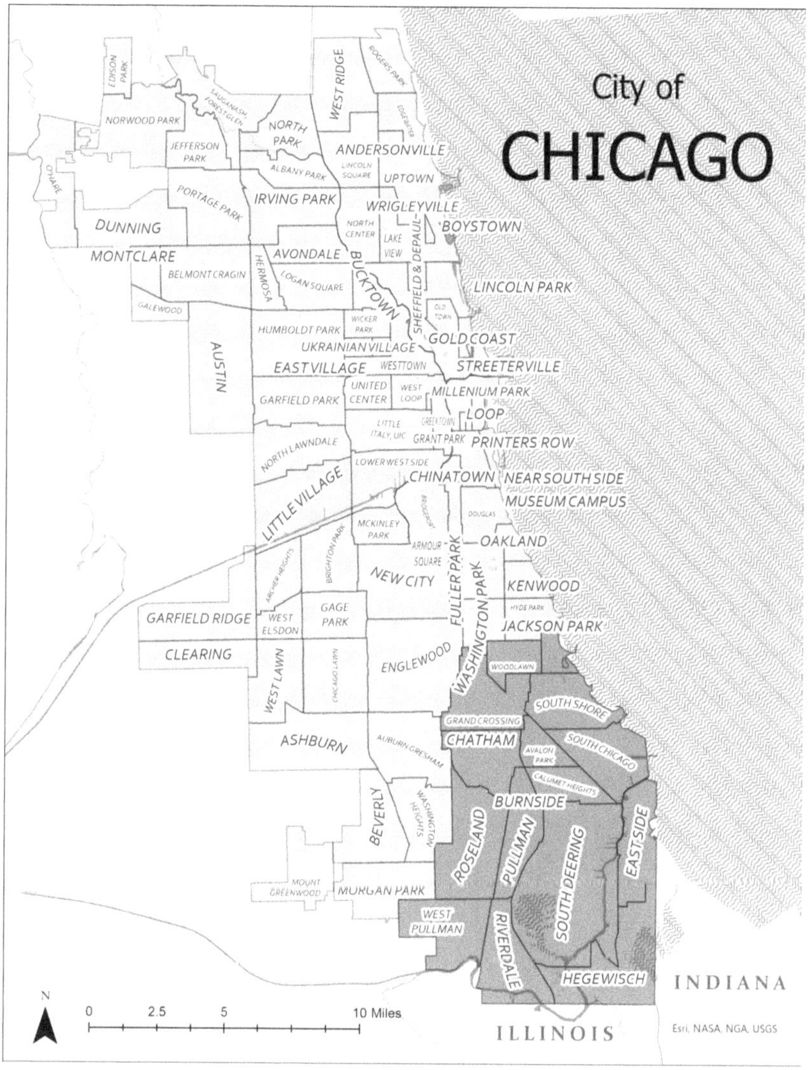

Map 1. The city of Chicago's municipal boundaries. South Chicago is located on the southeast side of the city, bordering Lake Michigan.

South Chicago consists primarily of working-class to middleclass families and has the following racial distribution: White (7.3 percent), African American (56 percent), and Mexican and Chicano (35 percent).[48] The South Chicago neighborhood is located south of downtown, near the border of the state of Indiana and Lake Michigan. To the north of South Chicago, we find a middleclass

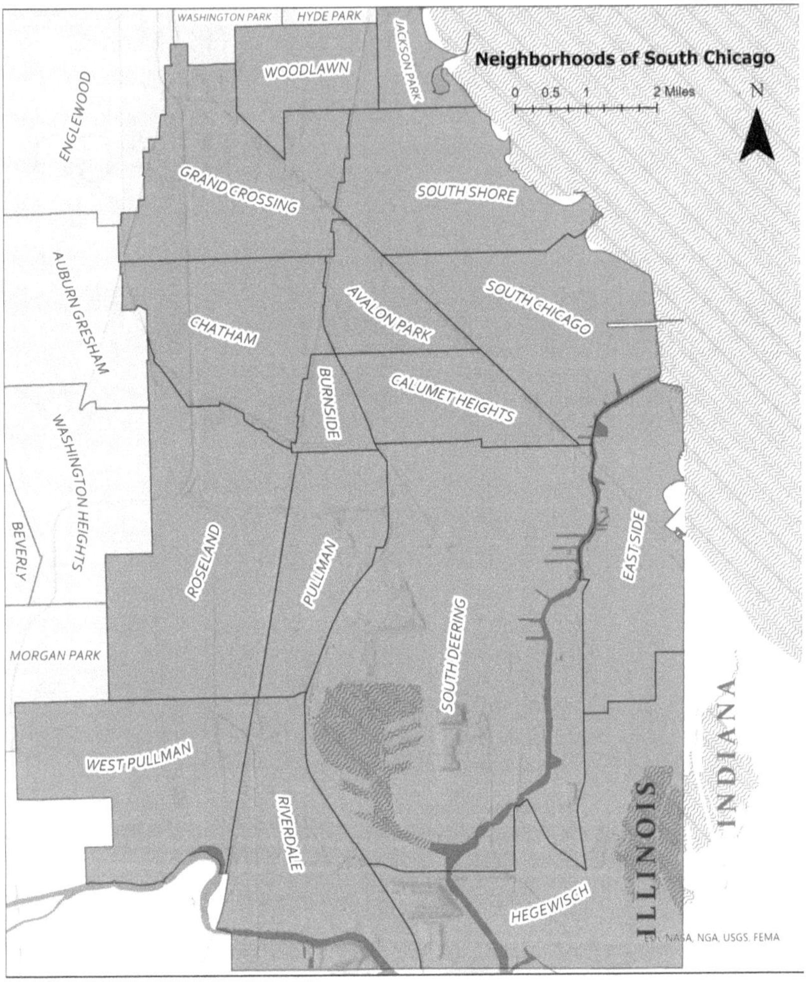

Map. 2. South Chicago streets and major boundaries.

African American neighborhood named South Shore, with 79th Street separating the two neighborhoods.[49] South Chicago also borders Avalon Park, Stony Island Park, and Calumet Heights to the west. The Chicago Skyway, which runs alongside South Chicago Avenue, separates South Chicago and these three neighborhoods. The residential streets do not cross through each neighborhood between 79th Street and 95th Street along South Chicago Avenue. Instead, six tunnels pass under the Chicago Skyway, and only two major streets connect South Chicago with Calumet Heights. To the south of South Chicago, we find a working- to middleclass Mexican and Mexican American neighborhood commonly referred to as the East Side. The Calumet River forms a border between South Chicago and the East Side. Just off the southwest tip of South Chicago, between the Calumet River and 95th Street, lies the neighborhood of South Deering. To the east of South Chicago lies Lake Michigan, next to which a $64 million extension of Lake Shore Drive has recently been added and where steel mills were located before closing in the early 1980s. The large strip of land where the mills once stood is now a lakeside park.

Today the South Chicago borders, whether physical or invisible, are saturated with meaning, power, and inequality. But amid these social and cultural processes, the hard labor of the yarderos beautifies the residential landscapes and lawns of Chicago neighborhoods that often go unnoticed and unappreciated (see chapter 1).

Organization of the Book

The ethnographic materials of *Los Yarderos* are organized into a preface, introduction, six chapters, and a conclusion. In the introduction I link the social, economic, political, and cultural processes to the *longue durée* of Mexican migration to the Midwest and the city of Chicago. For example, there is a slow but growing recognition of the historical connection between Texas and the US Midwest, and this book also attempts to capture that intraregional migration.[50] While that connection is present in the population I write about here, many of my collaborators came to Chicago during the early 1980s and subsequent decades, often avoiding the Texas borderlands altogether in terms of settlement but embodied as they traveled north and as they encountered them in Chicago and the Midwest.[51] After finishing my fieldwork, I have learned that many of the migrants I encountered have since moved to states such as Wisconsin, Ohio, Indiana, and Kentucky—and have even rediscovered Texas as a "new" destination; however, most of the folks I talked with have migrated to Chicago and are settled in the city.

Chapter 1 traces the emergence of yarderos in Chicago from the late 1970s to the present and documents the circumstances that led them to migrate from Mexico to the US Midwest. Learning why they headed north is the first step to understanding the complexity of the migration process and how they become yarderdos/as. In many cases, my collaborators came to work to support their families back in Mexico, sometimes because there were no other options in their hometowns or simply because of the precedent set by a long history of migration from their home states of Jalisco, Michoacán, Zacatecas, and Guanajuato to the United States.

Looking through the lens of the internal borders of class and culture, while providing a view of how Mexican migrants become yarderos, this opening chapter also examines how the family structure is fundamental to the success or failure of many yarderos in South Chicago.[52] Further, this chapter looks at the discourse of apprenticeship as an important cultural behavior relevant to understanding how capitalism reproduces class differences within ethnic Mexican communities. This is a significant contribution given that Mexican migration and immigration are often imagined within a monolithic class category. The stories I tell show how this oversimplification does not apply among yarderos/as.

In chapter 2, the focus turns toward relations of gender among working-class Mexicans in Chicago by focusing on how yarderos understand themselves as men in the context of a highly gendered cultural space. I argue that among men, and migrant men specifically, the desire to be seen as strong, independent, valuable, and the breadwinner, intensifies their need for material and nonmaterial goods. I engage here with specific cultural notions of gender and masculinity that disempower men through their active possession of material goods and the self-perpetuating system created through the logic of capitalism. Gender construction mirrors the capitalist process in that Mexican migrant men continually seek to fulfill an idea and practice of masculinity within a structural relationship of perceived class differences. In other words, gender does the work of class, and the approach applies in reverse. This chapter contributes to the scholarship on gender studies by theorizing a form of "dispossessed masculinity" to frame and explore the experiences of these men.

From gender relations, the book zooms in to offer a closer view of how power and the Mexican body become intimately connected within capitalism. To examine these mechanisms of power, chapter 3 documents how Mexican lawn service workers develop the discipline to control their physical movements, feelings, and functional necessities to perform lawncare service efficiently. Here, I examine how the yardero's body is key in the production process and how the effective management of workers and their bodies maximizes profit. This chapter draws on the notion of biopower to advance an anthropological analysis of how working-class life is lived in contemporary disciplinary regimes under late capitalism. The chapter concludes with a reflection on the hardships of the lawncare production process. It discusses the possibility of a limited agency that can be found despite the crushing feeling that there is no way out of the capitalist structures for the yarderos I write about.

Chapter 4 ethnographically utilizes border theory to examine how the category of "color" is central to scholars documenting the everyday lives of Mexican migrants in the United States. Here I argue that seeing daily working-class interaction as "color inspections" helps excavate ordinary and alternative forms of postnational subjectivity and document the use and misuse of the category of color and its hierarchies in the everyday lives of working-class Mexicans in Chicago. Ethnographically, the chapter looks at apparent colorblind social and cultural interaction areas to see how gender, masculinity, class, and power are experienced through the prism of a "colorism" that navigates between the white-Brown-Black spectrum.

Chapter 5 looks at the intergroup racism between Mexican working-class residents and their Black and African American neighbors in the greater South Chicago area. Relational studies posit that racialization happens dynamically; group-based racial constructions are formed in relation to whiteness, and other devalued and marginalized groups (e.g., African Americans, Native Americans, Latinos, and Asian and Pacific Islanders) whose own racialization is constantly at play. By studying race relationally, I argue, scholars can examine the logic that underpins the forms of inclusion and subordination a group faces when the gravitational force of whiteness is not visually present but structured in the American landscape. Thus, I show that the Mexican-Moreno dyad is a racial framework of mutual and often inseparable bonds that Mexican immigrants construct through anti-Black racism in urban spaces despite the antagonism already documented by other scholars. This chapter's main contribution is to grapple with the malleable, cultural characteristics of the term "Moreno/a" and get us close to better understand Black Mexico and the long legacies of anti-Black attitudes that Mexican migrants carry in their knowledge of who they are as they cross and later settle in the US Midwest.

In the past decade—and through most of the twentieth century—undocumented Mexicans have often been blamed for the perceived economic effects that have disenfranchised other working-class populations in the United States. However, despite the calls for their deportation or the creation of a regime of deportability, undocumented immigrants are central to advancing and reproducing the sovereign subject. Thus, chapter 6 tells the story of how the state of exception and bare life constructs and situates current state practices toward undocumented immigrants. I argue that the state apparatus refuses to ideologically incorporate undocumented immigrants into the polis by engaging in minimalist biopolitics to maintain migrants' bare lives in exchange for their labor. The final part of this chapter documents the politics of resistance that has emerged to challenge the current practices of Homeland Security. I contend that even as the state continues to impose policies against undocumented immigrants, this population has been able to combat state practices through a human rights discourse. While less ethnographically heavy, chapter 6 helps transition the reader from ethnography to the book's concluding remarks.

The conclusion brings together discussions from previous chapters to highlight how labor, colorism, gender, and power organize the lives of Mexican working-class folks—yarderos/as in particular—and how they have made a living in South Chicago despite less favoring structuring forces. I focus on the experiences of the migrant working class to explain the struggle, suffering, and subjection of living in a new land that can limit one's potential to live a fulfilling life. While my final analysis of the American dream is darker than other more positive renderings, there is hope (perhaps I am wittingly naive) for a better future for these families in South Chicago.

After you read this book, my hope is that every time you step out of your home, you are reminded that many Mexican, working-class folks are the people who provide many of the necessary services that bring our fruit to our tables, construct our new homes, clean our hotels, prepare our food, and mow our lawns.

The Method and the Writing

The stories that form this book are based on ethnographic research with Mexican and Mexican American populations in Chicago, Illinois. This book is also about how we experience our working-class lives and our resistance to systemic capitalism to imagine a better future for unprivileged sectors of society. During my formal fieldwork, I performed participant observations in Chicago from July 2012 through November 2013. During sixteen months of ethnographic research, I had the privilege of engaging with working-class Mexicans in the gardening and landscaping industries—people who proudly call themselves yarderos/as.

I consider my research methods ethnographic because I also worked as a yardero; I performed the work duties (mowing lawns) alongside the people I describe in this book, experiencing what Mexican workers are subject to daily. I spent hundreds of hours getting an intimate view of the spaces where yarderos interact, observing and taking notes after each full day of activities. While I attempted to become a yardero, I was never truly in their shoes. My account is inherently partial. My observations aim to be thorough, but I cannot fully appreciate what it feels like to organize one's life in relation to this work activity year after year. Nor can I understand how small company owners think as they need to exploit their fellow countrymen, often undocumented, to seek better profits. Nor can I experience how it feels to hire a Mexican landscaper and request their labor for a monthly fee as many African American or white lower- to upper-class folks do. Despite this, there was no other way I could have envisioned writing down the ethnography I wanted to capture than by being there and working with them.

The challenges to this research were numerous, but the insights proved rewarding. First, I had to talk to these populations in very demanding situations. Second, I followed an ethnographic sensibility of following my interlocutors, seeing what they do, working as they do, and making sense of the meaning of those activities. While working as a yardero, the amount of physical labor required during the day made it impossible to sit down and simply observe; the approach of following the subject conflicts with the classic ethnographic strategy of participatory research. My work involved being behind a lawn mower, picking up leaves, taking trash bags to the garbage can, filling gasoline tanks, trimming evergreen trees, erecting retaining walls, blowing debris off the streets, and cleaning clients' properties. I would often drive the cargo van for the company owner and drop the other workers at their homes in South Chicago before driving the truck to the boss's house and making my way home. Other activities involved helping yarderos by calling clients to inquire about payment, relaying messages, distributing monthly invoices, and reading the company owner's letters and other documents. I conducted my participation-based observations by working with two different lawn service companies for seven months and an additional ten of participant observation.[53] I worked an average of fifty to sixty hours per week. This translates to around 1,500 hours of working as a yardero and plenty of experiences with my interlocutors that I drew from to author this book.

Another pillar of my fieldwork experience involved formal interviews, which often took place in the late afternoon or on weekends. The interviews occurred in people's homes and in public areas such as McDonald's or the local Mexican restaurants of the South Chicago and East Side neighborhoods. Three dozen digitally recorded formal interviews form a central element of this book. Hundreds of informal discussions before and after my fieldwork added further depth to my ethnographic analysis. While I left the "field" formally at the end of 2013, I—like others who may have kin working in that space—will perhaps never leave. We are reminded of our interlocutors in the halls of our higher education institutions. Today, they are just one text away from us anthropologists.

In addition to toiling beside fellow yarderos, I also experienced their joyful moments of everyday life and festive events such as baptisms, first communions, birthday parties, and reunions during holidays such as the Fourth of July, Día de Las Madres, and Father's Day. I attended musical events where *banda* or *norteño* music was played and went to a Chicago flea market known as La Garra. My preoccupation with revealing or "witnessing" the economic, political, and cultural aspects of the working-class life of Mexican yarderas/os reflects my belief in an approach to anthropology that uses ethnography to challenge the hegemony of the dominant historic block, or "that sturdy structure," behind and beyond the actual US-Mexico border, in northern cities such as Chicago.[54] At the same time, this ethnography uses the limited stage of the landscaping economy in Chicago to understand cultural processes operating beyond the ethnographic site of South Chicago. To protect the privacy of my interlocutors, I have changed their names, altered textual representations from actual events, and avoided mentioning distinguishing locations. For example, sometimes street names are mentioned, but even these have been changed to reflect privacy concerns.

This book is written in the first person with interspersed dialogues with my interlocutors. This is not done for autoethnographic exploration or some type of reporting necessity; instead, I include myself to acknowledge that my presence in the ethnographic space indeed shaped what happened. To write myself out of the story would lead to a greater fiction than would an attempt to claim objectivity. Even objectivity is a moving horizon for ethnography.

My methodological approach of inserting my body, senses, and "native" understanding of the ethnographic space in which yarderos experience their everyday life follows newer approaches in anthropology, border studies, Latino studies, and cultural studies fields, which seek to position the subject and researcher at the center of the social analysis.[55] For example, objectivist modernist anthropology would seek out the subject and prioritize the spoken word, the linguistic interaction between the observer and interlocutor. Then the "Lone Ethnographer" would take the speech and utterances, return to the university, and write about that experience. After the crisis of representation in anthropology, two significant currents emerged, as described by Shannon Speed: one critiquing the actual text—that is, at the level of representation—and one where research is taken to an activist ground and the ethnographer co-shares the knowledge production with the interlocutors. Studies using this latter method suggest that the cowritten data collection offers a new decolonizing view of what anthropological research can accomplish. For example, the work by Mariana Mora, working with indigenous groups in the state of Chiapas, is an excellent ethnography among many that have emerged recently, following a decolonial anthropological approach we all should try to accomplish, Mora's work is an exception in the discipline of anthropology.[56] While I wish my interlocutors had been interested in looking over my documents, questionaries, or working conclusions—which I often shared—they rarely had the time to do so. Instead, I usually carry out many oral reports over conversations discussing what I thought was important from the interviews and the observations I was recording during my fieldwork.

When I sat down in the early mornings or late afternoons after work to write my notes, I did not feel that I was discovering something radically new. Instead, I often felt privileged to understand what was happening among yarderos. I could see flashes of how particular pieces fit together in the puzzle that surrounded me. My training as a scholar and my personal experience as a Mexican migrant served me well enough, but I needed ethnography. I knew and experienced Mexican migration to the Midwest (but not enough to understand how older yarderos experienced it in the 1970s, '80s, and '90s). I knew about gender relations (but not enough about women's experiences and the wives of landscapers). I knew how undocumented Mexicans experience their daily lives (but not enough to understand the fear that fills them when driving without a license). I knew about racism in the United States as it applies to Mexicans and Mexican Americans (but not enough to understand how darker Mexicans feel next to lighter-skinned Mexicans).

Indeed, we have wanted "natives" to speak for too long or even questioned if the "natives" could speak. In this book, we do speak; I speak. I write about yarderos/as because I hope to be a lens and lend my vision to you, the reader, to help you understand the lives of yarderos and walk the streets they walk. I want to allow you to see and feel the work of yarderos and experience what I experienced with my interlocutors. It retains ethnographic value even when I can offer only a partial view.

Some of this writing is unpleasant, especially when discussing the basic human necessity of eliminating, which for many working class people must happen in public in the back of alleys. At other times, it is dry and dull, when describing concepts like the differences between *chalanes* and their bosses. Many readers want action and suspense, but you cannot understand the working class without understanding their everyday lives and the cultural value they place on mundane work activities. How can we sympathize with their condition if we do not learn what others experience or what they put up with every day?

This book unearths an emerging working-class subjectivity—that of the yarderos—a concrete cultural production lived and experienced by Mexican immigrants within the context of Chicago. I did not make the category; it was one I found mobilized by my interlocutors. Beyond the scholarly specificity of documenting the lives of yarderos/as in my project, this exploration allows us to see how structural conditions and human agency, as limited as these concepts can be, are found in everyday life among this working-class population.

Indeed, this book focuses on those who left their homes in Mexico, traveled across both physical and imaginary borders, and faced intense inspections based on their color, perceived class, legal status, and gender differences as migrants once in the United States. Some may hope these migrants return to their countries of origin, but given the need for labor in the US, we are here to stay; this is home. We resist leaving, we insist on staying, and we persist. Mexican migrants are in many communities across the United States, and for many, our presence reaches back generations.

For Mexican yarderos, this book is an assertion that their lives matter; for me, it is a way to lend my expertise, both personal and professional, to tell their stories.[57] To those voices, we now turn.

CHAPTER 1

Becoming Yarderos

Migration, Capitalism, and Culture

> This more contemporary history of Mexican migration and racial formation in Chicago is likewise situated within the deeper historical framework of conquest and colonization in the U. S. Southwest, and the subsequent proliferation of interwoven ensembles of transnational relations between the United States and Mexico.
>
> —Nicholas de Genova, *Working the Boundaries*

> I do not see class as a 'structure,' nor even as a 'category,' but as something which in fact happens (and can be shown to have happened) in human relationships. . . . The notion of class entails the notion of historical relationship. . . . And class happens when some men, as a result of common experiences (inherited or shared), feel and articulate the identity of their interests as between themselves, and as against other men whose interests are different from (and usually opposed to) theirs.
>
> —E. P. Thompson, "The Making of the English Working Class"

It is July 2012, and Chicago's mornings are hot, sticky, and humid. During a typical working week *en las yardas* (at the yards), I would drive to Don Antonio's home in the East Side neighborhood and, from there, ride in a 1995 white Ford cargo van to the neighborhoods where we would be mowing. We pick up two other *paisanos* (fellow countrymen) on the way to work, Moises and Rember (short for Remberto). They live in different two-bedroom apartments in the South Chicago neighborhood, the same apartments that in the early 1910s had housed the first wave of Mexican migrants coming to work in the nearby steel mills. Moises comes from the state of Guanajuato, Mexico. He left his wife and two children to come to Chicago to work en las yardas. Rember was born in Chicago to Mexican parents. He did not pursue formal education, so he constantly tried to make ends meet by working in the informal economy. Like Moises, Rember, and myself (an academic turned yardero), many other Mexican landscapers start their workday early in the morning only to finish the day as the sun sets.

Scholarship on Mexican migration patterns has allowed us to see the importance of the informal sector as a source of entrepreneurship and at times as the only option available for work. For example, in his study of Latino informal networks in East San Jose, Christian Zlolniski argues that the growth of informal economic activities is indeed a common feature of Latino immigrant neighborhoods.[1] Zlolniski goes on to explain that informal economies are often viewed as remnants from past modernist projects or as integral to the current historical moment of capitalism. In my research of Mexican yarderos in Chicago, the ethnographic evidence supports the latter approach. If you look at their banking practices, modes of collecting payments, and many other economic interactions, they navigate between formal systems of economic exchange and the informal economy. On the other end of the spectrum is, for example, the work of Juan Thomas Ordóñez and his study of jornaleros in Berkeley, California.[2] In his study, jornaleros are the exemplar of a neoliberal subject embedded in a liminal state of precarity; they are unable to challenge the capitalist demands of the informal sector that takes advantage of them as vulnerable subjects vis-à-vis citizenship mechanisms.

En las Yardas, the mornings are usually light in job responsibilities because you settle into the day's work and schedule. Around 11:00 a.m. you feel good because you know that there is only one more hour of mowing before the boss starts figuring out a suitable time to eat lunch. The hour after lunch feels like a breeze with a full stomach. The most grueling hours of labor are often between two and five o'clock, as I experienced and as my interlocutors told me repeatedly. In the late afternoon, you realize that the day is not over and that you cannot escape the working-class relations or simply walk out from the job site. Rather, you could, but it would be at the cost of losing your job. Anxiety sets in, and you look for ways to slow the rhythm and intensity when performing your task. Once five o'clock arrives, there is a sense of relief, knowing that soon you will be on your way home. Imagine going through these same patterns of feeling for thirty years; indeed, it is extraordinary that yarderos can keep themselves centered under challenging late-capitalist conditions.

In the context of South Chicago, the "landscaping season" is a shorthand designation for the period when many Mexican migrants in Chicago are involved in providing lawncare services to residents in African American and white neighborhoods. The season typically runs from March 15 to the end of November. The story of how Mexicans in South Chicago became central actors in the lawncare industry is intimately tied to a global shift from industrial work to a service-oriented economy, as described by David Harvey in his study of neoliberalism in the United States.[3] This shift is expressed in local terms in South Chicago. The overwhelming majority of the labor force partakes in an economy emphasizing service jobs beyond the factory setting, as the introduction of David Harvey's book explains. This was the experience of groups of Mexican migrants who ended up working in the United States in the late 1970s but happened to find work in lawn care and landscaping as well.

This chapter traces the ethnographic presence of yarderos in Chicago from the late 1970s to the present and documents the circumstances that led these men to migrate north. I use three representative Mexican migrants, Andres, Cesar, and Don Antonio, to explore the life experiences that led them to choose Chicago as their relocation destination. Learning why they migrated is the first step to understanding the complexity of the migration process. My collaborators came to work to support their families back in Mexico because there were either no other options in their hometowns or simply because of the long history of migration from the states in western Mexico from which many of my interlocutors come. This chapter is descriptive at its core because it sets up the field of labor relations that allows us to understand other processes that Mexican yarderos experience while engaging in these economic activities. Similarly, this chapter theoretically unpacks the Mexican working class not as a monolithic category; rather, I argue that it consists of internal, fractured, and thinner classes of workers that researchers glossed over because of a tendency to emphasize working-class solidarity rather than conflict and change. I utilize a process of class deconstruction, much like a poststructuralist would do, but later focus on how we can still speak of a Mexican working class for itself despite these internal differences. As elaborated by Jacques Derrida, the original definition of *deconstruction* suggests the term should be understood as an "analysis" or "the sedimented structure which form the discursive element, the philosophical discursivity in which we think."[4] In other words, I do not dissolve the working-class subject but acknowledge its existence, as fractured as it may be, and look for ways (as small as they may be) where yarderos see themselves as part of a class for itself.

The chapter is divided into two parts. First, I discuss how state institutions such as the United States Department of Labor categorize work activities in relation to landscaping. I briefly offer an overview of the magnitude of the landscaping economy as documented by this institution and point to the apparent fact that the Department of Labor does not necessarily capture undocumented yarderos' role in the industry. The next section describes the story of Andres. His story represents the many other stories of Mexican migrants who come to the United States to work as yarderos to Chicago. The third section documents the life of Don Antonio, a yardero who became integral to my ability to gain access to these spaces and introduced me to other interlocutors. Don Antonio's story shows us that becoming a small lawncare-company owner takes time, energy, and resources. Often, that means being away from family for most of the week or even a year if the family still lives in Mexico. I follow up Don Antonio's migration story with a short account of his work activities during the landscaping season. This allows me to explore the centrality of work in his life and family. The fourth section engages with the story of Cesar. His biography represents the story of many other Mexican migrants who, given their skills, can rapidly become small company owners within five to ten years of arriving in the United States.

The second part of this chapter engages with the cultural practices of becoming a yardero, which hinges upon a worker's class position, as explored in the first part of the chapter. Further, by looking through the lens of the internal borders of class and culture and how my collaborators organize their work life, the chapter demonstrates how kinship is fundamental to the success or failure of yarderos in South Chicago. This section focuses on lawncare apprenticeship to understand how capitalism reproduces class differences between ethnic Mexicans and how these class differences are relevant for the production and reproduction of culture. The last section discusses how work ethic becomes an important and distinctive Mexican cultural practice used to define who will eventually become a successful yardero in Chicago.

Part 1: Migrating to Work *en Las Yardas*

YARDEROS LIVES FROM THE STATE'S OPTIC

The United States Department of Labor collects workforce occupation profiles from around the nation. The work that yarderos perform falls under the significant job group of building and grounds cleaning and maintenance occupations (labeled as 37–0000); lawncare service and landscaping activities fall under a subset data of landscaping and groundskeeping workers (labeled 37–3011).[5] The Bureau of Labor Statistics defines landscaping and groundskeeping workers as workers who landscape or maintain "grounds of property using hand or power tools or equipment. Workers typically perform a variety of tasks, which may include any combination of the following: sod laying, mowing, trimming, planting, watering, fertilizing, digging, raking, sprinkler installation, and installation of mortar segmental concrete masonry wall units."[6] In 2012 it was estimated that, nationally, the workforce consisted of about 830,000 workers with an average hourly wage of $12.44.[7] Most of the workforce provides services to buildings and dwellings, which accounted for about 25 percent. About 9 percent provided services to recreation industries, and the rest provided services to local government agencies, elementary and secondary schools, and general real estate agencies.[8] Geographically, the five states with the highest number of workers performing this work are California, Florida, Texas, New York, and Illinois, in that order. In Illinois, the landscaping and maintenance workforce ranges from 19,770 to 100,820 workers, depending on the time of year. During the summer months, the number of workers increases dramatically, and it declines as winter arrives. The Department of Labor's data also confirms that the metropolitan area of Chicago has one of the highest concentrations of workers performing this activity. There is a registered number of about 20,060 occupations in the city; in other words, five out of one thousand workers perform lawncare or landscaping work, which carries an hourly wage of $12.32 and an annual mean wage of $25,620. The next largest metropolitan concentration of landscaping and maintenance workers is Los Angeles, followed by New York, Dallas, Santa Ana, and Houston.[9] Other sizable areas where landscapers work in Texas are San Antonio and Laredo.

At a glance, the most current statistics suggest that, in 2021, the national estimate for folks working in this profession came to about four million with an average hourly wage of $16.23; however, the median hourly wage was lower: about $14.54. In terms of where most lawncare service workers are located, the list only changes a bit, with Texas becoming the state with the second-highest employment level.[10]

Studies of and about gardening work in the United States provide a well-balanced description of Mexican immigrants as they become active economic actors in this occupational niche.[11] These sociological studies, in concert, have highlighted the informal aspects of gardening work, their structural and occupational components, and their internal configuration across gender and class divisions. For example, scholars found that in the borderland city of Laredo, Texas, Mexican gardeners tended to be male, Mexican, and Spanish speaking.[12] In addition to this, they "work full-time as a gardener (through a sizable portion, 45 percent, parttime), [are] middle-aged, and possess middle school education. Three quarters can work year-round in the trade and have been doing so on average for more than 12 years."[13] In the context of Los Angeles, California, Alvaro Huerta found through personal interviews conducted in Los

Angeles that Mexican gardeners also benefited from social and kinship ties as they looked for work or started their businesses. In the context of Los Angeles, gardening work or maintenance is organized into "small crews . . . [that] usually consist of the owner and several workers, who are often nuclear family members or from the extended family, hometown associates, temporary day laborers, and/or hired from the available immigrant pool."[14] Further, in his study of day laborers in Berkeley, California, Juan Ordóñez tells us that in the case of day laborers we find the opposite: men are often severed from kinship ties whether in the United States or back in the home countries of Latin America. If they participate in gardening or lawn-service work, this often happens on a day's work activity or a few hours with someone who hires them on the spot at *la parada* (street corner).[15] Chicago's yarderos differ from day laborers in the sense that kinship is fundamental for them to obtain access to jobs in the lawn-service economy.

Other scholars studying and writing about gardening work in Los Angeles articulate the advantages and shortcomings of performing this economic activity. For example, Ramirez and Hondagneu-Sotelo conducted interviews and examined the occupational structure of the informal sector to assess the contemporary possibilities of socioeconomic mobility, thus asking, "Are these men exploited workers, toiling in a low-wage, dead-end, dirty, dangerous informal sector job, or are they acting more autonomously as small business owners who employ co-ethnics, strategizing risk and opportunity, and thereby enabling socioeconomic mobility?"[16] The research done among Mexican gardeners in Laredo and Los Angeles is remarkable and informs my work with lawncare service workers in Chicago. While a sociological perspective views this economic activity's structural and organizational nature, anthropological studies on Mexican immigration have not yet fully uncovered this working-class population. For example, we lack a complex understanding of what specific cultural transformations migrant men and women experience as they perform this specific work activity. Moreover, how does citizenship or immigration status allow Mexicans to reach for a better life in el Norte more quickly than those with a less privileged immigration status?

Anthropological studies offer opportunities to visualize how Latino migrants who come to the United States to perform farmwork and later gardening work, temporarily or on a permanent basis, conduct and live their lives in rural areas of California or major metropolitan centers. For example, in his study of indigenous migrants, Seth Holmes investigates the social hierarchies, health, and processes of naturalization from a transnational perspective. By examining the lives of migrant farmworkers, Holmes exposes the long-acknowledged experience of mental and physical injury and how social structures are reproduced by situating the workers, the growers, and consumers in a system where it is hard to blame one for the ills that folks experience.[17] Particularly relevant in this study is his concept of structural suffering and Holmes's concept of slow violence, which can take place in ubiquitous places such as the workplace. Holmes allows us to see, for example, that many of the first- and second-generation Triki indigenous folks from Oaxaca migrate to jobs such as construction, the services sector, and landscaping once they attain increasing levels of education or become exposed to other opportunities. For example, Lynn Stephen writes about indigenous Mixtec agricultural workers in California and Oregon and offers short but fruitful ethnographic interventions documenting the lives of yarderos in the United States. While examining the economic changes in Southern California in the late 1980s, Lynn Stephen came across a Mixtec yardero. She states that while many indigenous groups continue to work in the agricultural industry, "by the late 1970s and early 1980s they had moved out of agriculture into the service sector, primarily in the Los Angeles area."[18] In her ethnography, Stephen mentions Emiliano, a Mixtec indigenous migrant who returned to the United States in 1989 to pay for the costs involved in a formal wedding in Teotitlán del Valle, Oaxaca. Stephen tells us that Emiliano "returned and worked in a factory and then as a gardener in San Bernardino."[19] The following is an excerpt from Stephen's dialogue with Emiliano in which he describes gardening work. This work in Los Angeles is similar to how work is done in Chicago. Still, the yarderos I interviewed—in "Las Yardas"—did more labor-intensive activity and associated more with a working-class identity. But let us look at what Lynn Stephen documented about Emiliano's life.

> EMILIANO: I worked in the factory with my brothers for a little while, then I changed jobs. I met some guys who worked as gardeners in what they called "yardas." They worked outside, taking care of people's yards. I thought maybe I could make more money doing the work I did at the factory. They were going to pay me $300 per week in cash. I had a driver's license, and I knew how to drive. They put me in charge of a truck and a few workers. I went all around the Los Angeles area. We went to Long Beach, Corona, from Corona up to Anaheim, from Anaheim to Santa Ana to Orange, and then from Orange, I would go to Costa Mesa, Newport, and then I would return to San Bernardino. I worked from six in the morning and sometimes on Sunday. . . . I liked this work much more because I was traveling around. I had more freedom. I enjoyed it and was able to make money.[20]

Stephen elaborates that Emiliano's trajectory from factory work to gardening is "fairly typical." Still, given that gardening work, or in our case, "las yardas," was not her focus, she moves on to describe how Mixtec indigenous migrants use the skills gained in the United States to start businesses back in Mexico. Of interest in the case of Emiliano is how he describes a typical day performing gardening work in the Los Angeles borderlands. Here, as in the case of Mexican yarderos in Chicago, the intensity and complexity of gardening work activities are expressed through the idiom of freedom of movement. To enhance our understanding of gardening work, I located three stories of immigrants who have crossed the US-Mexico border. They provide us with a glimpse of the ordinary yardero experience in Chicago, Illinois.

ANDRES

It is the peak of the gardening season in Chicago, and the Fourth of July is around the corner. I sit at a kitchen table with Andres, a twenty-eight-year-old Mexican immigrant from the state of Zacatecas, Mexico.[21] I notice his hands are rough and deep brown from having done physical labor most of his adult life, mostly in jobs that require him to be out in the sun.[22] Andres grew up in Jalpa, Zacatecas, a region known for its canyons and arid landscapes during the dry season (September to February) and wet, green views during the rainy season (March through August). To the south is the state of Jalisco, to the north is the state of Durango, and to the East is the state of Aguascalientes. Traditionally, Zacatecas is one of the top states that sends Mexican migrants to the United States. As Nicholas De Genova has elaborated, beyond their "origins—beyond the village and city, province, and region—Mexican migrants to Chicago are incorporated into a racial order where they are *reracialized* as 'Mexicans.'"[23]

Southern California, Houston, Dallas, and Chicago have been magnets for migration from this state in western Mexico as well.[24] Nowadays, the migratory economic connections are so vast and intense that you do not even have to be in Zacatecas to build your home; according to some Facebook postings I would usually encounter during my fieldwork phase, you can do it from afar through companies that have in their ranks engineers, lawyers, architects, and the labor to make your home in an abbreviated time. A few older yarderos have taken advantage of this transnational opportunity and have built their homes from two thousand miles away. This newer experience contrasts with the older generation of migrants, as explored in Lynn Stephen's work among Mixtecs from Oaxaca.[25] For many of them, the need to construct a home in their hometown demanded they be present to direct *la obra* (the construction site).

Every year during December, *paisanos* travel South to enjoy the *Fiestas Navidenas* (Christmas holidays). But Andres, like many, has not been able to do that since he migrated to the United States in 2005. Andres is one of the many undocumented Mexicans who traveled to the United States after the 9/11 incidents in 2001. With the increasing policing across the US-Mexico border, the possibility of returning home and finding a safe crossing back to the United States is vanishing for the many who find themselves in the same circumstances as Andres.[26] For example, Jason de Leon documents the experiences Mexican and other Latin American migrants have while crossing into the United States through the Arizona desert.[27] For folks like Andres, the cost of crossing has increased so much that it has become almost wholly unaffordable to attempt to cross again. The border patrol policy of Prevention Through Deterrence (PTD) is becoming an inescapable reality for many migrants. Indeed, as documented by Ruth Gomberg-Muñoz in her study of undocumented busboys in Chicago, adding to the increasing price of crossing the US-Mexico border, those who "jump" face several dangers, "including: heat stroke, hypothermia, dehydration, armed property owners, immigration authorities, drowning, corrupt Mexican police, street gangs, [and] American and Mexican drug smugglers. . . . Any of these is a potentially fatal."[28]

At his South Chicago two-bedroom apartment, Andres welcomes me. Andres rents a two-bedroom apartment in a three-story home located on 88th Street and Baltimore Avenue. This home is owned by a Mexican landlord who is also from the same town in Zacatecas, Mexico, of Jalpa. The landlord decided to divide the three-story home in two apartments per level. Thus, he can rent each apartment for about $600, totaling a monthly rent of $3,600. Andres's apartment is simple, with few furniture items: a red sofa, a small TV, a wooden table in the kitchen, and a chair that does not match the table. As we talk, he prepares *ceviche* because his boss likes "Mexican" sea food, and he would give his boss a taste of this dish the next day. Andres tells me that he arrived in the United States in 2005 and talks about his current job working in a factory, welding the inside of railroad tanks. However, before working in his current position in the factory, from the day Andres arrived in Chicago in the late summer of 2005 until 2011, he worked in las yardas with a friend he had known since childhood from his hometown of Jalpa, Zacatecas. As the evening unfolds, Andres recalls how and why he came to el Norte and how he ended up mowing grass in las yardas for a living during his first couple of years in Chicago. The following is an extended excerpt from the interview I had with him.

SERGIO: Why did you decide to come to the United States?

ANDRES: You know, since you are little, you have heard about the North. I only wanted to help my family. In Mexico, I was studying but could not earn enough.

SERGIO: How did you cross the border? [The U.S.-Mexico border]

ANDRES: It took me about two weeks to arrive in Chicago. I took a bus from Jalpa, Zacatecas, to Aguascalientes, Aguascalientes, and from there to Nuevo Laredo, Tamaulipas. Once in Nuevo Laredo, we contacted a man who knew how to cross the river since I was traveling with my cousin. I recall that we stayed in a room with other people for three nights, until one day at night, they told us that we would cross. We arrived at the riverbed, and I bought a farm tractor tire. The other guys did not want to help me fill the tire with air, and they decided to swim. It took me about two hours to inflate the tire, and I crossed. Luckily, the guy taking us over the border decided to wait for me. He knew that it was dangerous to cross. He felt that we might need the tire once in the river. The other guys struggled in the water and rapidly got onto my tire when we were crossing. After we had crossed, we went to a nearby hotel and stayed there for another two days.

SERGIO: How did you travel then to Chicago?

ANDRES: I did not have any money by then, only [enough] to take a bus to Dallas, Texas, where my cousin said that he had another cousin willing to help us out and ride with us to Chicago. When we got to Dallas, his cousin did not even want to open the door. My cousin found another friend who said he would travel to Omaha, Nebraska. I told my cousin, "Well, I am going with him. I do not know what you are going to be doing, but I am going to Nebraska." I thought that Nebraska sounded close to Chicago, but now I realize that it is far!

SERGIO: How long had it been since you had crossed upon reaching Nebraska?

ANDRES: About ten days.

SERGIO: How did you then arrive in Chicago?

ANDRES: Well, I received food from my cousin's friend, who gave us a ride to Chicago.

SERGIO: So, your friend gave you a ride to Chicago from Omaha?

ANDRES: Yes, I remember arriving through [Interstate] 80—now I know its name—and he parked in a Walmart parking lot, and we waited for Rodrigo. Rodrigo arrived, and my cousin wanted to go with a friend of his to la 47 [47th Street], so Rodrigo took him there. Then, I went with Rodrigo to his house. There, Don Antonio and his wife were waiting for us, and for the first time in two weeks, I ate a homemade, warm meal, took a shower, and slept many hours. The following day, I went with Rodrigo to work mowing grass.

It has already been a decade since Andres arrived in the United States, but he feels it just happened yesterday when he recalls how he came to Chicago. The ability to work the next day Andres arrives is particular for undocumented migrants who actively use their networks to look for work and be hired quickly through friends and family networks. For example, in her study of busboys in Chicago, Ruth Gomberg-Muñoz tells the story of a Mexican named Chuy. This migrant took a plane to Tijuana and from there crossed into the United States. Gomberg-Muñoz recounts that Chuy was taken all the way to Los Angeles, and from there he and others took a bus to Chicago. As Chuy and the others arrived in Chicago, Gomberg-Muñoz says that Chuy told her that his friend from Mexico Mateo were taken to buy "food and beer, and took us shopping for clothes and shoes. Then, the next morning, my brother took me to Il Vino to start working as a busboy."[29]

Andres occasionally still works en las yardas, but he worked from factory to factory until he found a stable job in 2009 welding the inside of railroad track tanks. Toward the end of our conversation that night, I asked him why he did not just go ahead and start mowing houses on his own. Andres immediately replied that it was not possible. First, he says he does not have space to store his landscaping equipment, given that he lives in an apartment. Second, he would have to buy a truck or van and had no place to keep it. Third, and most importantly, what would he do without a driver's license if he got stopped by the police? The end of the formal fieldwork phase of my project coincided with an increasing and intense policing of immigration in towns and cities in the United States. This deportation regime, as that Nicholas De Genova has described so vividly, created real preoccupations for many undocumented immigrants such a Andres.[30] By 2012 they were painfully aware that if they were driving, they could be stopped for any small infraction and be taken to immigration authorities for further investigation. Undocumented migrants such as Andres would become attentive to figure out ways to maneuver outside of their apartments, often, thinking carefully how they interacted with society so as not to get caught by authorities. By 2012 simple activities such as shopping at a mall or grocery store or playing soccer in a public park could potentially trigger the optic of the state if someone deemed folks like Andres as not belonging to the sovereign space. For example, in his study of jornaleros in Berkeley, California, Juan Ordóñez documents similar strategies of visibility and invisibility. For example, jornaleros would be seen standing at la parada to get hired by private individuals and then turned into invisibility so as to not be seen as working without proper documentation.[31]

While the Chicago Police Department does not have a specific policy regarding calling immigration services when arresting an undocumented individual in the city limits, Andres is always worried that upon driving without proper documentation, he would be stopped and later deported to Mexico or, worse, be detained for an indefinite period. Migrants such as Andres come to Chicago because of preestablished kinship and migrant networks spread throughout Mexico and the United States. Once in the United States, their own specific experiences of migration channel them into jobs, in this case, mowing lawns for middle- and upper-class residents in the Chicagoland area. In 2018 Andres married a migrant woman from Austria, and he now has a one-year-old baby boy. It is important to note that marriage between racialized white women and undocumented migrants seems to be a cultural practice that has not been well documented and is an important potential research area. For instance, Ruth Gomberg-Muñoz discusses that most of the undocumented migrants she talked to while working at Il Vino, a local American-owned business, tended to marry or have white American women as partners. Indeed, Gomberg-Muñoz says that "such a high degree of social integration with nonimmigrant 'whites' is probably somewhat unusual among undocumented Mexican immigrants."[32]

DON ANTONIO

The story of how Don Antonio Flores ended up as one of the oldest yarderos of South Chicago and its neighboring areas begins more than three decades ago, when he first migrated to the Midwest in 1974. Don Antonio is a sixty-eight-year-old migrant from the state of Zacatecas with gray hair and bent posture from having done this work for almost three decades in the United States. However, Don Antonio, when working in las yardas, has the vitality of a twenty-eight-year-old.

I met Don Antonio through an acquaintance who told me he needed some *ayuda* (extra help) back in 2007, when I was still in my first year of graduate training at the University of Illinois and when I conducted preliminary summer research. Among yarderos, the Spanish word *ayuda* (help) is used in a subtle cultural way to hire someone and lessen the exploitative nature of the labor arrangement. In this context, when yarderos say "ayudar," the verb implies that the worker will help the small company owner, and it also avoids the discussion of the hourly rate of pay. Working for Don Antonio that year, I crafted the initial idea to study landscapers in Chicago. Since then, we have had countless conversations, which have allowed me to explore and value his way of life and worldview that many other yarderos I spoke with share. A respectful and respected yardero, Don Antonio is well known for helping other

Mexicans who have just arrived in Chicago, usually by giving them work and sometimes even shelter at his home. He has also trained his sons and sons-in-law to become yarderos themselves.

Don Antonio migrated to South Bend, Indiana, in 1974. He explains that he had already traveled within Mexico before migrating to the United States, *pal norte* (to the north). First, from Zacatecas he went to the state of Sinaloa and then to Sonora. Among Mixtecs from the state of Oaxaca, migrating within the Mexican nation-state was a common practice, as documented by Michael Kearney.[33] It was later in the 1990s that they started migrating to the US Southwest and the Pacific Northwest. In her study of transborder processes, Lynn Stephen offers an excellent analysis of how Oaxacan migrants crossed borders, both internal and international, along racial and ethnic lines, and in terms of gender.[34]

I first heard Don Antonio's account of how he arrived in South Bend, Indiana, in August 2012. It was a Saturday, and we had just completed the week's work when we stopped at the parking lot of a local store near 87th Street and Crandon Ave in Calumet Heights. It was one of those moments where the urgency to complete the work lessened, and we would have conversations about the past.

SERGIO: When did you first migrate to Chicago?

DON ANTONIO: I did not arrive in Chicago directly. I first arrived in South Bend, Indiana.

SERGIO: Why South Bend, Indiana? I thought that you came directly to Chicago.

DON ANTONIO: No . . . no . . . I first arrived in South Bend with Nena [short for Elena], *es pariente* (a distant relative). She is not related to me, but we all call her Aunt Nena. She had a house in South Bend and received many others like other families and me. It was like a guest-house so that you can understand me. . . . I stayed with my wife and three children for almost three years until someone called *la migra* [Border Patrol] on us.

SERGIO: So, someone called la migra to report that you were undocumented?

DON ANTONIO: Yes. We went back to Mexico because I received a letter that we needed to leave. I returned a year later to South Bend, Indiana, again by myself. By then, my brothers Pablo and Rogelio, who were also living with me in Indiana, had moved to South Chicago and began working with a man from our hometown who had a landscaping business. So I started cutting grass with Don Ramirez in 1978.

SERGIO: But did you work by yourself from the beginning?

DON ANTONIO: My brothers and I worked for Don Ramirez for the first two years. But he retired and gave *la ruta* (the route) to the three of us. We first began working together, cutting the grass of each other's houses, but then we split, and everyone began doing his own houses.

SERGIO: Have you been working in las yardas since then?

DON ANTONIO: Yes, every year. I began with only about fifty houses. My son Julio came to Chicago to help me in 1994 at the age of fourteen. He was born in South Bend. By the end of the year, I had about eighty houses. Then, by the end of the second year that I was working by myself, in 1996, I think, I ended the year with 120.

SERGIO: And why did you continue coming to Chicago every year?

DON ANTONIO: . . . [pause] . . . *a trabajar, que mas*? [To work, what else?]

Don Antonio's life as a Mexican migrant started briefly within the Mexican territory in the 1970s when he was in his thirties. By the time he was in his forties, the Midwest had become his preferred choice to migrate to during the landscaping season. However, as stated in the narrative above, during the early phase of his migration experience, he kept under the radar in South Bend, Indiana. Thus, a common phrase, "flying under the radar," becomes a central metaphor to explain the behavior of undocumented Mexicans as they travel within the United States. Just as jornaleros in California keep a low profile, Ruth Gomberg-Muñoz tells us about busboys' practices in the context of the service sector. For example, Muñoz says that fear of detection affects broader behavior. For example, if there is a social injustice at work, they would avoid confrontation with the boss. Indeed, as Muñoz further explains, "Undocumented people have little protection from unscrupulous employers who take advantage of them by not paying them, not providing required safety protections, or refusing to take care of undocumented employees who are injured on the job."[35]

Half an hour passed as Don Antonio and I continued to talk, and we were still in the grocery store's parking lot. I knew there were about ten houses left to mow that Saturday. A few months after our conversation, I heard that Doña Elena, who first sheltered Don Antonio, passed away. I attended her funeral in South Bend, Indiana, full of folks from the *Mexicano* community. Eighty to one hundred people attended her service, confirming her essential role in many people's lives, just as Don Antonio had described. As Don Antonio would often say, his life as a working-class Mexican was *una vida dificil* (a difficult life). He now works as much as possible, and Sundays, while often dedicated to the family, are still organized around his postwork activities that must take place before the following week. These activities involve making purchases at Sam's Club or taking a quick trip to the local landscaping retailer to buy the means of production he needs for the week. The early afternoons are often dedicated to swinging by the houses of older African American clients. As is customary, Sundays are the days that clients are with their families and, thus, they are more easily approachable to request payment for the lawncare services of the month.

After the landscaping season is over each year, Don Antonio travels to Mexico to stay during the winter season in Jalpa, Zacatecas. After spending three months in Jalpa, he returns to Chicago two or three weeks before the season starts in mid-March. Don Antonio starts the season power raking (*raqueando*) his clients' front and back yards, and it was because of this time-consuming and backbreaking task that he needed extra help. Besides power raking, the start of the landscaping season also involves deep cleaning and fertilizing clients' lawn areas. For example, he clears the bedding areas of debris, cuts plants near the root that have died due to the long winter, and trims branches obstructing any sidewalks and adjacent areas. As I learned quickly, to be a true yardero and be able to say, "yo soy yardero," *raqueando* is how you start to become one.

RAQUEAR (TO RAKE)

Raquear, as defined by Don Antonio and the other Mexican yarderos in South Chicago, involves various labor activities. Most yarderos start the season in the middle of March, and while some begin mowing right away, the majority power rake their clients' front and back yards. This activity involves using a power rake machine and passing it over the lawn areas of the client's residence. A power raker is about 26 inches wide, 33 to 39 inches in height, and weighs about 160 pounds. These machines usually cost between $1,000 and $1,500. The power rake machine has a rough system of free-swinging flail blades on the bottom that efficiently remove matted thatch with centrifugal force, removing old grass from the lawn. While the increasing use of high-powered machines has intensified the labor activity, Don Antonio would often recall that in the past, when he started, a handheld rake was the only equipment used to raquear his clients' yards.

The removal of grass accomplishes two essential tasks: first, it allows the grass to change slightly in color from light brown, exposing pockets of greenish color; and second, it allows grass that is barely beginning to grow in early spring space to "breathe," and according to yarderos, grow even faster. Thus, raqueando is essential to hold clients from the previous season, but it is time-consuming and hard to do. The power raker does not have a self-propelling mechanism, so one must push it forward. The centrifugal force of the blades helps move the power raker, but one must be careful with it. If pushed too fast, a yardero may run the machine over the grass without working on the lawn. On the other hand, if the power raker moves too slowly, the result reaps all grass from the spot where no forward movement occurred. Power raking a client's yard usually takes thirty to forty minutes, depending on the property's square footage. When a client's home is on a corner, we often work for an hour and a half on that property just to power rake it.

A substantial amount of "dead" grass emerges from power raking a client's yard. After producing small piles of grass and filling trash bags with it, power blowers are readily used to leave the lawns clean of debris. There are different blowers: backpack, electric handheld, gas-handled, and walk-behind. Among yarderos in South Chicago, backpack blowers are primarily used, but sometimes you see gas-handled blowers. Don Antonio says he likes to use the gas-powered backpack blower to direct air into the grass and get the smaller debris out. A gas-propelled backpack blower typically weighs about twenty-one pounds, has a fuel capacity of forty-seven ounces, and costs, on average, $360 to $650. The wind velocity can reach close to two hundred miles per hour. It is a powerful machine and beneficial for Don Antonio's work. As you may expect, *el soplador* (blower) is noisy, and its noise level can reach seventy-five decibels. In other words, a blower of this type is four times as loud as a vacuum cleaner or electric dryer. Now imagine carrying this noise with you for the entire day, rather than seventy-five feet away as the scale usually measures.

After the power rake has passed over the lawn areas, Don Antonio uses the blower to create small piles of grass. I would sometimes help him with this, but most of the time I did the first part of the task, pushing the power rake over the entire lawn area. After finishing my task, I would immediately help Don Antonio collect the grass, and finally, we would fertilize the lawn. The fertilization of the lawn has two purposes: first, it encourages strong root development and healthier turf and, in very practical terms, this is an opportunity for yarderos to add services to existing work activities, thus yielding an extra income when it is most needed at the beginning of the landscaping season. Don Antonio rarely charges for fertilization; for him, it is an investment given that if the grass grows, he will have work for the rest of the season. The amount and quantity of fertilizer used for a house depends on the lawn's size. Still, a twenty-pound bag of fertilizer, costing fifteen to twenty-two dollars, can typically be used for two properties. When fertilization was complete, we would blow the debris off the sidewalks, place the thirty-eight-gallon bags of dead grass into trash cans, and move on to the next house.[36] Once *la raqueada* is complete, starting in the first or second week of April, yarderos/as provide other lawn services. A yardero begins with a small crew of men and women during this period. Once the season begins to peak in late May, additional temporary help is hired from the Mexican labor reservoir of South Chicago. As Don Antonio often commented, it is as if yarderos start anew every year, given that new houses are added to the route or clients discontinue the lawn service. Don Antonio would often say, "Mowing for a living is a hard job." Indeed, that is the case.

Since 2012 many yarderos have turned to stand-on mowers because they save time when performing lawn services. Older yarderos such as Don Antonio do not like stand-on mowers because the thick, eight-inch-wide tires leave marks in the grass. Don Antonio prefers the twenty-one-inch walk-behind models with two-inch-thick wheels. The lawn mower I began to use early in the landscaping season was a thirty-two-inch walk-behind Bobcat mower. These heavy-duty machines can reach up to six miles per hour, have a fuel capacity of five gallons, and have up to sixteen horsepower. The machine's starting price is about $3,500, but the price is higher for increased product features. The hard part for yarderos is not necessarily directing the lawn mower to do what they want it to do but getting the machine out of Don Antonio's Chevy van for work.

It is also difficult to push the lawn mower to the cargo van deck. Don Antonio, just like many other yarderos, uses a Chevy 2500 cargo van, while the new generation of yarderos progressively incorporates a hauling trailer to carry most landscaping equipment. To unload the almost four-hundred-pound, thirty-two-inch lawn mower from his van, Don Antonio uses two ten-foot wooden boards to slide the mower down. His hired help, *chalanes* (employees), had to be careful; otherwise, they would drag the mower down instead of slowly guiding it backward. A wooden board can fall and leave one side of the mower tilted. If one is not careful, the four-hundred-pound mower can fall to the pavement from about four feet above the ground. Don Antonio is meticulous about how he wants the work to get done. For example, he likes to leave a client's house exceptionally clean. We make sure all grass clippings from the curbside that end up in the lawn area disappear from proximity to the concrete areas. Not all yarderos provide such a clean service; many blow the grass clippings onto the street or back to the grass again after mowing—*medio guandajos* (a little bit lazy), as Don Antonio would often say. He believes the cleanliness he is well known for is part of why he has maintained the loyalty of some clients for up to thirty years now. At the end of the week, the crew would mow whatever houses were left from the day before and finish the service to clients in South Chicago near 83rd Street and Yates Avenue. The residents of this area are a younger generation, and the yards are larger than those found farther south. While using the thirty-two-inch Bobcat lawn mower to mow the lawns is faster, a person walks the entire day. For example, along Yates Avenue Don Antonio would mow about twenty houses within just one block. The crew would finish the week's work at 83rd Street and Exchange Avenue, mowing the lawns at a funeral home and nearby houses.

CHAPTER 1

CESAR

Cesar Sanchez is a thirty-four-year-old Mexican migrant from Jalpa, Zacatecas, and has been in Chicago since 2002. Cesar tells me that back in Mexico, people used to say that he was from the family of *los gueros* (the blondies) because of his family's white skin tone. In Chicago he is still considered a Hispanic white, especially during the winter, but his skin looks white with a touch of light brown while working during the summer months. Before coming to Chicago, Cesar traveled during the summers to California to work at a family friend's carwash in Los Angeles. Cesar is five feet seven inches with a squared frame and is quick and outspoken about life in Mexico and the United States. Cesar is always in a good mood to talk about politics and culture in Mexico. He graduated as an elementary school teacher from a university in the Mexican state of Zacatecas. Presently, he owns a small lawn-service business, and during the end of 2012, I worked for him, mowing grass around the neighborhoods of South Chicago two or three days a week. While performing lawn service, there were short periods during which we would travel around residential areas, mowing lawns from house to house, and a small conversation would take place. During those moments, Cesar offered details about how he decided to migrate and why he became a yardero. Compared with Andres, Cesar has had a radical and different migration outcome. Much of Cesar's success in emerging as a yardero is because of the help he received from Don Antonio, Cesar's father-in-law. Thus, as Cesar's trajectory depicts, we begin to see that family plays a substantial role in providing economic development opportunities.

Cesar explains that after graduating from the Normal School in Zacatecas as a teacher, his mother did not want him to migrate because she had heard many bad stories of those who crossed *la frontera* (the border). Cesar recalls that he wanted to come to Chicago for a brief period. He moved into an apartment near East Side on 103rd Street and Ave D. Cesar stayed there with his cousins, who had lived in Chicago for over a decade. He later found a parttime job hauling cars for a local auto-repair shop and barely made ends meet to pay for rent and food. As soon as the landscaping season began in 2002, Cesar started working en las yardas.

From early March until the end of November 2002, Cesar would work six days a week, from eight in the morning to about seven in the evening, mowing lawns, trimming bushes, installing brick retaining walls, and performing other landscaping activities. Cesar often told me he earned enough money to marry his girlfriend, Beatriz. Both now live in Chicago. In Mexico he struggled to graduate with a degree in education. When he was ready to obtain a tenured position as an elementary-school teacher, he decided to migrate to the United

States. He would say with a smile, looking into the distance as if the images of his past decisions were before him, "*las vueltas de la vida*" (twist and turns of life). He migrated to the United States not to follow his career dream but for love.

In his second year in the United States, Cesar began performing lawn service independently as a yardero. Cesar started with only twenty-eight houses. He would mow his houses in three days, and for the other two days, he worked with Don Antonio as a chalan. Cesar tells me that he would often mow about fifteen houses daily, translating to mowing a yard every thirty-five to forty minutes. Cesar would work from early March until November. Eight years after arriving in Chicago, Cesar provides lawn and landscaping services to more than 350 houses every week and can now provide work for two chalanes during the busiest months of the landscaping season.

In early September 2012 I began looking for a lawn-service company to work with for the remainder of the landscaping season. I knew that Cesar Sanchez had scaled up since I initially met him in 2006, so I asked him whether he needed any help. It was essential to be treated like any other worker, even though he had known me as an acquaintance since 2006. In documenting the lives of working-class populations, it is critical to start where many workers do, asking around to find out who may be hiring. There are other ways to study working-class populations; for example, Christian Zlolniski would help his interlocutors with "immigration-related paperwork; job applications; government, school, and other official forms . . . which contributed to [his] visibility in the neighborhood."[37] Cesar confirmed that he was looking for help because he had difficulties with the current chalan. I learned on the first day that migrant labor as a yardero is hard—seriously, it is. Thus, I started working with Cesar from early September until the end of the landscaping season, in late November 2012. Not all yarderos work through the end of November in Chicago, when temperatures average thirty-five to forty-nine degrees Fahrenheit. Many finish the season at the end of October. Usually, yarderos with many years of experience mowing grass are the ones who have work at the end of November.

In the three months that I worked for Cesar Sanchez, in 2012, I learned of the differing practices of structuring lawn service. Cesar often told me that part of his success is due to the fact that clients see the name of his company, Sanchez Lawn Care, and believe he will provide better service than other non-Hispanic companies. In other words, he believes that by attaching his Hispanic last name to the service he provides, customers will request his service from better-established companies. Moreover, Cesar thinks that clients believe he will charge them a cheaper rate, and they know Mexicans will do a better job. Cesar's suggestion is concurrent with what I documented while mowing lawns during fieldwork. I often saw other yarderos passing by with banners and names like Gonzalez Landscaping, Jimenez Lawn Service, Hector's Lawn Care, or Mendez Lawn Care.

Indeed, anthropologist Arlene Davila writes about the "hotness" of Latina/o or Hispanic names in marketing and advertising.[38] Thus, central to the field of cultural analysis is the argument that the reconstitution of individuals into consumers and populations into markets requires cultural work and the logical underpinnings of market-driven ideas. Davila argues that "Hispanic marketing is particularly revealing of the relationship between culture, corporate sponsorship, and politics, and can illuminate how commercial representations may shape people's cultural identities and affect notions of belonging and cultural citizenship in public life."[39] For lawncare companies such as Sanchez Lawn Care, the purpose of marketing with a Latina/o last name is to transmit the idea that one's company would do the work better than other racially marketed companies within Chicago.

Part 2: Cultivating Work Ethic en Las Yardas

SI DEJA LA HIERBITA

The phrase *sí deja la hierbita* (wild weed gives) is a common linguistic expression I often hear among my interlocutors. This phrase represents the merging of two cultural domains—the media-exalted discourse of the drug industry and the lawncare service. Yarderos would express this phrase when, for example, they would buy a new vehicle, a new lawn mower, or move to a better home. I learned that "*sí deja la hierbita*" signifies that working as a yardero has benefited the person so that there is now additional income, thus signaling the genesis of class differentiation vis-à-vis the hired workers by the small company owner. Of course, we know that class consists of much more than income, but in a constrained economic niche such as lawn care, having extra income to spend on pleasurable activities makes substantial cultural differentiation among workers. This phrase can sometimes be considered an insult and create a class fracture depending on the linguistic inflection. Or, as José Limón reminds us, it can be a form of working-class solidarity when expressed among *vatos*.[40] Often, when a yardero expresses this phrase, the reply can be, "De que te admiras, andamos en lo mismo?" (What are you surprised by? We do the same job?). Both yarderos will recognize a nonaggressive tone in a playful linguistic fashion, making the conversation friendly. To illustrate the internal class differences ethnographically, the remainder of this chapter discusses how yarderos such as Andres, Don Antonio, and Cesar experience internal borders of class. These sociocultural constructions are structurally enforced and consciously cultivated through entrepreneurial expertise to develop a robust understanding of how capitalism operates to reproduce power differences as fractured processes to show how internal class differentiation within a perceived homogenous working class—los yarderos—matters to my interlocutors.

Early in the twentieth century, anthropologists theorized culture as embodying dialectic dual life through beliefs and practices. Since then, the concept of culture has been instrumental in explaining how and why human beings behave in multiple social, political, economic, and geographical landscapes. For example, in the 1970s, culture was imagined as being composed of "symbolic structures and collective behavior," structure and agency, human action and intention, culture as constituted, and culture as lived.[41] Renato Rosaldo reminds us that recent anthropological concerns have radically changed because the discipline's "agenda has shifted from the search for structures to theories of practice that explore the interplay of structure and agency."[42] More specifically, Rosaldo calls for a remaking of anthropological analysis that is also attentive to the workings of culture and power. Applying some of these suggestions to the lives of yarderos in Chicago, I investigated what circumstances or experiences are relevant for migrant men to become and feel like yarderos in Chicago, offering my social analysis of their experiences as workers crossing multiple borders and being inspected as they attempt to cross them. Not everyone can cross borders, as Ruth Behar reminds us. Later, Michel Foucault argued that a new plane of reference or a unique assemblage is needed that can, from my perspective, envelop the ethnographic study of populations and move beyond "economic actors" by maintaining culture and power in late capitalism and its fragmenting effects central in our analysis.[43] The following cultural exploration of the yardero class structure examines how culture and power operate in spaces where yarderos work as they become yarderos.

CHALANES

When a Mexican migrant starts working en la yardas as a chalan (at the yards as extra help), it usually means that this migrant is a beginner or apprentice in this work activity. For many yarderos, working as extra help is often temporary, like the *paleteros* (ice cream street vendors) that anthropologist Christian Zlolniski encountered when examining the subcontracting economy and informal sector in Silicon Valley in California.[44] A chalan is also a well-known category among construction workers in Mexico and the United States. In general terms, it denotes an apprentice to the work activity. While the chalanes described here enjoy a stable contractual relationship with their employers—that is, other Mexican owners—anthropologist Christian Zlolniski further mentions that many Mexican working-class folks often "receive few if any working benefits, have limited access to state and welfare benefits, and are denied most of the political rights of legal citizens."[45]

At other times, a chalan will work *podando* only (bush trimming evergreen trees) or work in temporary positions for one to two days *contratado de palabra* (word of mouth contract) when a yardero has acquired a well-paid landscaping contract that will yield profit and needs to get the job done quickly. For example, Cesar Sanchez has specifically dedicated himself to mowing lawns, but other yarderos often perform larger landscaping jobs such as building retaining walls, planting trees, or installing decorative rocks. Within the yardero company owners, there is a hierarchy among lawn-service providers between those who only perform mowing and those who carry out larger landscaping contracts. Typically, those yarderos who acquire landscaping contracts tend to increase their income more rapidly, but contracts often do not arrive steadily. For example, a yardero might land two or three landscaping contracts in one month, but they will pass another month without a single contract. On the other hand, when an owner concentrates on just mowing residential homes, the number of house lawns needed to make ends meet increases exponentially to about one hundred houses per day. Thus, there is a steady income stream at each month's end.

Few chalanes become small company owners, and not all company owners are documented. However, owning a small company marks a cultural difference even as they perform the same job. In practice, it is also about domination and control. Chalanes often struggle anywhere from one to three years before becoming full-time yarderos or small company owners. Becoming a small company owner signals that you are an accomplished entrepreneur in many ways. You are smart enough to understand how to make money, provide for your family, and be a man. In numerous conversations with Andres, we often discussed the constraints that prevented him from becoming the owner of his labor and starting a small lawncare service company. I learned that Andres is not afraid of being unsuccessful but of the legal constraints and subsequent criminalization that comes from not having *papeles* (proper documents).

Another chalan, Guillermo Solis, the nephew of Don Antonio Flores, is a United States citizen by birth. At the same time, his father, José Flores, the brother of Don Antonio, was born in Mexico and migrated to Chicago in the late 1970s. Guillermo is currently married and has a young daughter. He has worked with Don Antonio, helping him mow lawns since the early 1990s. During our lunch breaks, Don Antonio recalls that Guillermo would get out of high school early, drive to where Don Antonio would be working, and help him mow grass, sometimes even until eight or nine in the evening. Like Andres, Guillermo has not become an independent small company owner, despite having many years of experience working as a yardero. Instead, he works as a full-time chalan to one of Don Antonio's sons, who owns a separate landscaping business.

While we find exceptions, such as Guillermo, who have American citizenship, most chalanes are *sin papeles* (without proper documentation). By the end of the 2013 landscaping season, I learned that Guillermo had quit working as a chalan and would become a full-time yardero with his brother Arturo. Indeed, after almost fifteen years of working as a yardero for someone else, "Memo" finally became independent. A chalan or gardener apprentice has a few options when becoming an independent yardero. Many, if not most, of the chalanes I spoke with rarely became yarderos. In many instances, kinship ties structure these options. For example, when a chalan works for his father or uncle, an older family member will typically help secure the means of production for the would-be yardero. A twenty-one-inch mower usually costs about $1,500, a blower about $350, and a line trimmer about $180. If chalanes buy a full set of new equipment, they need to invest at least $2,000. Buying lawncare equipment is usually one month's salary for a chalan. Other workers will save income and go to Sunday flea markets or openair markets to buy used lawn-maintenance equipment. Thus, a would-be yardero must invest energy, money, time, and effort if they want to become a full-time yardero and earn enough to make ends meet. There is a marked difference between working as a yardero and accepting this working-class identification as part of everyday life. This cultural identification in a worker's life often occurs as lawncare service workers become full-time yarderos like Cesar Sanchez or Don Antonio. Indeed, work activity directly affects one's sense of belonging to a particular group of individuals who perform the same work activity, as a part of a specific working class. Once you become a full-time yardero, your life revolves around las yardas (the yards). Likewise, your yearly cycle of cultural events becomes structured in relation to the environmental changes and seasons of the yard work.

DON RAUL

Don Raul Mendez is a seasoned yardero in the East Side neighborhood of Chicago. Don Raul came to Chicago from the municipality of Huitzila, Zacatecas, in 1992. Huitzila is a town located in the municipality of Teul de Gonzalez Ortega in the southern part of Zacatecas. Within ten years of the fall of Tenochtitlan at the hands of Hernan Cortes in 1535, Nuno de Guzman sent Pedro Almidez Chirino to the area. Historically the area has maintained itself through agricultural and livestock production. The main economic activity in this area revolves around the cultivation of maize, cattle ranching, and the planting of mezcal. However, according to Mr. Mendez, there were times of the year when participating in illicit agriculture was customary practice, sometimes by force, and sometimes by individuals seeking to earn income rapidly. The Mendez family runs one of the most prominent Mexican family-owned lawn-care companies in South Chicago. However, Don Raul often does not want to be associated directly with the Mendez family because of personal feuds between family members. Thus, he has a different logo on his truck. The following conversation occurred at his East Side home in early November of 2012 when I asked him to tell me how he ended up as a yardero.

SERGIO: How did you start working as a yardero en la yardas?

DON RAUL: Well, I first arrived in 1992. Let me tell you, Sergio, I came here . . . [pause] without a pair of shoes. When I arrived, a cousin gave me a couple of pairs, and as soon as my cousin gave me money after having worked cutting grass for a week, I went to buy a pair of boots. I continued working with my cousin, from the Mendez family, for almost three years. I am telling you we would work from sunup to sundown, *no parabamos* [we would not stop]. By the end of the day, my legs would hurt so much that I would go home, shower, eat, and fall asleep. And the next day, we did the same all over again.

SERGIO: Where did you arrive first? At this house on the East Side neighborhood?

DON RAUL: I first arrived at an apartment building near Ewing Avenue and the park [Calumet Park] by 98th and Ewing Avenue. We stayed there, my wife and kids [and I], for almost eight years. Then we moved to this house.

SERGIO: And have you worked all the time en las yardas?

DON RAUL: I worked with my cousin for the first three years, until I decided to go on my own one day. I began doing the lawn of only ten houses and went up to about thirty for the next three years or so. In the fourth year, I started going up, but only like ten houses per year. Now I have about a hundred clients, but the number varies yearly. One thing that I do differently than other yarderos is that I charge more than the regular price. In this way, with a few houses, I can obtain more income. Nowadays, some yarderos are doing the same work for much less money. That does not help us all.

SERGIO: How did you make ends meet with thirty houses to mow a month?

DON RAUL: I would work during the week with another guy from Huitzila, Don Carlos, and then do my houses during the weekend. I would also do deliveries for a Chinese restaurant located on 106th Street whenever I had the chance.

SERGIO: And what about during the winter?

DON RAUL: Well, the snow. I worked shoveling snow. I will ask them if they want me to come and remove the snow in the same houses I had for the summer to mow the lawn. It works for me since many are older and cannot shovel the snow out of their driveways. I charge them just like the regular lawn service. When it snows a lot, you must clear it every time it snows for the same price.

Don Raul continued recounting his difficulty when he began as a yardero. Sitting in his kitchen drinking coffee and holding a piece of *pan dulce* (Mexican pastry), Don Raul conversed about his struggles while starting his lawn-service company. For example, there were days when he did not receive any client phone calls to mow lawns. Don Raul was highly active in promoting himself and his company. One of the most common activities for a would-be yardero is designing and printing flyers, a one-page document with essential services, and contact information to distribute in the neighborhoods he would like to provide service in. For instance, Mexican migrants would order flyers from a small printing business and distribute them at people's homes by placing them on their door knobs or in their mailboxes. Don Raul tells me that he is continuously engaged in this marketing strategy to increase the size of his clientele. He would often take his two sons, Rogelio and Enrique, so distributing flyers door-to-door would not take much time. Today, like other yarderos, Don Raul returns to Zacatecas each year for a month at most. I asked Don Raul when he knew he had made it. He said that it dawned on him when he began to see more people calling and requesting his lawn service. Quite simply, he did not know. Don Raul said he started noticing a stable list of eighty clients about five or six years ago, in 2009. He said that with that number of clients, he could take care of the necessities for his family and have some income left for the winter season when he does not mow lawns but instead provides snow-shoveling service to his clients as described above.

Indeed, many Mexican migrants experience periods of unemployment that they combine with additional odd jobs. For instance, Christian Zlolniski documents the life of an interlocutor named Gustavo, a Mexican in Silicon Valley. To compensate for the limited and precarious opportunities, he "usually sold flowers in the streets and in nightclubs, combining this occupation with day jobs such as cleaning, gardening, truck loading, and unskilled construction work."[46] Indeed, "most households of the immigrant workers met in Santech were involved in informal income-generating activity to make ends meet."[47]

A good yardero knows another yardero's class status within the work hierarchy by asking the simple question, "How many houses do you have?" If a family member asks the question, the answer tends to be part of a normal conversation. But if the question comes from a nonkin yardero, often there is an implicit understanding that with this question, the yardero that asks it is attempting to locate the other yardero within an internal cultural and class hierarchy. Differences matter: even minor differences among yarderos enable class identification or disidentification from everyday labor struggles. Among yarderos, I most often saw an intense sense of class fractures as something that, in fact, happens.

Yardero apprenticeship	*Years of work experience*
Chalan (Extra help)	0–1 years
Trabajador (Full-time help)	1–3 years
Yardero (Independent yardero)	3–5 years
Patron (Full-time yardero; usually hires chalanes)	5 and above

Income potential dictates the amount of energy devoted to this work activity. For instance, when yarderos would tell me that they provide lawn services to about thirty houses, their monthly income would average $1,900 per month, as was the case with Cesar Sanchez and Don Raul Mendez when they entered the lawn service. However, this figure is not all net income. Doing the lawn service of about twenty-eight houses a week, I learned that a yardero would spend about $50 per week on gasoline for the Ford cargo van, lawn mower, blower, and line trimmer. That comes to about $200 per month, just for gas expenses. Also, a small company owner would often mow the lawns of these houses in two days, and as many yarderos do, eat at a fast-food restaurant such as McDonald's, spending around $56 per month just on food. Additional expenses include water and insurance for the van at $65. Thus, $1,900 would become $1,500 in monthly income for about thirty clients at the end of the month. Given the lawncare service sector structure, yarderos/as always fail to receive this entire amount in a lump sum at the end of the month. Some clients would send their lawn-service payment at the end of the month via regular mail, which often takes one week to arrive at the postal service station. Thus, the true monthly income of a yardero doing lawn service for thirty houses per month is $1,200 on average. A yardero will end up with 25 percent of their clients paying for the service two or three weeks behind. This work is frustrating for the yardero, who depends solely on this income to sustain their families.

In many ways, this entrepreneurism is a prime example of the neoliberal condition many working-class populations in the United States find themselves experiencing. Yarderos are not the exception. For example, Don Raul Mendez would often mention that he reached the point where he began to consider himself a full-time yardero when he could provide lawn services to about eighty clients. In terms of income, that means a yardero will make $5,200 per month on average. Again, this figure is elusive. About 20–25 percent of the clients do not pay on time or end up not paying at all, given that there are no written contracts between the Mexican landscaper/yardero and the individual who hires them. Thus, the actual net income obtained at the end of each month will be approximately $3,900. Likewise, as a yardero scales up, additional expenses also rise. I also saw that Mexican migrants tend to supplement their income through additional odd jobs on the side. As we know, the landscaping season is only eight months; therefore, the yearly salary of a yardero will end up being a net take-home income of $16,000. Then we must divide this amount over twelve months, and the final theoretical figure goes down to about $1,300 per month, or a salary of $325 per week. In theory, if you recall, the yardero is making the same amount of money as the chalan helping him do the work. However, the yardero needs to offer additional services to make a good living. Otherwise, many will find themselves without income saved for the winter season when it ends in November. Thus, the yardero will provide extra services to the clients whenever possible. These other economic activities may include fertilizing, bush trimming, planting flowers or trees, and cleaning gutters. This is where the actual additional net income can be collected.

As Don Raul and Cesar Sanchez told me on many occasions, few yarderos want only eighty clients; *muchos quieren muchas mas* (many want many more). This first significant profit threshold enables the yardero to scale up when serving one hundred clients or more. Typically, a crew of two workers—the boss and a chalan—work the entire week, except on Sundays, and can provide lawn service to two hundred clients. If a yardero increases the number of clients to more than two hundred, there is a risk of not increasing profit. If the work is not done with a crew of two workers, hiring another worker can potentially hinder the net profit after the means of production are covered. For example, Cesar Sanchez's company currently provides lawn services to about two hundred clients. While providing service to all his clients, there were times when I worked for him that he had to hire extra help to do the work effectively. By calculating total income minus means of production and labor, two hundred clients will leave Cesar with an income of $10,300 per month. This is an elusive number if we get into the details and literally "follow the money."

When a yardero/a scales up, they also must scale up in equipment. Insurance costs for the pickup truck and hauling trailer come to about $150 per month. Gas expenses add up to about $500 per month. On-the-job food and water consumption come to something near $400 a month. Here you must add the additional cost in terms of labor. A permanent worker's salary will come to about $2,000 per month, plus extra help for two days at about $160. Thus, adding the means of production and labor costs, the net profit for the patron (boss) will be about $6,590 a month. Suppose we multiply this by eight months, which equals $52,700 for the season. Keep in mind that this is only for eight months of the year, and since many yarderos do not work during winter, you must divide this amount by twelve months. That brings his salary to $1,647 per week.

However, let us consider that *el patron* (the boss) starts work well before picking up the workers and dropping them off. The owner will work around sixty to seventy hours in a typical week. Thus, an actual value income calculation will average twenty-two to thirty dollars per hour for the small company owner. The question becomes, Is it worth it? The answer is a definitive yes for many of my Mexican migrant collaborators. However, let us remember that it is hard to say whether they have other options, as the structural constraints they find themselves in do not allow them to escape their class positions from one day to the next.

MEXICAN WORK ETHIC

Much will be lost in translation if this hierarchical presentation of a yardero's work structure and cultural development is left as it stands in the structural realm only. Becoming a largescale yardero takes time, effort, and a work ethic not easily found, even within the Mexican population. Based on the time I worked for Don Antonio, I learned the work ethic instilled in the worker was actively cultivated. For example, the issue of time was very central. Not a single day would Don Antonio wake up late during the landscaping season to prepare for work. He expected the same kind of commitment from his workers. For instance, if it rains, many yarderos wait until the rain stops and then pick up their workers afterward. In the case of Don Antonio, this was not an option—if he had work, he would expect you to be ready whenever he came to pick you up. This approach toward time management is not always intensely instilled in other landscape business workers.

In his study of jornaleros in Berkeley, California, Juan Thomas Ordóñez discusses the type of work ethic among day laborers and the "moral economy" produced among these migrants. Ordóñez problematizes this term, which recently has come to be understood as a type of paternalistic reciprocity, on the one hand, and an elegant term to label forms of cooperation, organization, and mutual support, on the other.[48] In this context of precarious neoliberal conditions for day laborers, Ordóñez documents a moral economy that developed among the workers that would hang out at la parada as they sought employment. Guided by certain ethics of comportment, they would share one another's opportunities for work, challenge one another to ethically respond to carry out the work, and be *humilde* (humble) so as not to be excluded from circles of cooperation.[49] Among the yarderos I talked to, I felt a deep commitment to carrying out my work tasks diligently when I worked with Cesar and Don Antonio. Otherwise, if you were not *humilde*, or even grateful for the opportunity, you risked being labeled as a lazy (*huevon*), which is another cultural metaphor also used to dominate working-class populations and communities of color historically in Mexico or the United States.[50]

Indeed, a key to becoming a well-known yardero, according to my interlocutors, was approaching the work seriously. For example, the system utilized by Cesar Sanchez and Don Antonio was to mow the lawn every week and *wirear* (edge) every other week. There were weeks when the grass would not grow—especially in April, October, and late July. Sometimes we would pass a house that seemed like the grass had just been mowed, even though it was done a week ago. Some yarderas/os would be tempted to skip the house and move on to the next. Don Antonio does not like to do that. If Don Antonio got behind schedule because of rain, an equipment malfunction, or a personal problem, he provided consistent service to all his clients. This work ethic contrasts a bit with Don Raul Mendez's approach. For example, if it rained, Don Raul would skip all his clients for the day and not mow until the following week.

Don Antonio was extremely strict in the way he approached ending the workday. We quickly learned that the end of the day came when Don Antonio told us to load the lawn mower into the cargo van—otherwise, we would continue mowing. During June, there were days when we stayed after six in the evening and did additional jobs, such as bush trimming. We all knew that we were working past the regular hours, but we also knew that if we were to say anything or question why we were working past six in the evening, the boss would not say anything. Instead, he would let you go and hire someone else within a couple of days.

There are very few cases in which a chalan who has worked for many years mowing lawns transfers to another work activity. One of the sons of Raul Mendez is Enrique. He is tall and skinny with thick eyebrows and pale skin. Enrique began working as a yardero with his father's lawncare company, where he learned the basics of mowing, edging, and trimming bushes. I met Enrique in the summer of 2009. He was younger, only seventeen years old, and attended one of the City Colleges of Chicago. In 2010 Enrique transferred to the University of Illinois at Chicago to study architecture and graduated in 2012. Even as a college student, as soon as his studies ended in the middle of May, he would start working with a lawncare company with whom his father had contacts. Enrique worked all summer mowing grass, and in the last year before graduating, he became the driver for the company for which he was working. I met him at a nearby fast-food restaurant in an East Side neighborhood, and we talked about his expectations after graduating from college.

SERGIO: Are you still working with the boss from last year?

ENRIQUE: Simon [yes, of course].

SERGIO: How is it going?

ENRIQUE: It is fine—he has me driving the route. He has two routes, and I take care of one.

SERGIO: Who do you have working with you?

ENRIQUE: This week the owner's daughter is helping me mow the houses.

SERGIO: How? You mean you have a chalana?

ENRIQUE: I guess so. But she is still the boss's daughter.

SERGIO: Well, as long as she helps you? Does she?[51]

ENRIQUE: Well, she only mows with the standing lawn mower. You know, the one that you mow while standing. She also uses the blower when I have not finished edging the houses.

SERGIO: Do you find it challenging to work alongside her?

ENRIQUE: Not really.

SERGIO: What are your plans after graduating from the University of Illinois at Chicago

ENRIQUE: I do not know. *Tu sabes* [You know], *no seguro, no trabajo* [no social security, no job]. . . . I am applying for a temporary work permit to get a driver's license, but I am not sure how long.

Not long after I had this conversation with Enrique, he applied for the Deferred Action for Childhood Arrivals (DACA). He could get his permit, social security number, and driver's license by July 2013. Later, in June, he texted me and told me that he had an interview with a company from Lombard, Illinois, that wanted him to perform some architectural-related work. Enrique got the job in the last week of August and started working full time with health insurance benefits.

Conclusion

In this chapter, we have seen the underlying class structure and form of the yardero activity. As we followed these men in practical terms by discussing how they became yard workers, we saw that ethnography is central to observing other cultures and telling their migration stories. The significant difference between myself and the men I spent time with is that I could easily refuse to continue working as a yardero. Given my privileged status, I could escape las yardas anytime I wanted; they could not. Still, despite this academic privilege, I gained a deeper understanding of the lawncare economy, class relations, and varied cultural forms.

Don Antonio's lawncare company has been built on constant, dedicated, hard labor for twenty-eight years. When examined diachronically over an extended period, Don Antonio's story shows that yarderos adjust their service according to client's demands and that clients adapt themselves to the social and cultural condition of yarderos. For example, as observed, for Don Antonio, *tu palabra* (your word) had the value of gold, sometimes even more than any legal enforcing agreement. Those who worked for him ensured they never missed a day. Missing a day would be unacceptable. Work ethic within a moral economy of reciprocity is the crystallization of proper cultural behavior and the masculine expectations explored later in the book. Likewise, *la palabra* encompasses a cross-culturally functional relation to yarderos and their clients. If Don Antonio or Cesar said they were planning to do a job at a specific date and time in a client's home, they fulfilled their promise and arrived at the expected time. In this sense, work ethic added value—that is, a Mexican value, in capitalist terms—to the service offered to clients.

Indeed, we have also ethnographically captured the "normal" working routines in the lawncare service. Beyond the actual work practices, work itself is fundamental to social and class relations that emerge among yarderos. Thus, the elasticity of the "normal" working day becomes a product of the class relation between the yardero/a and the chalanes that is, in fact, expressed in the actual work activities and cultural relations they both form. While the two companies examined in this chapter did not necessarily force their workers to stay longer hours, chalanes sometimes resisted, thus slowing the production toward the end of the day. A worker might walk slower or take additional time to unload the equipment. On the other hand, if we follow the chalan beyond the regular working hours, we will inevitably conclude that the entire day is composed of the workday. While we can articulate the intricacies of exploiting capital in the working class's lives, the yardero/a and the chalan/a do not always necessarily experience it as an exploitative regime of domination all the time. Sometimes, though, working hard every day and week is a way to get ahead in life, to get closer to a better life in the north, and to reproduce their ways of life in the United States, thereby reproducing the same structures of exploitation. These are the contradictions left unresolved in a capitalist system full of traps that tell us that to get ahead in life, we must work even harder, even when the system does not allow us to live a decent life.

Once in the United States, escalating through the inner class hierarchy is seen as a process that takes time, effort, and cultural work. It is a process of constant cultural reproduction as a working-class subject. But before yarderos become adept at navigating the class hierarchies in the migration process, we should look at how gender identity is also a central cultural aspect of how they see themselves as Mexican workers. Thus, in the next chapter we will consider how ideas about the market influence the performance of these gender identities as part of the larger structural forces of capitalism. In other words, as they manage to become yarderos, they must also figure out how to reproduce their sense of men as men. After all, being a man still matters, and gender differences matter as well for these Mexican yarderos/as.

CHAPTER 2

Dispossessed Masculinity

The Market and the Cultural Production of Migrant Mexican Men

> In the construction of our own ethnographic narratives, we are inevitably faced with the problem of rhetorically managing what we are pleased to call "the data." How much is enough so as to persuade and not bore or overwhelm? And, where do we place it in the structural development of our own text? What is the proper relationship between the data and our interpretive analysis?
>
> —José E. Limón, *Dancing with the Devil*

> There are but a few of the numerous men and women whose lives may at first glance appear too mundane to merit attention but in whose everyday activities, if we look closely, we may glimpse the creative efforts of people coping with the gender relations they have inherited from past generations while simultaneously striving to fashion new approaches as best as they can.
>
> —Matthew C. Gutmann, *Meanings of Macho*

Ignacio "Beto" Quintanilla was a well-known Mexican singer who sang *corridos* (folk ballads) for more than twenty years in Monterrey, Nuevo Leon, and other cities and small towns of northern Mexico. Quintanilla wore a mustache, a cowboy hat, and boots while performing to symbolize his ranch lifestyle. Known as "El Mero Leon del Corrido" (The One and Only Lion of the Folk Ballad), Quintanilla sang about violence, love, courage, and working-class life in the US-Mexico borderlands.[1] Telling tales that are set along the Texas-Tamaulipas border or in cities such as Matamoros, Monterrey, Ciudad Juarez, and

Chihuahua, Quintanilla's songs include "El Deportado" (The Deported), "El Calabozo" (The Dungeon), and "El Sapo" (The Toad). In March 2007 Quintanilla passed away from a heart attack, but his corridos still play in ballrooms along the US-Mexico border and beyond.

While performing corridos, Quintanilla's style was rustic and flamboyant, and he constantly challenged death, or *La Santa Muerte* (Saint of Death). In his lyrics, masculinity becomes one of the central themes that allows his music to touch on the role of Mexican men in the market and in capitalist consumption. In this global context, however, notions of masculinity linked to acquiring particular types of goods are not limited to Mexican immigrants.[2] Car brands such as Chevy and Ford have long marketed their models using imagery of cowboy life, emphasizing the freedom that can be achieved by purchasing one of their vehicles. An example of the so called "crisis of masculinity" can be found in the Super Bowl XLIV ad in 2010 announcing the Dodge Charger. The commercial, titled "Man's Last Stand," portrays the car not as "a mode of transportation but as a lifestyle choice and last defense against manhood."[3] The genre of *narcocorridos,* on the other hand, emerged out of a long history of folktales and Spanish romances, which are central in later narratives of the Mexican Revolution, narco traffickers, and manhood, especially in the 1980s.[4] These are the folk narratives of Quintanilla and many others along the US-Mexico border region.

Quintanilla is part of a lineage of Mexican folk singers that includes Miguel and Miguel, Lorenzo de Monteclaro, Los Baron de Apodaca, and Los Cadetes de Linares. These songs are often enjoyed over carne asadas (a barbecue-style gathering).[5] In most of Quintanilla's songs, a border subject or bandit heroically challenges society's norms, much in the way that Americo Paredes described it in his book *With His Pistol in His Hand* (1958) discussing the context of South Texas. Eventually, this bandit fights the state apparatus to legitimize his illegal activity and perceived deviance. Mr. Quintanilla's heroes are often the small-town individuals involved in the narco economy. These subjects eventually rise to become bosses of the cartels and oversee largescale businesses. Indeed, Mr. Quintanillas's characters often resemble other historic legends, such as Gregorio Cortez.[6]

For example, the lyrics in the song "El Camaro" tell the story of a Mexican father who buys a Chevy Camaro for his son so that he can become an authentic Mexican man. The song, however, also portrays driving a brand-new car as the ultimate expression of having made it as a man. The details described include the shine of the paint, the soft touch of the new leather seats, Los Cadetes de Linares blasting from the speakers, and the smell of newness that sparks the imagination about what you can do as a man. As the lyrics further explain, the father is unaware that he is buying the gift of death because his son will eventually get into a fatal accident. The song also warns fathers not to accelerate their children's development. Its themes draw a clear link between masculinity and how it is fulfilled by purchasing a car that draws respect from others. Again, it warns what can happen if one pursues such a model of masculinity.

In this chapter, I argue that among the Mexican migrants in South Chicago, the desire to be seen as a man and feel like a man intensifies cultural notions of gender and masculinity, which both empowers and disempowers men through their actual (at times apparent) possession of material goods. Thus, let us begin by demystifying ideas of "the market" and how cultures of capitalism are developed through gender normativity or heterosexual conceptions of masculinity. Regarding the lives of yarderos, the ethnographic evidence suggests that while dispossession is pervasive, the performance of gender identities is central to their way of life in South Chicago. Sometimes it is a way for these men to feel that the world makes sense.

Thus, to explore Mexican masculinity among yarderos, the first section of this chapter deconstructs our idea about the market and engages with how las yardas as a mode of production generates market-driven ideas about masculinity for yarderos. This section discusses how the neoliberal turn in Mexico—and its subsequent effects on Mexican migration—at times allows Mexican men to explore their gender subjectivity while at other times constraining them to perform specific masculine identities based on dispossession and ideals about how the comportment and performance of migrant men is expected in their transborder lives. The second section of the chapter descends into the ethnographic spaces in South Chicago and surrounding neighborhoods to document events among Mexican yarderos that manifest ways in which masculinity works. Often yarderos tease each other by boasting who is a better landscaper and, by extension, a better man. In this section, I further analyze the ways in which material dispossession through the act of possession is interconnected with the performing of their masculine roles as yarderos and this game of possession that leaves yarderos with few options to maneuver. The chapter concludes by recognizing this multilayered gender subjectivity through what I term "dispossessed masculinity" as it produces specific Mexican masculine identifications, and dangerous behaviors and fulfills market-driven logics rather than alternative or egalitarian ways of being and becoming a Mexican man.

The Market

The relations between gender subjectivity and how market forces reproduce suggest that these categories are not a priori cultural notions. These sociocultural categories are rather created by and emerge through engagements with the market in an ideological and material sense. In other words, gender takes cultural work, requiring both symbolic ideas and material ones to exist and to dialectically influence and produce each other. Understood within the ethnographic context of las yardas, Mexican masculinity emerges as men interact with the market, including the mode of production—las yardas—and spheres of social interaction beyond it. We can, for the moment, consider Mexican masculinity as a process that is continually performed.[7] In the context of yarderos in Chicago, I argue, these gender processes take place through the acquisition of material goods and the performance of gender norms in relation to the market economy.

Theories about the market navigate within the range of perception of and about human nature. For example, as explained by Marion Fourcade and Kieran Healy in their essay "Moral Views of Market Society," the *doux commerce* thesis held "that market relations made people cordial and less inclined to fight one another for most of the eighteenth century."[8] This view has a long history in economic theory, including the following claim: "It is not from the benevolence of the butcher, the brewer, or the baker that we expect our dinner, but from their regard to their own self-interest. We address ourselves, not to their humanity but their selflove."[9] At other times, the market is represented as a place where creative and liberating forces act in harmony. The market's wisdom arises through the competition among various actors battling out of self-interest, slowly moving toward better solutions. This view tends to favor the relation between the market and the protection of individuals as consumers; in other words, it is by buying goods that your identity acquired cultural relevance in society. The story goes that the empowerment of the market enables individuals to empower themselves and links them as actors of desires, emotions, and individual investments. It is a market that pushes individuals to compete selfishly and to consume. Further, in regard to the competitive nature of capitalism, this second view suggests the following:

> [Capitalism] pushes individuals, even those with little money, to consume wastefully as means to acquire honor and reputability. . . . This drive for conspicuous consumption, in turn, has a profoundly degrading effect on individual judgment and conduct. It transforms the canon of ethics, aesthetic taste, and the sense of devotion by replacing them with general respect for wealth . . . [and] expense.[10]

While it is easier to critique the perils of capitalism in the potentially harmful production of gender subjectivities, this chapter aims to elaborate, examine, and discuss how the possession of goods may disempower Mexican migrants through specific gender meanings linked to the post-1980 logic of neoliberalism. Indeed, although there may be no emic discourse of neoliberalism at the worker's level, even more, they may not call their cultural practices "neoliberal"; the workers objectively experience the market's transformation in neoliberal terms. To be more precise, they understand and experience these conditions as *el jale* (labor work) and las yardas and develop their gender ideologies, discourses, and practices to make sense of the world in gender terms, not in terms of neoliberalism as it is academically understood. Gender dispossessions, as used here, speak to the tensions between gender performativity—or displays of Mexican masculine behavior—and the intimate ways that capital uses gender to exploit these men who work as yarderos.

In traditional agricultural societies, dispossession and land ownership are used as explanatory frameworks to capture the relations that make specific populations landless and thus dispossessed of their means of production; that is, for the purposes of analysis here, it is the social condition in which we find many Mexican men who must travel north to gain their subsistence after becoming landless due to structural reforms in the 1980s in Mexico. As explained by Julia Elyachar, the concept of primitive accumulation as elaborated by Marx refers to "the state's use of direct force to evict peasants from their land and separate them from ownership of their means of production."[11] Indeed, one of the most critical developments in the history of capitalism is the creation of a large contingency and supply of workers to be used by the capitalist at any time. In other words, dispossessing folks of their land forces their modes of production to change. Now, as landless peasants, they must be the principal agents of a wage economy and, in many cases, must migrate to seek subsistence. To make a living, peasants now must sell the only thing they have: their labor. In simple terms, when folks are dispossessed of their only means to generate the goods, they consume in their everyday lives, they have to find ways to reproduce themselves. As the previous chapter highlighted, becoming yarderos is one way to manifest these processes among these Mexican workers. In this classical dispossessed scenario, for example, this means that the landless peasant, by engaging in a wage economy, earns money to buy items that he would not have consumed had his land not been taken from him.[12] While this may be a theoretical exercise, the applicability of dispossession theories makes sense in different historical and contemporary contexts. For example, in 1994, the North American Free Trade Agreement (NAFTA) was signed by the United States, Mexico, and Canada. The idea was to open the markets for investment between the three nations. The Mexican market would fully open its borders to multinational corporations from the United States to invest in the agricultural, manufacturing, and service sectors. Among the many political leaders and the economic elite who lauded the agreement, US president Bill Clinton declared, "We have to create a new world economy. . . . This is our opportunity to provide an impetus to freedom and democracy in Latin America and create new jobs for Americans. It is a good deal, and we ought to take it."[13]

Indeed, the necessity to engage in free trade had been promoted for more than a decade before NAFTA was signed. Carlos Salinas de Gortari gained power in 1988 after a disputed election, and the reaching of this economic agreement became a central policy direction for the Mexican state distinct from previous economic frameworks. Until the mid-1980s, most of the Mexican economy had been based on agricultural products and the export of primary goods. When NAFTA became institutionalized, many small landowners lost their land because they had borrowed money to compete with multinational corporations and placed their land as collateral. On top of this, in 1991 Salinas de Gortari reformed Article 27 of the Mexican Constitution such that the land long held by communal, rural communities was to be sold, and multinational corporations bought large properties, taking up the land of indebted property owners.[14] For many dispossessed Mexicans, the most viable option was migrating to the United States.

By the early 1990s in the United States, Mexican migrants and US-Latina/o groups had become a significant presence in the informal economy in the United States.[15] Scholars suggest that the informal economy represents an essential source of employment for Mexican migrants and is vital to the survival of these working-class families. Thus, in many ways Mexican migrants have been central players in Fordism's shift to decreased formalization of the US economy, focusing on third world immigrants' survival strategies in cities such as New York and Los Angeles.[16] As aptly argued, the informal economy supplies goods in low-income neighborhoods, fulfilling a critical function unmet by the formal economy. This point has already been made by Christian Zlolniski's work on the informal sector in Silicon Valley. Similarly, the informal economy is a form of entrepreneurship for immigrants who have been left out of the formal market.[17] Indeed, most scholars agree that the informal economy, of which we still have an obscure view, despite the increasing number of studies, represents an essential source of employment for migrant workers.[18] The landscaping or las yardas economy in Chicago likewise comprises formal and informal sectors in which Mexican men and women participate to make a living.

Chicago also experienced an influx of migrants from Mexico in the mid-1990s. Many became workers in the service industry, restaurants, construction, manufacturing, and landscaping. Historically, much of the Mexican migration to the United States has been composed of males, especially in the early 1920s.[19] In this urban space, gender is actively mobilized and performed among market forces that operate within a dualist system or heteronormative frame. In other words, performing gender subjectivity is emotionally fulfilling and produces pleasure; however, carrying out these gender performances in the long term may not benefit people economically, culturally, or politically. Thus, how Mexican yarderos become men and understand themselves as males in relation to their work is a central component of their gender subjectivity. If gender matters, then masculinity matters.[20]

Latino Masculinity

Theorizations of Latinx masculinities invite us to venture into areas of gender stereotypes, thick descriptions of working-class behaviors, and localized expressions of being a male. Recent anthropological and sociological approaches to studying Mexican men as men highlight the current dearth of representations that allow for a straightforward reading of gender identification and its cultural significance within the context of nationalism. Some studies on Mexican masculinity interrogate the macho stereotype. The term *macho* has a complicated terrain, history, and cultural formation.[21] Matthew Gutmann mentions that contemporary Mexican men see themselves *ni macho, ni mandilon* (neither macho nor apron-wearing); they do not practice the harsher behaviors associated with being macho, nor are they entirely submissive to their wives or female partners. Others have commented that ranchero masculinity dominates portrayals of Latino men among immigrant groups. An excellent analysis of this "ranch" metaphor is found in the work of Alex Chávez, who theorizes the "rancho chronotrope"—that is, a metaphor that has come to form a central organizing mechanism in the lives of Mexican men and women in the United States, especially within the context of migration.[22] For instance, the ranch chronotrope relies heavily on nationalistic ideas from country living, which many migrants seek when relocating to the Midwest or the Latino South. Sujey Vega, for example, in her work on Latino Hoosiers in Indiana, further elaborates on this as being one of the reasons why some of her interlocutors enjoy the rural life that places like central Indiana offer.[23] Other scholarship by Chicano scholars has challenged stereotypical portrayals of Mexican men that have heavily influenced cultural understanding of Mexican masculinity. For instance, José Limón documented how *vatos* (young men) engage in behaviors to develop *communitas* (a sense of community), given the structural constraints around many Mexican and Mexican Americans vis-à-vis Anglo capitalist structures in

South Texas.[24] I agree with the previous analysis; as we know, workplaces tend to be key places where Mexican manhood and masculinities obtain cultural meaning. At work, gender identities and displays are constructed, affirmed, challenged, and negotiated.[25]

Following the work of Robert Connell, Mexican yarderos also practice active forms of masculinity.[26] For example, Hernan Ramirez theorizes what he terms *jardinero masculinity,* a type of masculinity where danger and dirtiness are features of *jardineria* (gardening) work in Los Angeles.[27] According to Ramirez, this theorization offers a nuanced understanding of how being a man, carrying out hard work, and performing *chingaderas* (making a mess out of ordinary activities) expand our knowledge of working-class life among these men. Jardinero masculinity also questions the homosocial dangers of performing *relajo* (behaving with a lack of seriousness), posturing, and the kind of macho behavior that is damaging for these men in the same way that Juan Thomas Ordóñez found it to be among jornaleros in Berkeley, California.[28] As further discussed by Ramirez, this type of masculine identity offers us a glimpse into how jardineros construct, affirm, and challenge masculine identifications through their work routines.

In the context of Chicago for Mexican yarderos, gardening or landscaping is not associated with the Spanish noun *jardinero,* even though that is the literal translation. For my interlocutors, *yardeando* or working *en las yardas,* are more appropriate emic descriptions of their work activities. Yet there is a short but distinctive and different theoretical, practical, and metaphorical distance between what Ramirez calls "jardinero masculinity" and what I term "dispossessed masculinity." My term calls attention to other damaging behaviors among Mexican men in Chicago. It emphasizes the structural conditions that shape the type of masculine behaviors I see occurring among yarderos. It also calls attention to interclass masculine behaviors by focusing on the capitalist structural forms that leave Mexican men disempowered. It calls attention to an aesthetics beyond dirt and hard work. In short, as my interlocutors understand their working-class subject formation, they do not consider themselves jardineros but yarderos. This difference, I argue, calls for dispossessed masculinity as a more accurate framework to understand the lives of Mexican migrant men who mow lawns for a living in South Chicago. The following ethnographic vignettes offer an elaboration and expose the theoretical relevance of the ways in which I see dispossessed masculinity taking place among yarderos of South Chicago as well as how they manage to challenge these structures through their own individual actions and collective imagining as working-class men.

Pablo

In late 2012 I met Pablo Garcia, a Mexican migrant from the state of Zacatecas. At five foot six, Pablo is well known for using short figures of speech in a playful way that is endearing. In 2005 he was diagnosed with diabetes and since then has struggled to work as a full-time yardero. He loves his hometown of Tlatenango and made sure to travel there each year at the end of landscaping season before returning to the United States in early March for the next work season. Having arrived in the United States when he was young, Pablo attended high school in South Chicago in the late 1980s and for his entire life participated in the informal economy as a yardero. When I discussed the idea of an interview, he initially resisted. But then, in early June 2013, he asked me to spend a day with him while he mowed his houses. It was a way for me to talk with him, but he also wanted extra help. I said yes. A week later, he asked again. He picked me up in a white cargo van, and we began mowing in South Chicago.

While we mowed lawns, Pablo told me that in 2006 he lost his left leg due to an infection he had neglected to take care of. While moving from house to house, he told me that he wanted to earn enough to return to Mexico and marry his girlfriend. While we ate lunch in the van, usually McDonald's, Pablo shared his longing to return to Mexico for good. Being inquisitive, I asked, "Why don't you just go?" Pablo paused, chuckled, then got serious and replied, "*No, te imaginas . . . dirian todos que soy un perdedor, que no la hize como en los Estados Unidos*" (No, can you imagine . . . everyone would say that I am a loser, that I did not make it in the United States). This was a powerful statement on how working-class masculinity organizes not only past decisions to migrate to the United States but also decisions about the future and how, in many ways, working-class masculinity reproduces the class relations in which young men—in this case Pablo—find themselves in las yardas. Let me explain.

The yarderos I talked to widely rejected the idea of returning to Mexico permanently, whether voluntarily or via deportation. A few scholars have nonetheless started documenting the effects of deportation on Mexican immigrants, especially those who are undocumented and a part of the "1.5 generation," a term that often denotes migrants that came to the United States at an early age. For example, on her study of busboys who migrate from the Bajio region (Jalisco, Michoacan, Zacatecas, and Guanajuato states) to Chicago, Illinois, Ruth Gomberg-Muñoz writes that some do go back to Mexico but encounter a difficult and challenging return. Indeed, in discussing the story of Alejandro, a Mexican who eventually traveled to the United States to work in the service industry, Ruth Gomberg-Muñoz recounts that Alejandro told her "I had a job in Mexico making shoe boxes. With that job you can buy food for your kids, but if you want to go to the park or something you have to think. . . . You always live day to day, with just enough to pay your household bills."[29] Given the degree of economic dispossession, Alejandro decides to travel to the United States wanting to "buy something, a little business." He says, "[I want this] just so we have something." Every time he returns to Mexico, he finds himself needing to return to the United States for a slightly longer period.[30] Thus, every time he migrates, he becomes a bit dispossessed of the love of his family by having to be away and work as a busboy in Chicago.

Furthermore, for example, Jill Anderson writes that young people have capitalized on their English fluency and are finding jobs "at the transnational call centers alongside near-native English speakers who were deported after incarceration."[31] For young people, the cultural effect of experiencing deportation is the formation of what Anderson calls a "semantic place(lessness)"—that is, a paradox as a "place where meaning collapses."[32] The participants' productive dialogue that Jill Anderson describes says that, despite being criminalized in the United States and then in Mexico, the familiar cultural spaces of what linguistics would refer to as "language-speaking communities" provide support for those who have been deported despite the apparent traumatic dislocation of being in forced displacement. Focusing on transnational undocumented migrants and their gender and family relations has provided a productive ground for examining policy as a restrictive mechanism of social and political control.[33] After 2016, due to the Trump Administration's "zero-tolerance" policy, the focus slowly shifted to renew a commitment to criminal immigration enforcement against both attempted illegal entry and illegal entry into the United States by an alien. The voices of those who return rarely come to light. Accounts of displacement show how people turn suffering and profound loss into resilience and flexibility, despite the chaos that impacts undocumented Mexicans as they return.[34] In many ways, undocumented migrants continue to define themselves primarily as *hombres de trabajo* (working-class folks) and not as "bad hombres." Despite efforts to follow a strict work ethic, the market also consumes the work life of many migrants.

As we completed the day, Pablo recalled struggles when friends frequently joked about his missing leg, suggesting that he is less of a male and that it inhibits his ability to have an intimate relationship. Despite these difficulties, he plans to marry his longtime girlfriend and return to Mexico to fulfill his dreams. Thus, we can imagine here, for a moment, that dispossession not only takes place as a material condition but also concerning love as a cultural practice and sentiment.

Vamos al Russo

In the last two weeks of February, before the landscaping season begins, yarderos spend afternoons in the garages where their equipment has been housed for the winter. There they fix their lawn mowers and other power equipment, organize supplies, and prepare to start the new season in full swing. After fixing whatever needs to be fixed and getting their trucks and utility trailers in order, a yearly question is asked: *Cuando vamos al Russo* (When are we going to the Russo)? One morning in early March 2013, Cesar Sanchez woke up early to travel to a landscaping supply center known as El Russo, in the Schiller Park neighborhood of northern Chicago. Officially called Russo Power Equipment, the company started around 1970. From the parking lot, it looks like a small one-story building. Inside, however, the amount of power equipment for sale is hard to believe. This location offers everything needed to upgrade or replenish one's supply of lawn mowers, line trimmers, bush trimmers, fertilizer, weed control, and grass removers. As its website states, the supply store began on the northwest side and has grown into the premier supplier of power equipment and landscaping supplies in the Midwest.[35] The store maintains a robust product line of major vendors such as Bobcat, Echo, Honda, Kawasaki, and Stihl. In most cases, landscapers ride a yellow or orange stand-on lawn mower. If it is yellow, it is likely a Stander B Standon mower (thirty-two inches). These are considered entry-level commercial mowers. Once a yardero reaches the one-hundred-client mark, as discussed in the previous chapter, they go to El Russo to finance one or buy one with cash.

From the perspective of a yardero, buying your first Stander (thirty-two or forty-eight inch) is a milestone and a material representation of having made it, of making it as a man. In the many conversations I had with my interlocutors, this lawn mower emerged as a specter of class mobility as well. The details of when and how one could obtain this type of lawn mower would be discussed at lunch or on the ride home. For example, Cesar Sanchez spent a year saving for his. He told me that he would charge clients extra whenever possible and ensure that this additional income remained untouched despite the financial constraints that the winter months would bring.

In 2013 Cesar bought a thirty-two-inch Stander B at the start of the season. It did the job twice as fast as his walk-behind mower and required little maintenance. The only problem was that, with such intense vibration, at the end of each day, even when he was sitting in his living room, Cesar still felt tingling in his extremities as if he were standing on it. Moreover, he was the only one able to handle it. But having a lawn mower that would do the work twice as fast meant that he would now acquire even more jobs to help pay for the lawn mower. This is an example of how possessing an item such as a high-end piece of commercial equipment both empowers Cesar and dispossesses him of his time and income in fundamental ways. Cesar Sanchez was one of the many Mexican yarderos who I would see using, purchasing, and acquiring this type of power equipment. Meanwhile, he worked all day from sunup to sundown to pay for it by completing additional contracts.

At higher levels of this economic hybrid collectif, Russo Power Equipment has become a company with around $7 million in net worth annual revenue. In 2015 there were discussions about opening a new location in Elgin, Illinois. This new location would create forty to sixty jobs and generate city tax revenue roughly equivalent to that of a local car dealership.[36] According to the newspaper reports, by the end of its fourth year in operation, it is expected to generate a revenue of around $10 million.[37] At the back end of this economic hybrid collectif, the countless yarderos will continue to purchase their power equipment to find a better life in the north. As I authored this book, Russo Power bought the Elgin location and was operating. Certainly, it will only be a matter of time before more and more Mexican immigrants stop by to purchase equipment and become yarderos and, in the process, become dispossessed materially.

El Numero Uno

In late 2012 I met Julio Gonzales, who owned a small company that would hire two or three employees during the summer's busiest months. Julio grew up in Chicago and attended George Washington High School in Chicago's East Side. However, he did not finish the four years and decided from an early age to dedicate himself to becoming a full-time yardero, like his father, Don Ernesto, who had migrated to Chicago in the early 1980s. He was born in Hidalgo, Mexico, and his wife, Dona Maria, was also from that area. They have three sons. They are not the typical transnational family that travels to Mexico every year, but the phrase "long-distance nationalism" applies in this case; such a view involves "a set of identity claims and practices that connect people living in various geographic locations to a specific territory that they see as their ancestral home."[38]

Julio asked me to help him mow. Seeing an opportunity to expand my number of interlocutors, I called to work for him one Saturday in July 2012. We had just finished planting three tall trees at an apartment complex on the West Side of Chicago when Julio's brother Roberto stopped by to chat. Like Julio, Roberto was born in Chicago. When they were little, they would help their father mow lawns after school. Now twenty-six years old, Roberto owns his own lawncare company. Roberto used kinship ties to become an entrepreneur, initially receiving a short route of houses to mow and growing his client list from there. Roberto is outspoken and continually switches between English and Spanish.

Frequently when we encountered other lawncare companies while driving around town, we would raise our hand in a quick greeting and continue on our way. This behavior did not occur, however, when we encountered other family members. When encountering a family member en las yardas, the practice is to stop, chat for a few minutes, and then move on with work. The cultural practice is to take time out of your workday to greet (*saludar*) someone properly. While this practice may seem insignificant, it in fact provides explicit recognition of Mexican masculinity when done as expected. When one yardero stops to greet another, the cultural value mobilized is respect. In other words, from that moment of social interaction emerges a class recognition that both family members and friends belong to or work in the same profession.

As family members, Julio and Roberto would often see each other and stop—talk for a few minutes while the *chalanes* waited in the truck. God forbid you should overlook another yardero in passing, especially if that yardero is a family member. Sometimes, I would hear of such instances when one family member encountered another around the neighborhood and did not stop to greet them. Instantly, rumors would arise regarding why he did not stop. Indeed, a greeting can be culturally relevant for many different groups or irrelevant cross-culturally. For example, among the Ilongots of the Philippines, when kin visit each other, no apparent social or personal recognition is given by the host or the visitor. Only after the visitor has settled in the host's residence and can rest does the host make initial contact.[39] But let us return to the Gonzales family.

The Gonzales family owns a spacious lot near 95th Street in South Chicago and runs a large landscaping company, but individual family members manage their own contracts with clients. These contracts are not enforced by law but through *la palabra* (by spoken agreement). When you mobilize your *palabra,* you put your manhood on the line, which speaks to your work ethic, as mentioned previously (chapter 1). To put it another way, to use your *palabra* is to use your manhood as a form of agreement, or in many other instances a form of credit.[40] The Gonzaleses' way of operating their business is not very different from how other small lawncare companies operate.

But to return Julio and Roberto's encounter, I noticed that Roberto drove a new Ford 450 that must have cost between $40,000 and $50,000, depending on the luxury options selected. As Julio's brother left the work area, I asked the price of the truck, hoping he would quote a range, but Julio responded, "It does not matter, the goal at the end of the year is to exchange it for the newest model, and we have it just to impress our clients." Although I accepted his statement, it took me a while to realize the tremendous effort they invested in developing a particular image among their clients. For Roberto and Julio, driving a big truck symbolized their ability to impress clients and denoted the health of their landscaping business. Julio elaborated, "Now, with our big trucks, [clients] think twice about talking shit to us. They see us as a real company, unlike those small landscapers just starting." Julio was referring to the landscapers or yarderos who often use, according to Julio, rudimentary materials such as twenty-one-inch lawn mowers and cheap blowers and string trimmers. Small landscapers start with trucks, not Ford 450s, vans, or old pickups. On the other hand, professional landscapers like Julio and Roberto, who have been in the business for almost twenty years (since their father first migrated to the States), use more sophisticated equipment. However, sophisticated equipment does not necessarily translate into a strong work ethic or a sense of manhood.

Empezando el Pobre

When I mowed for Don Antonio the next year, in 2013, we often cut grass in the Calumet Heights area. Given the high density of lawncare service workers in this area, big and small Mexican companies would pass by often, and many opportunities would arise to comment on other yarderos' work ethic and performance. If we saw a rusted pickup with a lawn mower and a line trimmer on the side, Don Antonio would say, "*Mira, apenas esta empezando el pobre.*" (Look, that poor little fellow is just beginning). At other times, when a large pickup passed with one or two stander lawn mowers, two or three blowers, and three line trimmers on the side, Don Antonio would exclaim, "*Mira, pa que tantos wiros, que un wiro para enfrente, otro para atras y el otro para que.*" (Look, why so many weedwackers? One weedwacker for the front, another for the back, and the other for what?) In the first instance, on seeing the rusty pickup with the old lawn mower, the phrase *el pobre* (poor little fellow) might seem condescending, depending on the tone that Don Antonio used. Often, though, it was said in admiration that this yardero would have the courage to start from nothing.

These interactions between workers were moments when yarderos would challenge each other and, in turn, try to find out who was the best man at the job and, by extension, in their business. For instance, during the summer when I worked with Don Antonio, I would often be sent with Gabriel to help mow his homes. Thirty-seven years old, standing at six foot five inches tall, Gabriel is particularly skilled at managing his lawncare service business. Gabriel first migrated to Chicago from the state of Zacatecas in his early twenties. He was studying in Mexico to become a physical education teacher. Knowing that a permanent position in Mexico's public education system is hard to find, though, he traveled, in the summer of 2000, to Chicago to work en las yardas with his father, Don Antonio. Now, ten years later, Gabriel is a full-time yardero in Chicago and has become an expert in the business.

On Wednesday afternoons, the only day I was sent to help him, we would mow around 87th Street and Stony Ashland Avenue. This area of Chicago is a mix of low-income, middle-class families living in apartment buildings ranging from two to six floors. This neighborhood is traditionally an African American residential neighborhood. Before beginning lawn service for about twenty houses in a two-block radius, we decided to grab a bite at Wendy's. Someone would usually run in and order for the crew, but this time we used the drive-through. It rarely happens that yarderos enter an establishment and dine inside for lunch. Reasons for this range from the way the work is organized, the particularities of the route, cultural perceptions of hygiene, and racialized perceptions of bodies within spaces of transgression. There is often not enough time to eat lunch with Don Antonio's son, Gabriel, so we would either eat in the truck or find a big tree near the sidewalk of a client's home and eat on the curb.

At first we parked in a spot that was not at all shaded. Given the scorching summer heat, the shade is a better place for lunch. Most of the time, any shaded area is about ten degrees cooler. As it happened, we were uncomfortable, so we moved closer to the end of the block. As we were relocating, however, a white pickup from Gonzalez Landscaping passed, and someone shouted in English, "We are the number one." Gabriel was visibly taken aback. In his more than fifteen years mowing in this area, no other yardero had dared to engage in such chingaderas.[41] As soon as they passed, Gabriel looked at me in disbelief, as if to laugh, but instead, in his classic style, spat out an expletive and said, *"Pues quien se cren estos?"* After muttering a few more words of disbelief, he continued, *"Que huevos para pasar y decir esas chingaderas?"* (Who do they think they are [. . .], what balls do they have to pass and say such *chingaderas*?) After ten or twenty seconds, we all laughed aloud. We felt challenged, mocked, and hurt. From then on, the phrase "the number one" became part of our banter and play within the crew. When we wanted to praise ourselves, we would mock the Gonzalez crew and suggest that we were "the number one." I often teased Gabriel by asking why he had remained silent, thus demasculinizing his reaction. He would laugh and say that "those took him by surprise." I would then say playfully, "*Ehh, ehh, te dijeron* number one" (ehh, ehh, they said number one to you), and we all would laugh.

Following John L. Jackson's suggestion of mobilizing the conceptual framework of "thinness" in ethnography, this interaction between two landscaping crews, while encompassing just a moment, carried deep symbolic significance for the crew. When the Gonzales crew suggested they were "the number one," it questioned the harmonious relations between Mexican landscapers, especially those related through kinship. Furthermore, suggesting that the Gonzales crew was "the number one" announced a challenge regarding which crew better exemplified the working-class *hombre*. If you are not number one, then you are number two, and a hierarchy is implied that can challenge gender ideas. If the Gonzales crew was the number one crew in mowing, then they, by the same cultural association were also "better men" and thus able to claim a class-based Mexican masculinity.

Gabriel had two options. First, he could find the Gonzales crew in the various areas where they often encountered each other during the week and directly ask Julio Gonzales why his crew had said what they said. This altercation would likely bring further animosity between the families. Or Gabriel could let it go and just laugh it off. In other words, given the structural constraints in which Gabriel and Julio found themselves en las yardas, he could turn that aggressive behavior into a sense of communitas, as José Limón suggests.[42] Gabriel would turn serious over the following week whenever I mentioned the "number one" event, but by the second week he began to laugh at our own *chingaderas* regarding the notion of being "number one."

La Troca

Contrary to the experience of many Mexican workers who migrate to the United States as undocumented, Agustin migrated in the early 2000s, after his father had finally obtained visas for his family. Agustin was born in Zacatecas, in Villa de Guadalupe, part of the town of Villanueva. Like Julio, he left high school to become a full-time yardero. He is twenty-two years old. Agustin works in the summer months, and if he stays in Chicago for the winter, he shovels snow. One evening after work, Agustin told me he wanted to buy a new truck. I asked whether he could afford monthly payments and insurance, considering that he is not married, as marital status affects the cost of insurance. Agustin told me he would have to work side jobs on Sundays to pay for the vehicle. For yarderos, a typical side job usually means working on a landscaping contract or doing construction or other skilled service. One afternoon as I was sitting on my front porch, a beige Chrysler Hemi pulled into my driveway. From behind the wheel, Agustin proudly invited me to cruise around Little Village. Visiting this

Mexican neighborhood in the summer is common for Mexican working-class folks *pa' pasarla* (to pass the day) and grab a bite in a traditionally decorated Mexican restaurant. It is also a chance to see members of the opposite sex and possibly socialize across the gender terrain as well. I later saw Agustin in April as he was preparing for the new season. He still needed to work Sundays to pay for his truck. Agustin later employed another Mexican worker on Sundays and doubled the number of houses he served in order to pay back the debt he had incurred with the new item.

Thus, we see that Mexican masculinity is reproduced through specific engagement with the market and the economies of dispossession that disempower or empower immigrant men. In the context of Chicago, Mexican immigrant men in the landscaping economy engage in specific gender performances. As my interlocutor Julio told me, it took him many years to be able to afford the latest vehicle models and $7,000 lawn mowers.[43] Indeed, as Julio made it clear, his mind was already set on increasing profits by acquiring better equipment and generating more efficient ways to carry out the daily work activities anticipated the next year. Typically, there is a marked difference within the internal dynamics of working-class yarderos between those with walk-behind mowers and those with stand-on mowers. The cost difference between the models ranges from $3,000 to $5,000. With stand-on mowers, the work is performed faster and in greater quantity. With a couple twenty-one-inch mowers, a crew of two can complete three to four properties per hour. The internal competition among workers of different companies is genuinely palpable when they encounter each other throughout the city.

This competition intensifies when workers meet on the same block or street in South Chicago. When, for example, two crews start mowing within one or two properties of each other, they often compete to finish first, potentially implying to the other crew that they are slow or lazy.[44] This intensifies when landscaping crews are small or when women work in their ranks. Seeing yarderas was not common in Chicago in the early 2010s; however, more recent stories that I have heard from follow-up interviews suggest that a small percentage of landscaping crews are entirely composed of Mexican women with the same duties as yarderos.

Indeed, in Chicago Mexican immigrants engage in economic behaviors by pursuing material goods to achieve the American dream. For example, when I asked Agustin why he wanted to go into debt by buying a $28,000 pickup, he did not see the purchase that way. For him, purchasing the truck was an improvement, representing the fulfillment of a desire he had worked hard to acquire. Among yarderos, risk-taking can be seen as an asset because those who achieve are seen as masculine models to emulate. As soon as they reach a goal, there is always another step, and the desire to increase their buying power compels them to incur more debt. But the more they purchase, the more manly they are perceived by their families and friends.

The market is not just an entity neatly mapped into cultural practices and everyday social interactions. When we envision the market with clear boundaries and characteristics, we lose sight of the fact that this entity comprises men and women interacting with one another through multiple cultural terrains. The market is, as a classic Marcel Mauss expression has already suggested, such a "total social fact" that, in my rendering, it touches every aspect of working-class Mexicans' lives. In this chapter, I highlighted how Mexican masculinity is produced and reproduced through practices of dispossession.

Indeed, the eighteenth-century *doux commerce* thesis, which argues that market relations make people less inclined to fight one another, suggests that there are varying degrees of politeness and hostility when people compete with one another, at least within capitalist relations among workers mowing lawns for a living. The other pervasive liberal assumption describes the market as a place of creative and liberating forces acting in harmony and is indeed a complicated theoretical claim to uphold. Small landscaping companies regularly engage one another on a macro level to fight for clients, contracts, and neighborhood business opportunities. At an individual level, Mexican immigrants engage in risk-taking through the possession of accounts with higher trading limits and material goods, each person making sense—within their universe—of their position as capitalist subjects. Again, while the market promises to empower individuals who purchase an item, the underlying fact is that empowerment goes hand in hand with dispossession, not only economically but also in terms of gender. Yardero men engage in a game of possession that dispossesses them of the power to structure their lives more beneficially. From an emic perspective, it may well be the case that possessing material goods and displaying specific masculine subjectivity is a valuable cultural asset in everyday interactions and in terms of making sense of their lives. Still, one wonders whether the behaviors they see as fulfilling only serve those who benefit from the landscapers' work.

Conclusion

To make sense of how Mexican migrants are dispossessed through the possession of specific material goods—of dispossessed masculinity—David Harvey's theorization of dispossession through accumulation is useful and can serve as a fitting conclusion to this chapter. For Harvey, accumulation by dispossession always exists in tension with accumulation by expanded reproduction. In my reading of Harvey, I argue that, through the drive to possess certain goods, people are being dispossessed of their already limited choices and are forced to manufacture more egalitarian forms of gender subjectivities, as limiting as these can be. For Mexican yarderos, despite not seeing the damage that performing dispossessed masculinity incurs, it still makes sense to possess material goods. Yarderos still perform their identities based on acquiring those items. Thus, in the landscapers' engagement with the market, with conditions not of their own making, we can see how power expressed by the yarderos in their gender terms (for example, the ability to possess material items) comes to accentuate the harsh conditions of capitalist accumulation through dispossession.

We must also recognize the multiple layers from which dispossession and masculinity arise. Here, we focused on how capitalism affects the construction and production of Mexican identities through the practice of dispossessed masculinity. Michel Foucault once made clear that the mechanism of subjection cannot be studied outside of its relation to the mechanisms of exploitation and domination. We have done so precisely by highlighting how Mexican men are manufacturing and constructing gender subjectivities within and against specific markets that are, by nature, exploitative and disempowering but that at the same time enable these workers to reproduce their gender subjectivity. As Foucault further clarifies, the mechanisms of subjection—in this case, gender ideologies and market structures, or economic hybrid collectifs—are not fundamental mechanisms of capitalism; they entertain complex relations that sometimes are moved by the subject itself and have a life before or beyond it. We can hope that yarderos eventually see that possessing the latest vehicle is indeed dispossessing them, even if possession allows them to feel happy and be seen as men in the short term.

Discussions of and about power within working-class populations often emphasize the punitive elements within economic regimes; however, often these classic readings are not accurate, or rather are too economic reductionist. The next chapter shows the dual impacts of power and complex relations that are entertained by focusing on how Mexican men discipline their own actions and bodies, even when the owners of production are absent. In other words, Mexican culture is actively and strategically mobilized by the yardero owners to make their workers work.

CHAPTER 3

Performing Power

The Body, Capitalist Discipline, and Laughing Hard

> The fundamental, essential problem, anyway the first problem which arises when one wants to analyze labor in economic terms, is how the person who works uses the means available to him. That is to say, to bring labor into the field of economic analysis, we must put ourselves in the position of the person who works; we will have to study work as economic conduct practiced, implemented, rationalized, and calculated by the person who works. What does working mean for the person who works?
>
> —Michel Foucault, *The Birth of Biopolitics*

> The workers must still eat, they must still go to the restrooms, and they must still try to find themselves; they still joke, they still complain, and they still strategize to keep their human agency—all of this in the context of their dehumanization.
>
> —Alejandro Lugo, *Fragmented Lives, Assembled Parts*

Starting in the month of March, many Mexican yarderos in Chicago begin the ritual of fixing their lawn mowers, leaf blowers, and trucks and buying landscaping materials as discussed in the last chapter when they visit the famous Russo Power Equipment. Then, as the season begins, each morning for the next nine months they can be seen traveling around middle- and upper-class white and African American neighborhoods in their pickup trucks and construction vans, searching for the American dream.

Don Antonio works six days a week mowing for a living. Don Antonio's work involves mowing the yards of residential homes, but the work activities range from planting trees to curing the grass of earthworms to trimming ornamental trees. Working as a small company owner, he can make his living when regular work is out of reach for many migrants, especially after the increasing normalization of deportability of the state apparatus. He would always say, "*Yo no quiero que nadie me mande*" (I do not want anyone to direct me), in a way resembling an entrepreneurial spirit that he passed to his sons, who also perform lawn service in the city of Chicago. The yarderos indeed are a population of migrant working-class men that emerges concomitantly with the space they inhabit, their historical circumstances, and their desire for success in a new land despite the capitalist regime that seeks to organize their everyday lives.[1]

This chapter focuses more specifically on the experiences of yarderos as they perceive their labor relations to their work to better understand working-class life and the ways in which working-class bodies become a vehicle to sediment identity as Mexicans. Metaphorically and in practical terms, this chapter descends even farther down, to the grass level, where workers labor hard every day of the landscaping season in Chicago. Through this discussion, I examine how yarderos perform power en las yardas, the first section theorizes how, within a capitalist economy, a class analysis explains how power at both the population and individual level is culturally mediated through specific work activities. The second section describes the work activity of bush trimming, typically known as *la poda*. Discussing la poda highlights how having front landscapes adorned with evergreen trees carries class references across neighborhoods in South Chicago. More specifically, this section uncovers how la poda is more than just the trimming of evergreens; it carries aesthetic and artistic forms that are cultivated among high-skilled yarderos. The third section focuses on edging as a major second task that yarderos constantly perform while working. There I provide a brief account of how edging became a central work activity for the lawn-service owner as well as clients who desire to have their front and backyards looking beautiful and neatly cut. The fourth section details the real difficulties that yarderos face as they work in areas where access to a restroom is unavailable. Sometimes the only option is to find a place in the back alleys, as these become liminal spaces that materialize as workers find a place to urinate or defecate. You, the reader, may find this discussion difficult. Still, suppose you are not confronted with the brute facts; then it becomes hard to understand the difficulties that working-class Mexican migrants face in their everyday lives as they beautify the green landscapes of America.

CHAPTER 3

Power as Marx, Class as Foucault

In this chapter, the ethnographic engagement with capitalism and techniques of control and domination transcend and connect with more extensive historical discussions about the role of capitalism and class formations. More precisely, it is argued here that through controlling the body, workers become subject to capitalist discipline, or in the worker's understanding, *por el jale* (the work activity), which is the key problem to untangle if we want to envision forms that lessen the exploitation of the Mexican body and to inquire on the presence or absence of agency, as limited as it can be.

Specifically, these ethnographic materials engage with the Marx-Foucault borderlands—that is, the theoretical intersections between capitalism and its mechanism of control—which is understood as it relates to individualized capitalist subjection rather than formal state coercive enforcements.[2] In both theoretical domains, two main modes achieve control of bodies. First, processes are exerted on populations with no intrinsic essence but rather have been created through state logics (e.g. indigents, aid recipients, police, the hospital, etc.) on the one hand, and how individuals reproduce the inequalities as workers where domination and control of the body on the other (the care of the self). An ethnographic example of the first mode of control emerges when, for example, the small company owner attempts to direct workers to perform labor tasks. The second mode of control materializes when the individual works so diligently that the small company owner does not have to be nearby for the worker to perform equally or better. Bush trimming and edging are examples where workers will train their bodies to perform the work tasks so impeccably that they learn the upper thresholds of perfection in performing these tasks.

En las yardas, satisfying social and personal needs clashes with capital needs. The goal of capital is to make production a constant so as to absorb the greatest possible labor from the worker. In many instances, culture and ethics are mobilized to increase productivity, as Christian Zlolniski reveals through his discussions with janitors and subcontracting laborers in San Jose, California. At other times, as discussed by Alejandro Lugo in his analysis of an electronics factory in Ciudad, Juarez, this intensification of capitalist production is achieved through metaphors of laziness. In other words, calling someone lazy meant that other coworkers were pressuring folks to do the work faster, and if they did not, they were called lazy.[3] Despite this mobilization of culture and capitalism, there are moments when laughter becomes a necessary mechanism to ease the tension between the demands of capital and the demands of the worker's bodily necessities. Indeed, the centrality of the body and capital and its modes of governance emerge, as managing the body becomes an instrument-vector of specific techniques of control and a consistent element in the production of value. Thus, workers' activities, such as podar, *wirear,* and mowing demonstrate how capital's efforts to exert control of the worker's body operate at multiple levels. At times this control is exerted in very intimate spaces. Indeed, refusing the mechanism of power is a strategy that Latino/a workers continue to utilize en las yardas, as in other places such as the poultry industry in Mississippi and in the farms of Southern California and Eastern Washington.[4]

In his celebrated economic account, Karl Marx writes how capitalism structures the workday in the production process. For Marx, the workday had two limits, a minimum and a maximum. While the minimum does not have a limit for capitalist production, the maximum is conditioned by two things: first, by the "physical bounds of labor power . . . [and second, by] moral ones," which Marx more accurately described as "social bounds."[5] Despite the crushing weight of the economic sphere, the worker must satisfy needs such as sleeping, eating, washing, and dressing. From this perspective, an underlying problem in production emerges when the worker must perform a "physical" or "social" need that disrupts the utilization of the worker's "sold" time to the producer. In other words, within capitalist logic, the time purchased from the worker must be utilized for profit "to make its constant factor, the means of production, absorb the greatest possible amount of surplus labour."[6] This constant factor leaves little room for the capitalist to see workers as constrained or limited by their physical needs, much less by their social desires. Marx's diagnosis of the centrality of the body in his theory of capitalism instructs border theorists to pay close attention to how a worker's physical and social bonds and borders play out within their lived experiences. In other words, a Marxism focused on the issues that matter in border contexts may seek to answer the question of why class matters in border studies and studies of power as well.

The proposition of the centrality of the human body as a government mechanism was intensely examined by Michel Foucault. For Foucault, disciplining techniques from state and nonstate apparatuses now work "to rule a multiplicity of men to the extent that their multiplicity can and must be dissolved into individual bodies that can be kept under surveillance, trained, used, if need be, punished."[7] Similarly, a vital component of capitalist development is the surveillance and training that takes place within the economic spaces in which workers' activities occur. From here, the processes that direct individuals toward specific disciplining behavior can become a target for the analysis of biopower and capitalism. For example, it is Foucault who argues that "the growth of a capitalist economy gave rise to the specific modality of disciplinary power, whose general formulas, techniques of submitting forces and bodies, in short, 'political anatomy,' could be operated in the most diverse political regimes, apparatuses or institutions."[8]

Thus, it seems that a yardero's "political anatomy" is at the center of the production of capital and is part of more extensive disciplinary regimes (coercive or self-disciplining) that derive techniques from biopower that then become critical to developing capitalism. For example, working-class Mexicans first exercise a form of biopower on themselves (voluntarily internalizing the discipline imposed by their employers). Next, this lived experience becomes culturally mediated, acquiring specific meanings defined as "Mexican" by the workers. Indeed, this cultural appropriation of the workplace becomes present by labeling gardening work as "las yardas," a Spanish phrase to define the new space from which yarderos now work for a living. Just as yarderos label their work activity and space as "las yardas," these workers develop a cultural repertoire to speak about their experiences as working subjects. Indeed, it was not common then to see that when men and women talk about everyday life at family reunions, there were many references to las yardas.

The story of power in las yardas shows that the workings of biopower are culturally mediated and not restricted to state or nonstate institutions but are lived, experienced, inhabited, and include the body as a central mechanism for reproducing power, capitalism, and profit.[9]

La Poda (Evergreen Trimming)

Between May and the first two weeks of July, yarderos reach the peak of the landscaping season in Chicago. There are a few reasons for this. First, most yarderos acquire and add new clients to their routes in May. Second, many potential new customers have side jobs that they want Mexican landscapers to do, and in the process, these side jobs eventually become consistent work.[10] The harsh Chicago winters affect the grass and may break a tree branch or two; just the amount of debris in clients' yards is a hard-enough task for people, motivating them to hire a landscaping or lawncare company to do the work. During this time, demand increases for the yarderos' services—trimming bushes, building retaining walls, fertilizing, and controlling weeds—on the South Side of Chicago. In my experience, and from what I heard in the countless discussions with yarderos, the Fourth of July celebration is an important date that often decides the fate of the rest of the year. If a yardero has accumulated enough clients for the remainder of the year, the later months of August, September, and October remain stable in terms of income. Once November arrives, there is no telling how many clients will keep the services, cancel ahead of time to save a fee for that month, or not pay until the start of the following year.

While working for Don Antonio, who has more than thirty years of experience as a Mexican yardero in Chicago, I learned that he does the labor practice of trimming the evergreens of his clients' homes in late May and early June every year. Mexican yarderos working in South Shore and Calumet Heights find a high demand for trimming evergreens in these areas. The structural aspects of the houses show the differences between these two neighborhoods. For example, most of the homes in South Chicago are at least one hundred years old, and very few new houses have been constructed in this working-class space. The lawns in South Chicago are about twenty-five by eight feet in the front yard, and the backyards are twenty by twenty feet, on average. Most front yards in South Chicago lack the extensive landscape features such as retaining walls, ornamental trees, or plants, that are more common in Calumet Heights. Usually, having a front landscape is considered a symbol of higher-class status within South Chicago.

On the other hand, Calumet Heights is primarily a middleclass African American neighborhood and is newer than South Chicago; almost all homes are adorned with front and back landscapes. A prime characteristic of these homes is that clients like to have their front and backyards adorned with ornamental evergreen trees. These four- to ten-foot trees need to be trimmed annually to maintain the landscape's attractiveness. A few blocks south of Calumet Heights is the area known as Pill Hill. This area was known as the affluent portion of Stony Island Heights, and by the 1970s many African American doctors from the nearby hospital became the main residents of the area. The cultural importance of this area for local African American folks remains central. For example, Samuel Lawrence Kelley is well known for writing and producing Pill Hill's critically acclaimed play of the same name. Set on the South Side of Chicago, the play speaks of the failures, successes, and relationships of six African American steel-mill workers transitioning from blue-collar jobs to white-collar professions between 1973 and 1983. In a recent memoir, author and former First Lady Michelle Obama writes about her childhood years when her dad would drive her around this neighborhood on Sundays. Obama comments that sometimes they would, "end up in a neighborhood to the south, an area known as Pill Hill due to the large number of African American doctors living there. It was one of the prettier, more affluent parts of the South Side, where people kept two cars in the driveway and had abundant beds of flowers blooming along their walkways"[11] Indeed, it is more than likely that the same walkways that Obama saw in these yards of her youth were planted, cared for, and maintained by the older generation of Mexican yarderos that started mowing in this area as well.

When I worked for Don Antonio from early in the season until late August, we trimmed most of the evergreen bushes and tall trees for his clients. Trimming evergreens involves several processes and tasks. The details of the work itself matter because working-class folks and the cultural production generated from this mundane activity matter; more importantly, the nature of the work allows exploring in detail how the body becomes a conduit to speak about larger structural problems. For example, in his study of Triki Oaxacan migrants to California and the Pacific Northwest, Seth Holmes offers an excellent analysis of the ways in which the body becomes a critical site where politically organized subjection by private interests and state policy manifests through illnesses and chronic pain. In the case of yarderos, while at the beginning of the fieldwork phase, I did not pay attention to their medical experiences with chronic fatigue or pain; it was quite clear that their suffering from working long hours mowing grass did have an effect on their bodies. Thus, it is only by examining their job mechanics in detail, in the same way that Holmes did with farmworkers, that we can explain how strenuous amounts of work causes harm on the bodies of lawncare service workers.

For example, when yarderos carry out la poda, if the tree had not been trimmed the year before, giving it a nice, round shape would be more challenging. In other words, the worker struggles less, only cutting the upper layer that had grown (usually three to five inches), to maintain a tree that had previously been shaped than to maintain a tree with years of growth, requiring more intensive work. Don Antonio ensures that he trims most of his clients' trees and evergreen bushes each year; thus, when the next season comes, he does not have to spend much time on this assignment. Early in Don Antonio's career as a landscaper, he would acquire clients by telling them that the trimming of their evergreen trees was included in the service. Other yarderos do not include this task in their service now. Part of their reasoning is because if they pushed themselves to trim the evergreens leading up to the Fourth of July celebrations, they would need to work on Sundays to keep their clients happy.

When trimming evergreens, a worker takes the hedge trimmers and holds them waist-high, slowly brushing over the evergreen shape, cutting only the greener tips that have emerged from the past winter. Next, the worker shakes the evergreen tree or bush with extra force, so all the debris falls to the ground. Yarderos, with a strong work ethic, spend a few minutes before trimming, covering the area around the bushes with plastic to stop any debris from reaching the mulch or the decorative rocks. Other yarderos, who are often critiqued by the older generation, do not cover the area underneath the bushes, and when they finish the trimming, they only blow the tree clippings away and pick them up with a rake. Taking debris from the tree's body is essential; otherwise, it will wither within a day or two and the tree will look as if it had been sprinkled with brownish debris. After the first cutting of evergreen tips, a worker then gives it shape. Giving a pretty shape to the evergreen bushes is a skilled process. The worker must be careful not to cut the tips too low or they will sever growth points on the crown. Lastly, the evergreen is shaped a final time. During this process, the worker is usually standing, holding the hedge trimmers, and using the force of his arms to cut the evergreen tips, as if brushing the tree, to finalize its shape. When yarderos perform this activity for a long time, they develop a beelike movement, moving, circling, and shaping in a rhythmic fashion, operating the hedge trimmers as an extension of their bodies.

Evergreen trimming is not backbreaking work unless one does it for more than one hour. For example, when performing work for Don Antonio in June 2013, we had to work the last three Sundays before the Fourth of July carrying out this activity. On Saturday morning, we would finish *la ruta*—the houses we provided lawn services for—and then trim the evergreens for two or three houses. Then, on Sunday mornings, we would go out to Calumet Heights and the Pill Hill area to trim the evergreens of all the properties we could. When we dedicated all our effort to trimming bushes, we would do about ten properties. When I would trim for more than an hour, my body began to feel the effects of the work. This was felt through a continuous and persistent pain in my lower back. The pain felt as if two knives had been pushed into each side of my body. There were times when I had to bend down to trim evergreens from three feet off the ground or lower, and just standing straight would cause even sharper pain in my lower back. This feeling was also recounted by my interlocutors, especially the older yarderos who tended only to trim the taller evergreens. Indeed, as documented by Seth Holmes, farmworkers in California and the farms of Eastern Washington would tell stories of pain in their stomachs, backs, hands, and feet; however, little was done from a medical standpoint because doctors could not interpret their pains as part of the social structure but rather as individual choice.[12] Thus, by individualizing pain this practice did not raise an awareness of how working-class conditions affected their lives as part of a working-class populations. As we know, when folks see themselves as part of a class, then this allows for a social movement to emerge.

All gas-driven equipment produces vibrations, which adds more discom fort. For example, during the summer months, between May and August when substantial mowing or bush trimming was done, I would wake up to start work, and my hands would be so swollen that making, and even grabbing, a cup of coffee while having breakfast would bring pain to my joints. Likewise, evergreen trimming creates a significant additional vibration in a worker's hands to the point that by the end of the day, while driving home, other workers also would comment that they would feel as if they were still holding the hedge trimmers.

On one occasion, I asked Don Antonio about la poda.

SERGIO: When do you start la poda this year?

DON ANTONIO: *Poco a poco* (little by little). You see, we begin when they want.

SERGIO: Who, the clients?

DON ANTONIO: Yes, but I do not wait for them to tell me. I know which clients I can safely start with. I know which ones do not mind. I know which ones will pay me.

SERGIO: Do you include la poda in your service?

DON ANTONIO: Look, before, when I started in the late 1970s, it was included. I tried to follow the practice, and I did. In the past years, this has changed. Trimming all the evergreens takes a lot of time, especially in this area. If you see, all the houses have evergreens.

SERGIO: Why do not you hire someone else to do only that task?

DON ANTONIO: You cannot. In this job, the owner must supervise the job. Sometimes, when I trust the worker to do the job right, I leave him trimming a few houses, and I go and do other tasks. But not everyone can trim bushes the way I want. It requires time.[13]

Edging

While working lawn service with Cesar Sanchez and Don Antonio, besides becoming an expert on trimming evergreen trees, I also learned to *wirear* (line trim or edge). Just like hedge trimming, edging is a skill that is not easily acquired; it takes considerable practice to perform it correctly. As I discussed earlier, lawncare service companies in Chicago typically provide edging as part of their lawncare service package. For example, Cesar Sanchez uses Don Antonio's system of mowing grass every week and edging every other week. In the case of Don Raul Mendez, he also edges every other week, but sometimes, especially when the grass gets overgrown in the early months of the season (May and June), Don Raul edges every week. Other lawncare companies, such as that of another Mexican immigrant, Ricardo Garcia from Zacatecas, edge every week. According to most yarderos I spoke with, the idea of edging every week is to diminish the time spent at each residence. For example, while working for Don Antonio, I noticed that the work became very time-consuming in the weeks of the month we edged because edging lawn areas creates additional grass clippings on the client's sidewalks and driveways and, therefore, substantially more debris to collect.

Edging is a specific kind of work and cultural practice within the context of Chicago. For example, edging is a new work activity, done very rapidly through gas-powered equipment using a line trimmer most of the time. In our multiple conversations, Don Antonio mentions a fellow countryman from the state of Zacatecas, Mr. Ramirez, as the first Zacatecano that worked mowing grass for a living in South Chicago. According to the story, Mr. Ramirez was the first Mexican to own a lawncare company in South Chicago. Mr. Ramirez was the man who originally gave work to Don Antonio and his two brothers, Alberto and José Flores, back in the late 1970s when they first arrived in South Chicago, as I mentioned in the first chapter. In those days, recalls Don Antonio, the three brothers worked together as chalanes. Mr. Ramirez retired in the early 1980s, and in 1982 he handed down *la ruta* (the list of clients) to them. Don Antonio discussed how edging was not done as fast as it is today during that time. In the early 1980s edging was done by kneeling and using a sharp knife to edge around most clients' front yards.

Today, all yarderos use a gas-powered edger or line trimmer. The other less-used method is a blade-powered trimmer, which is mostly used at the beginning of the landscaping season, when the line of separation between the sidewalk and the grass area is hard to distinguish. Given that all of Don Antonio's clients were within a one- to two-block radius, the work was finished quickly, usually within an hour or less. In the early 1980s, as told by Don Antonio, it would take him fifteen minutes to an hour to edge with a handheld knife. Then a crew of about four workers would clean up behind him, not with a high-wind-powered blower but rather with a simple house broom. During a typical workday, a crew of two or three workers would do about five to eight houses. Nowadays, some lawncare companies, like Rick's Landscaping, mow the lawns of nearly one hundred homes per day.

Yardero Hoosiers

In a classical approach to the study of anthropology, the field site is located far, in a distant place, the "field" is left behind.[14] In 2017, as I began to work on this book, I wanted to understand how Mexican landscapers in a Midwestern college town, such as Bloomington, Indiana, would go about their work, and the kinds of relations that they would develop. I tapped into the Mexican working-class network that we know exists in almost all aspects of service-sector economies in the United States by frequenting a few local Mexican restaurants and asked about working as a landscaper to find a comparative cultural space where yardero hoosiers worked. I was curious about the type of techniques utilized in this context. It did not take long for someone to point me to Ernesto from the state of Tabasco. I called him and asked him if there was an opportunity to join him en las yardas. He said, "I call you later; I need to ask the permission." I was not expecting him to call me back, but he did within a couple of days.

Ernesto said I needed to talk to his boss and asked me to go to the shop where they met every morning to start the day. I went on a Monday morning in mid-May 2018. The boss was John Carver, and he owned a landscaping company. Later I learned that most of the workers were undocumented and came from Tabasco, as had Ernesto, or from San Luis Potosi. I asked John about the opportunity to work for a few days. He responded, "When can you start?" Taken aback by the upfront questions but wanting to get a sense of the structure, form, and local culture of the lawncare service sector in Bloomington, Indiana, I hesitantly said, "Whenever you want." Upon further reflection, I realized that my working-class background emerged when I answered. In my head, I decided that I would work a day or two in the next two weeks, and that would be it.

I showed up on a Thursday, and to my surprise, they did not start me with a twenty-one-inch lawn mower as the companies I had worked for in Chicago had but instead with the wiro—line trimmer. They also did not tell me beforehand, but Thursday was the day they completed the bulk of the yardwork for the week. I was in a crew of two other paisanos, and a second crew also came to a subdivision in an area west of the local university. I counted the houses as we worked, and we completed about 140 properties by the end of the day. Later I learned that they made a bet about when I would give up and ask to go home. My "college-based" fieldwork paid off this time. I endured that grueling day and showed up for the next day to their surprise.

While this was only a short, two-week experience, it allowed me to see the backbreaking work of edging to confirm my previous ethnographic observations. This company in Bloomington would edge every week. While the properties were larger in size than in Chicago, the intensity of the work remained a constant factor in both locations. But let me go back to Chicago in 2013.

While conversing with Don Raul at his home on the East Side, I asked him why he edged (*wireaba*) each week. He told me that his clients do not like the grass tips on the sidewalk; edging it looks neat. Don Raul discussed how he learned to edge while working with his cousin for the Mendez Lawn Care company. Don Raul shared the story of how the edging service began in his family. His older cousin, Carlos Mendez, from the Mendez family, started this practice. Don Raul said that before edging was provided as a regular service, the wiro was only used to clear up large and tall weeds in people's yards. The grass would grow a lot in one month, and Carlos Mendez began using the wiro to cut the grass tips that fell onto the sidewalk, leaving a clear distinction between the grass and concrete areas. According to Don Raul Mendez, clients said that edging with the line trimmer looked so lovely that more homes began to request their lawns be edged regularly.[15]

Edge trimming is a product of cultural preference, a necessity of the labor process, and a way for company owners to offer additional services and make additional money. Once this work activity was brought into the labor process, it was normalized as part of the process itself. However, at the end of the day, the worker's body suffers the consequences of this taste for better-looking grass in Chicago. For example, edging, or *wirear*, is done with a gas-powered line trimmer with an average weight of thirteen pounds. A worker must carry this piece of equipment around the perimeter of the lawn throughout the day while performing the task. Then, if the backyard or front yard has one or several trees, the *wireador* would go around the perimeter of the tree trunk and trim any grass inconsistent with the level of the rest of the lawn. The front end of the line trimmer consists of an "edge head" with two plastic lines emerging from it that can easily cut weeds up to three or four feet tall when running at high speed.

The wiro is set horizontally to cut tall weeds. Suppose a worker wants to cut vertically, as in edging between the concrete and lawn areas. In this case, the line trimmer is turned to a ninety-degree angle. Then a worker needs to be careful not to cut too much inside the lawn area or not to cut it at all. The size of a line trimmer, on average, is fifty-nine to sixty inches from the shaft to where the worker holds it. Given the length, the worker must hold the line trimmer in a particular position to cut vertically between the concrete and the lawn areas. To properly do this task, a worker places their right hand (if righthanded) on the accelerator to control the speed of the head. Typically, in the beginning, a worker uses this accelerator control frequently, but an experienced worker uses the accelerator at full speed while they are edging. The faster he can walk while edging, the better. The left hand is placed on the handle of the line trimmer. The function of the shaft handle is to turn the line trimmer and hold it up to avoid cutting too close, which could cause the grass to be ripped up from the root. In short, to edge around the lawn's perimeter, a worker must bend sideways, then walk in a straight line, placing one side in a bent position to modify the axis of his body so that the upper body is bent. In contrast, the lower body walks forward in a line. It is a highly uncomfortable position that takes time to get used to. Suppose a worker is line trimming for the entire day, on a regular ten to twelve-hour schedule; in that case, a worker's right hand, typically the hand that holds the weight and controls the line trimmer's acceleration of speed, can hurt to the point that it can become numb for hours after work.[16]

As observed, working as a chalan or yardero is much more than merely walking behind a lawn mower to cut grass. Mowing and other related activities require substantial skill and levels of understanding, not only of how nature and the environment operate and grow but also of how certain activities provide cultural taste for clients. Yarderos are aware of these preferences and will create work activities to instill other taste preferences in their clients. However, at the end of the day, the individual who must do these painful work tasks is the chalan who works for the yardero. Ultimately, workers must train and modify their bodies to perform these work activities as the *patron* (boss) demands, which is demanded by the *patron*'s clients.

Bowel Movements and Laughing

While working as a chalan and yardero myself, I learned that one must train the body and the inner, sometimes involuntary, bodily functions to do certain work activities. For example, when I worked for Cesar Sanchez from October through November 2012, at times, right after lunch, I would have to go to the bathroom. Working as a yardero means mowing different neighborhoods through most of the workday, and a restroom is rarely available since workers mow residential areas most of that time. Given how work is organized, around noon, *el patron*—the boss—will search for a nearby fast-food restaurant to bring the workers something to eat for lunch. The fast-food establishments are often McDonalds, Burger King, Subway, Wendy's, or nearby Mexican food places. Given that this kind of food is barely nutritious, sometimes it does not digest well, and one must find a place to eliminate waste after eating.

For example, one of Don Antonio's workers, Julio, came a bit late to work one day, driving his car from the East Side neighborhood to 89th Street and Phillips Avenue in South Chicago. After just an hour, Julio asked the boss if he could use the bathroom. The next day, Saturday, we continued mowing grass in this area, this time near 89th Street and Anthony Avenue, which is close to the Chicago Skyway, a toll road connecting two larger highways. Again, Julio suddenly disappeared within a couple of minutes of having lunch. He came back to where we were mowing half an hour later. As soon as he disappeared, Don Antonio and I knew he had gone looking for a place to use the restroom. We asked him where he went, and he pointed toward the Chicago Skyway, near street level, and we both began to laugh. Right on the top of the Skyway, at the pay station on 87th Street, is a McDonald's that is only accessible by car. We asked Julio, "How did you end up there if there is a ten-foot wall and the McDonald's is on the Skyway runway?" Julio said he walked two blocks to one of the tunnels connecting South Chicago and Calumet Heights, and there is a ramp toward the toll booth where McDonald's is located. From that point on, when he would come to help us, we would continually make jokes about this incident. For example, when we picked up Julio from his East Side home at other times, right after he climbed into the van, we immediately asked him, "Did you go to the bathroom?" or simply, "Did you bring toilet paper with you?" Of course, the point of the joke was not to insult him but to acknowledge that he still could not control his bodily needs.

Since there are no public restrooms when one is out mowing residential neighborhoods, when a worker decides to use a "proper" space to eliminate, he creates production problems for the owner of the small lawncare company. In other words, the houses may not be mowed at the rate they are supposed to, and the work will slow down. This creates problems for the boss because they must recalculate the labor expenses. For example, deciding to eliminate in "proper" spaces takes a worker at least half an hour of lost time, as the closest restroom could be anywhere from five to ten blocks away, depending on the location the crew is working in. Julio left to find a restroom three times in the first week. The second week Julio helped us work, he decided to bring his car so the boss would not get annoyed when he requested the cargo van to find a place to use a restroom.

While eliminating is a bigger problem for lawncare services workers, urinating is an effortless process, at least for men. If a worker needs to pee, there are various practices. For example, when workers must throw out the grass clippings, they are often placed in trash cans provided by the city. Thus, if a worker needs to urinate, he often volunteers to throw away the garbage in the ally, and as it tends to happen, when the rest of the workers wait longer than usual for someone to come back to the front of the house, they know that he was probably peeing in the back. They ensure that the owner does not come out of the house; otherwise, the worker may get into trouble. It is typical for workers to urinate in an alley or a backyard, hidden in a corner during fieldwork. If I saw the owner of the house coming out, I would simply shout, "Aguas!" which means literally "watch out!" At other times, if someone wants to urinate, the task is easily accomplished if the company owner drives a closed hauling trailer because the worker will get inside the trailer and no one would see him.

Indeed, as my fieldwork progressed, it became obvious that the worker's body is centrally located within myriad relations of labor, power, gender, and mechanisms of control. While controlling the body and redirecting its mechanisms was an essential task that a worker needed to master, there were far-reaching consequences, as Seth Holmes describes in his discussion of farm workers in California and Eastern Washington. It often takes years after a worker has left the "field" to begin to experience less pain. The physical manifestation and generational traumatic effects of being part of a working-class population is an important intellectual task to capture the complexity of the Mexican working-class lives in the United States. A task still incomplete.

Conclusion

This chapter has documented how governing and controlling working-class migrants takes cultural work, often done by Mexican working-class folks and their self-inflicted capitalist internalized power assemblages. I further examined how the body is directly and indirectly affected by capitalist demands that leave little room for a worker to experience this domination outside the confines of capital. I further showed that workers are culturally creative and experts in knowing the capitalist demands embodied through the work activity and how to challenge them or further intensify the effects of power differentials. The fact that workers continue to perform work activities in the absence of supervision is a clear manifestation of self-disciplining techniques being internalized by the worker themselves through the physical routine required to succeed as yarderos. For example, workers are often left alone for the entire day when trimming evergreens, and the boss will come back around midafternoon to help clean up.

The ethnography presented in this chapter thus engages with the relations between class and power as experienced by these workers. The lawncare maintenance and gardening work, or las yardas as my informants call it, is a demonstration of the power regimes to which Mexicans become adapted given the opportunities that migrants seek in the United States. The critical intervention that this chapter proposes is that workers are controlled by capitalism's logic, practices, and organized activities, and by their own selves who want to be seen as good, hardworking Mexicans. The worker's self-governance is the best evidence that capital has achieved its goal of mechanizing, modifying, and changing the subject, even at the expense of their wellbeing. In many ways, the discussion in this chapter (like the previous chapter) descended at the level of the work activities themselves rather than a focus on the social relations to examine working-class folks as they engage with various forms of power at the level of production.

As we have known for some time, the lives of Mexican migrants and diaspora populations are lived transnationally as scholars such as Juan Thomas Ordóñez and Seth Holmes clearly articulate in relation to day laborers, farmworkers, and in this ethnography the lives of yarderos.[17] Thus, decentering the nation-state reveals fractures and opportunities to use other lenses to understand Mexican migration. The lives of Mexican migrants encompass many other processes that are fundamentally transborder.[18]

Additionally, a critical aspect of working-class life is workers' engagement with race, racism, and discrimination across physical and social borders. Indeed, the problem of color in Mexico also travels to the Midwest, but it changes, modifies itself, and acquires additional layers of meaning in everyday life. The next chapter looks laterally within working-class Mexican yarderos culture to examine how colorism among Mexican migrants is experienced in the second decade of the twenty-first century. To you, reader: please be patient. While I would like to offer a clear map of how yarderos understand their racial subjectivity concerning or in distinction to white residents and African American clients, the aim of the next chapter is to analyze how Mexican migrants racialize each other through the logic of a "transborder colorism" rather than to discuss how they understand color through the American racial system, which scholar Tanya Katerí Hernández has termed "racial innocence." Indeed, Mexican ideas about color matter in las yardas as well because matters of color have cultural value for my interlocutors in transborder Chicago.[19] To that discussion I now turn.

Migrant Sunset, the city of migrant dreams on the horizon of possibilities, July 2012.

Migrant Intersections, marching in Chicago for immigration reform under the Obama administration, May 2013.

Families on the Fence, the border fence as encountered for many migrants as they attempt to cross into the United States, May 2013.

La Torito. Acquiring a twenty-one-inch commercial lawn mower is the first step to become a successful yardero in Chicago. March 2013.

El Chalan, turning around to see the beauty that labor leaves on people's front yards, April 2013.

La 32. As yarderos become successful, thirty-two-inch lawn mower sediments a worker's identity en las yardas in South Chicago. April 2013.

Borders en Las Yardas, a daily chalan's view in that backyards of Avalon Park in Chicago, May 2013.

Precision. Clients and the yardero boss demand precision as a worker mows in the Pill Hill neighborhood in South Chicago. March 2013.

At the Grass Level. A worker takes a picture when resting after lunch in a client's backyard where beauty is hidden in plain sight. May 2013.

La Poda, trimming client's evergreen trees as they prepare to celebrate the Fourth of July, June 2013.

Yardeando, beautifying Pill Hill, a middle class African American neighborhood, July 2013.

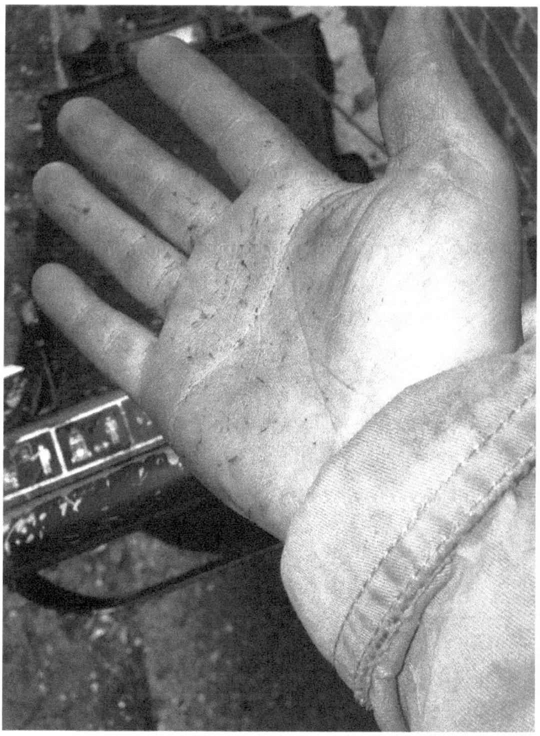

Manos Rasposas (Rugged hands). This is the bodily effect that many workers suffer from as they do the labor that others refuse to do. August 2013.

CHAPTER 4

Color Inspections

Alternative Imaginings of Racial Landscapes among Yarderos/as

> Anatomy is not destiny. . . . As human beings we divide this world up into socially relevant continua. The shading of colors of human beings is one such continuum
>
> —Nancy Lindisfarne and Jonathan Neale, "What Gender Does"

> What happens when you stay long in the sun?
> To what degree do you turn brown?
>
> —Questionnaire from a gym in South Chicago

As yarderos enjoy a reunion over a carne asada in Chicago on a Sunday evening in early August 2013, a song by Mexican singer Pepe Aguilar plays in the background. At a carne asada (barbecue-style outing), *cerveza en mano* (beer on hand), and with a good sense of humor, these men are ready to enjoy an evening of friendly conversation, which helps erase the week of demanding work doing lawn service and recharge for the new one the following week, and for the remaining of the summer.

Radio, music, and television are some of the mediums associated with intensifying national identity aside from newspapers as one of the early forms of mass media communication.[1] For example, in Mexico in the 1920s and the following two decades, Mexican cinema appeared and intensely promoted the metaphor of "el rancho" to explain Mexican national identity. Indeed, songs later added into films such as *Aya en el Rancho Grande* (There in the big ranch) played in almost every region of Mexico; later, this song successfully crossed borders as Mexicans settled in the various communities in the United States, as anthropologist Alex Chávez explains in his work on *hupango arribeno* and migration.[2] Today, most ethnic Mexican folks know cinema stars such as the classic Pedro Infante (191757), Jorge Negrete (1911–53), Maria Felix (1914–2002), and the more recent Antonio Aguilar (1919–2007), the father of Pepe Aguilar. The Aguilar family has become famous for returning to Mexican rodeo shows, or as known by Mexican yarderos, "*jaripeo,*" and is currently showcasing its music throughout Mexico and the United States under the banner, "Jaripeo Sin Fronteras."[3] Indeed, this proliferation of the "charro" image has been suggested as the master symbol of Mexican culture by anthropologist and Latino Studies scholar Olga Najera Ramirez in her study of identity and discourse which focuses on the engendering forms that the image of the charro creates, produces, and reproduces in Mexican nationalism.[4] This master symbol of the charro is also embedded in larger structures of what I call color inspections. Indeed, as the two epigraphs at the start of this chapter and the following discussion will explain, the focus on color hierarchies is a key area to investigate if we want to understand how Mexicans and Mexican migrants understand their place in the world.

For example, in his song, "100% Mexicano," Pepe Aguilar prides himself on returning to a truer Mexico, which he tries to express it exists through his musical lyrics and mariachi songs. The lyrics describe a male, said to emerge from a *raza de bronze* (a race of copper), a poet, and a peasant. The first two lines alert us to the known folkloric relevance of populations in producing cultural and poetic expressions.[5] The song's protagonist tells us that *sangre de indio* (indigenous blood) runs through his veins.[6] Within Mexican culture *indio*, depending on the context, is often and almost always a derogatory term to refer to someone of indigenous descent. The more proper term is *indigena*, or the cultural group with whom they associate locally (e.g., *purepecha*, *yaqui*, etc.). Still, in this case, the term indio, despite its often-negative associations, is praised for having a heritage that the song's protagonist wants to obtain as essential. Indeed, in Mexican society and often among yarderos in Chicago, when individuals suggest they are somehow related, connected, or come from an indigenous background, it is a way to claim the past from a traditional indigeneity. This use aligns with what Renato Rosaldo calls "imperialist nostalgia," in other words, longing for what one has destroyed, whether through direct or indirect cultural practices.[7]

Pepe Aguilar's song, then, engages with Mexican nationalism and regional identities. First, the lyrics suggest that the protagonist fully identifies with his origins from the state of Zacatecas by singing that he is not just a Zacatecan but a pure Zacatecan. The adjective *pure* signals the notion that there is a deeper and rooted regional identity of being from that state in Mexico; that is, he is claiming a deeper authentic identity. The following line tells us that he is Mexican through heredity and utilizes biologized metaphors to discuss national identity. The song's next lines recall a distant past where the Aztec empire reigned over Mexico City. Here, skin color becomes gendered as the protagonist describes, in color terms, how he wants and wishes his woman to look. The protagonist explicitly says that he wants a "*morena*" (brown-skinned) woman, like the women in his homeland. He intends to adore her as he worships the Virgen de Guadalupe.[8]

Moreover, in this song Mexican "whiteness," as a discourse on and about the light-skinned Mexican population, has been hidden for a preference for *mestizaje* understanding of identity. The skin discourse around the term *moreno/a* is also part of the racial grammar used to understand Mexicans' color subjectivity, at times denoting "Brownness" and, in other transborder contexts, "Blackness" (next chapter). In reference to whiteness, anthropologist Claudio Lomnitz reminds us that the emergence of the term *Spanish* as a linguistic and religious category also shaped the spread of identities based on color in Spanish America early in the 1600s. For example, to secure better control of the colonial state, Spaniards (*españoles*) began labeling other populations as *indios*, *mestizos*, and *morenos/as*. The creation of the "other" category can be explained to designate who would eventually belong in the "colonist" category. The colonized term, in Spanish America then, encompasses both Blackness and Indianness. This is addressed in the recent ethnography by Laura Lewis, which highlighted the *moreno* populations of the Costa Chica in Guerrero, Mexico, and the complex relation that they have had to *mestizaje*.[9] This preference at the level of discourse does not easily map on the ground; of course, Mexicans come in all forms, shapes, and colors. However, those with lighter skin complexions tend to overwhelmingly benefit more, in their families and work, as they seek political posts, apply to public or private universities, or even enter higher-end bars in downtown Mexico City or Ciudad Juarez.[10] These are some of the complexities we encounter when color is centralized, and *mestizaje* is strategically refused to understand the varied racial landscapes Mexicans in Chicago experience in the second decade of the twentieth century.

This chapter captures the complex and often contradictory "color" meanings among Mexican migrant men and women in South Chicago. Specifically, I argue that the phrase *color inspections* helps us capture subjectivities based on color. The ethnographic mobilization of this concept, both at the analytical and ethnographic level, emerges from realizing that the processes that shape the

US-Mexico border affect communities north in the Midwest. Gloria Anzaldúa distinguished early on the difference between a "border" and the "borderlands;" later, Renato Rosaldo suggested that the "borderlands" are spaces of creative cultural production. Following this line of inquiry, Alejandro Lugo commented that, despite the celebratory nature of the "borderlands" in relation to culture, there needs to be an account of how power operates and that the "borders" need to be inspected.

My contribution to this theorization is modest but of deep implications to better understand how Mexican men and women experience racism in Chicago, the Midwest, and beyond. I am arguing that, for Mexicans in Chicago, *color inspections* is a more appropriate descriptive term because Mexicans encounter not only a US-based racial binary system but have actively overlaid their understanding of Latin American forms of colorism in their postnational or diasporic context of migration much in the way that Katerí Hernández has recently helped us to understand the ways in which discrimination takes place within Latinx populations in the United States.[11] Moreover, by grounding the term *color inspections* in everyday life, I position it ethnographically to explain better how color emerges as a structuring, cultural force, or regime of power in working-class people's lives, despite some calls that suggest we live in a postracial society and culture. Ethnographically, *color inspections* exist because, in many ways, this concept achieves operational legibility within the multisided spaces of power and culture. Yarderos' *color inspections* are, as we may expect, lived through class, gender, labor, and culture. This concept touches all aspects of everyday life and operates as cultural sediment overlaid from earlier racial logics. Indeed, Chicago's racial landscape is a space, place, and cultural context suited to document how color is lived and experienced by Mexican working-class folks laterally.

To elaborate on this argument and discussion, the first section of the chapter looks at the borders of color by examining, in broad strokes, the way state officials charged with the task of creating a national culture for the Mexican nation had to rely on or come to grips with the problem of color in postrevolutionary Mexico. Indeed, despite nationalistic calls that suggest that Mexico is a nation of mestizos, when the mestizo subject is destabilized or refused, color hierarchies can be used to explain either how particular groups were able to become Mexican or which groups were still in need, from the optic of the state, of modernization through hygienic practices and de-Indianization policies. The second section engages with the colonial debris of colorism, or the problem of color in Mexico, a topic recently addressed through the studies focused on pigmentocracy in Latin America. Then, as colorism travels north along with Mexican migrants who become yarderos in Chicago, it acquires additional layers of meaning. The following section focuses on how colorism emerges in conjunction with other cultural domains within Latinx populations in the United States. The fourth section comments on the *color inspections* that both men and women are subjected to, at times viscerally, as they travel within the boundaries and borders of South Chicago. I specifically comment on how colorism is a prism that can be used to uncover the problem of color and how colorism is culturally expressed across local, national, and transborder lives. In other words, it appears that, given the structural and cultural positioning of Mexican subjects, there is not an outside to color, that is, to racialization processes whether influenced by Spanish, later Mexican, and now the American racial system, the presence of color hierarchies cannot be erased. The conclusion assesses the theoretical weight of the term *color inspections* as it helps us examine Mexican race relations where color subjectivity is a central, organizing, cultural mechanism, one that is put into practice every day by Mexican yarderos/as in Chicago.

The Colored Color Frame

The association between the term *gachupin*—a noun from the Spanish language derived from a noble surname of northern Spain, the Cachopin of Laredo—as a way of both "othering" and reclaiming a sense of Mexicanness cannot be overlooked in Mexican culture and folklore. For example, the song "Juan Guerrero," popularized by the Mexican norteño group Los Tigres del Norte, recalls the story of a man who lost his girlfriend in a battle with her family members who did not want him as her partner. In the corrido, Juan Guerrero is captured by the mounted police and, the police ask him who he is and what his trade is. The following stanza speaks to the presence of the "gachupinismo" in contemporary Mexican folklore:

Me preguntaron ¿Cuáles son tus credenciales?
Ocupaciones y mi nombre verdadero
Llevo por nombre y apellido Juan Guerrero
Soy delegado de la Unión de Aserraderos

Comisionado de la Agraria Campesina
Llevo expropiadas cuatro haciendas gachupinas
Me preguntaron ¿Cuántas veces has matado?
Y yo les dije cuántas veces me han buscado

Translation
They asked me: "What are your credentials?
Occupations and your real name?"
I go by the name Juan Guerrero.
I am a representative of the Union of Sawmills
Commissioner of the Agrarian Peasant Organization
I have expropriated four Spanish estates.
They asked me, "How many times have you killed?"
And I told them, "How many times have they come after me?"

The corrido is a lyric and folkloric space where cultural practices are explained and given meaning and allure among the social relations in everyday life, a life often defined in color terms. In this case, *gachupin* stands for those who once were landowners. This tended to be the elite *peninsulares* and *criollos* who belonged to a "whitened" colored caste in colonial Mexico. Thus, this colored worldview allows us to see the complexity of color imaginings which was readily present later to those taking part in the formation of the post-1910 revolutionary state. For example, José Vasconcelos became the chancellor of the National Autonomous University of Mexico (UNAM) during this period. He became Mexico's secretary of public education a year later. Mexican *mestizaje* ideology served no other means in 1810 (as well as in 1910) than to support the hegemony of those who gained power. For example, in the early 1920s, José Vasconcelos wrote one of the most well-known texts promoting Mexico's racial and color erasure, *La Raza Cosmica*.[12] Vasconcelos begins this text by arguing that, in history, there were four racial "stages": the Black, the Indian, the Mongol, and the white. He argues:

> Clearly, white domination will also be temporary, but their mission is to serve as a bridge. . . . The civilization developed and organized in our times by the whites has set the moral and material basis for the union of all men into a fifth universal race, the fruit of all the previous ones, and amelioration of everything past. . . . The transcendental mission feeds upon the two most daring branches of the European family, the strongest and most different human types: the Spanish and the English.[13]

As a state-sponsored ideology and practice, the discourse of *mestizaje* also served to accelerate the de-Indianization process, despite being an incomplete state project until today and a literal erasure of the presence of Black descendant communities.[14] Indeed, *mestizaje*'s discourse does not erase racism but instead becomes a permutation of futile efforts to produce national and nation-state building projects because of the always present "Mexico profundo," as anthropologist Bonfil Batalla argues.[15] Furthermore, Beatriz Urias Horcasitas explains that, after the Mexican Revolution of 1910, the political elite wanted to implement a "cultural revolution" that sought to change the mentality of its citizens. One of the first areas where the Mexican state intervened was in fomenting a secular orientation rather than a religious one. The second area of intervention at the population level was the elimination of aspects of the population considered degenerative. In a classic example of this campaign, according to Horcasitas, the state invested itself in a gendered discourse of "El Nuevo Hombre" (the new man), which was envisioned as follows:

> Socially, [a mestizo] would combine a lifestyle from proletariat to peasant, middle class customs . . . free of addictions such as alcoholism, a hard worker, a good parent. . . . He would be an ideal candidate to diffuse the new nationalistic doctrine and secular ideas emanated from the state apparatus."[16]

"El Hombre Nuevo" discourse was marked in class and gender in specific ways. It appears "El Hombre Nuevo" embodied the ideals of the political elite and the ruling classes, meaning those with a monopoly on private property and those who directed Mexico's national project as a modernist project. The idea of the perfect citizen, specifically within the postrevolutionary context, emphasized a public discourse on the material and discursive production of skin-color erasure. In other words, it was an ideological program that sought to modernize, educate, and control the population. It is, then, a contention as I move the argument forward that "Mestizo privilege" in colonial, national, and postcolonial Mexico was achieved through several politically organized means. Just like hegemony and language, it is incomplete, partial, challenged, and uneven.[17]

In this context, despite state efforts, colorism, while negated in state projects and Mexican nationalism, has remained present in the lives of Mexicans in Mexico and the United States. Indeed, a recent study that examined ethnicity and race in Latin America surveyed four major countries and the project titled, the Project on Ethnicity and Race in Latin America (PERLA) concluded that "skin color is a central axis of social stratification."[18]

Erasing Colorism, Erasing Blackness

Mexico during the national period demonstrated a relative absence of Blackness within the national imagination. As Mexican independence was settled, the nation shifted the continuum of color to a narrower skin-color spectrum analytically, at times ideologically, but not so much in practice, and mestizo became the prism to understand relations between Mexico's populations. Black Mexico, as some recent scholars have pointed out, has always been part of the fabric of the Mexican racial state formation, and calls to recognize the Afro-Mexican population have been louder since the early 2000s.[19] For example, Blackness as an ethnic or racial category has been recently documented as central to how Mexicans think of themselves as Mexicans.[20] However, for both, regardless of the space from which skin-color designations are labeled as such, the lighter-skinned person has been historically privileged over the person with darker tonalities as an observation made by Latino scholars among either Black versus Latino relations or the relation of Latin America population toward darker-skin populations from former Black descendant communities.[21] In other words, I suggest that in a capitalist system, gender and color have served to naturalize class exploitation and further reproduce domination. At other times, gender speaks for color, and class speaks for gender.[22] Indeed, race is different from color analytically; still, it is hard to disentangle the two categories in practice, especially in the United States, given the long history of assigning value to skin color. At other times, however, examining racism does clarify color hierarchies and power differences, and color hierarchies' obscure accurate descriptions and racist practices.[23] The ethnographer's role is to begin peeling back and uncovering, layer by layer, core meanings associated with perceptions of color among Mexican migrants and academics alike, and in the process, dismantling the power grid that does not allow working classes to work and only distract them.[24]

The examination of skin color and the attention paid to color hierarchies concerning class inequality and the migration process is such an embedded academic practice by anthropologists, historians, and Latino Studies scholars trained in the United States who, through their writings, expose and undeniably attempt to grapple with color expressions in the lives of Mexicans in the United States. In the process, they reproduce the same ontological categories scholars seek to deconstruct. For example, in the late 1920s, Manuel Gamio, an anthropologist and a student of Franz Boas, published one of the first studies of the experience of Mexican migrants in the United States. He described his participants in striking skin-color imaginings. The hierarchy of color that Gamio imagined is one in which the continuum starts with Mexican migrants with "Indian" features, then moves toward mestizos, and ends with white (blanco) Mexicans. Not surprisingly, his participants' physical descriptions and skin-color classifications neatly map lower-, middle-, and upper-class mobility within the Mexican population that travels to the United States. For example, we find Gamio describing maladjusted Mexicans as matching the Indian type and sometimes the mestizos, but he rarely mentions a white (blanco) Mexican as a lower-class subject. Interestingly, but not surprisingly, a mestizo within the skin-color hierarchy portrayed by Gamio is rarely described as a white type; thus, we find a specific *colorismo* that does not map well within a white-Black dichotomy of the racial order in the United States. Gamio was one of the first Mexican-born scholars to describe Mexican migrants by considering Mexican-based ethnic and racial classifications and how these classifications adjusted as Mexicans navigated the US racial order. I do not believe he was critical of how his racial bias colored his analysis of the life of Mexican migrants in the United States; still, the study he carried out allows us to visualize the kind of preoccupation Mexican scholars have with issues of color and race.

Within the historical context of South Chicago in the early twentieth century, racism based on skin-color and its meanings toward the Mexican population inevitably fractured the group's sense of identity by making Mexican workers battle colorism within Chicago's steel industry. Given that Mexicans were specifically hired to work in factories, owners found ample cultural metaphors to sustain class relations that inevitably harnessed color descriptions and color and class became two sides of the same coin. In more philosophical terms, class and color engaged into a kind of dialectical capitalism where class did the work of color, and color did the work of class, to produce a kind of racial capitalism in South Chicago. For example, according to Innis-Jiménez, the skin-color hierarchy overlaid on the Mexican population attempted to make sense of their skin-color differences by placing them in the "less-than white" category early in the twentieth century. Moreover, even though Mexicans are also white in skin color, they are not considered *racialized* white Americans (Gueros) among the Mexican population but white (blacos) within the historical context of colorismo. However, within Chicago's skin-color hierarchies, their Mexicanness or "otherness" became a prime factor in defining their racial status within the skin-color hierarchy. A skin-color hierarchy made legible through class relations placed them as "less-than-white" but not "too-close-to-Black" because they were viewed as desirable workers within the steel industry.[25] A similar process in American capitalism is making populations "white," but this sociohistorical move often emerges out of labor demands or capitalist necessity and a desire by those of European descendant populations to keep their class status and privilege. For example, early in the twentieth century, Irish, Italian, and other eastern European folks were not considered "white." But as the influx of brown populations to different areas of the United States increased, white populations needed to create social distancing mechanisms embedded in racial logics, as all groups began fighting for the acquisition of jobs.

In another case, we also see that class is, in very definitive ways, clearly marked by skin-color designations in the context of contemporary Mexican Chicago. Historian Gabriela F. Arredondo, in her monograph on Mexican Chicago, comments that she experienced a color inspection at a school playground early on. Gardening was marked in color terms, as it is now among yarderos. In that playground experience, as she was interacting with other kids, they told young Gabriela about her identity: "You can't—you're not dark enough," and "Yeah, we should know. Our gardener is Mexican." This phrase captures a racialization process in which class and color form a mutually supportive relationship. By examining the early decades of the twentieth century, Arredondo focuses on race, identity, and the nation to problematize the historical constructions of *Mexicanidad* while pointing out the differences across gender. Arredondo wrote one of the first historical analyses that argued that Mexican racialization as experienced by Mexicans in Chicago remained focused on matters of skin color. According to Arredondo, there was an increasing push to create a colorblind society through Americanization programs. Secondly, a Mexican *mestizaje* ideology was functioning beyond Mexico's boundaries. In Arredondo's words, "The ethnoracial dynamics of Chicago—namely, the presence of these groups and the strength of their individual group histories in the city—provide a distinct and fundamentally unique circumstance for Mexican settlement."[26]

Colorism Crosses Borders

Ideas and ideologies cross political and international borders. As a state-sponsored ideology and a dispersed power assemblage, *mestizaje* evolved among Mexicans located in the US Southwest and farther north into the US Midwest. For these populations, while the Mexican state apparatus may not have been directing their everyday lives, its state-sponsored ideology of *mestizaje* was. This was especially relevant for communities just north of the Rio Grande River.[27] For example, in her pioneering work on borders, Chicana writer Gloria E. Anzaldúa challenged stereotypical portrayals of Chicano homo-nationalistic claims in her critique of Mexican American history, culture, and gender relations. Anzaldúa's work offers an alternative understanding of the Chicana experience as a border-queer subject against Chicano masculinity among Mexican and Mexican American communities. Her work represented a direct challenge to patriarchy as an organizing form and cultural logic.

Anzaldúa drew attention to the centrality of borders and borderlands.[28] *Borders*, for her, mean "the actual physical borderlands" at the US-Mexican border; *borderlands*, on the other hand, refers to "the psychological borderlands, the sexual borderlands, and the spiritual borders [which] are not particular to the Southwest."[29] Anzaldúa makes a key distinction here. The border is an actual geographic space for her, while the borderlands deal with aspects of everyday life's less material production. She writes, "Borders are set up to define the places that are safe and unsafe, to distinguish us from them. A border is a dividing line, a narrow strip along a steep edge. A borderland is a vague and undetermined place created by the emotional residue of an unnatural boundary. It is in a constant state of transition."[30] These two definitions allow us to realize that there is always a tension between attempting to fossilize a border to a territorial space and imagining a border's influence in its de-territorialized formations. This chasm should not be seen as a problem but as an opportunity to visualize the processes that make us actively and productively move from the US-Mexico border to its multiple and often complex areas of influence, affect, and materialization farther north.

From Anzaldúa's analysis of borders emerges a query: Does a border subject need to be, as in our case study, close to the US-Mexico border to be a subject of its effects?[31] Social scientists, Latinx scholars, and anthropologists working inside the United States on issues pertaining to the study of the lives of Latina/o or Latinx populations have critically reminded us that borders, as well as their creation and reproduction, are relevant to how these populations think of themselves in relation not only to the US-Mexico border but also to many other internal borders and boundaries.[32] The emotional residue of the US-Mexico border—its nightmarish character and its thickening power matrix—are indeed felt all the way north to Chicago. Anzaldúa also reminds us that those who pass the border patrol checkpoints "find themselves in the midst of 150 years of racism in Chicano barrios in the Southwest *and big northern cities* [emphasis added]. Living in a no man's borderland, caught between being treated as criminals and being able to eat, between resistance and deportation."[33] For Mexicans in transborder Chicago, to be more precise, it is a century of racism, given that the first Mexicans who arrived at the steel mills in South Chicago came in the second decade of the twentieth century and encountered a highly racialized order based on perceptions of color differences.[34]

Scholars seeking to understand border dynamics as they apply to migrant and Latino communities in the United States filtered into anthropology. For example, Renato Rosaldo writes that in the classical period of anthropology, an anthropologist would "emphasize patterns at the expense of processes of change and internal inconsistencies, conflicts, and contradictions."[35] Thus, as Rosaldo comments, "Cultural borderlands appear to be annoying exceptions rather than central areas of inquiry."[36] Rosaldo explains that in some instances, "such borders are literal. . . . Cities throughout the world today increasingly include minorities defined by race, ethnicity, language, class, religion, and sexual orientation. Encounters with difference now pervade modern everyday life in urban settings."[37] More specifically, Rosaldo calls for the remaking of anthropological analysis attentive to the workings of change, practice, and history. Arguing against and complicating the work done by classic anthropologists, Rosaldo gives theoretical attention to the borderlands, those areas that should be regarded "not as analytical empty transitional zones but as sites of creative cultural production that require investigation."[38] For the social analyst, as for the border theorist, the borderlands have moved from the margins to the center of research, theory, method, and inquiry. This shift was especially relevant during decolonization and the decades after the 1960s, when social protest, movement, and the fight for civil rights were present in the West.

Drawing on Gloria Anzaldúa and Renato Rosaldo, anthropologist and Latino Studies scholar Alejandro Lugo writes about borders in Mexican society and theorizes about its relevance to Mexican migrants in the United States. For Lugo, "border crossings" are often theorized from those less privileged subjects as they experience passing through inspection stations in their everyday lives, which "are pervasive and, therefore, more common than border crossings in the lives of such unprivileged subjects as factory workers and other working-class people." Thus, drawing from the theoretical texts of border theorists and theories of power, as well as ethnographic accounts, Lugo provides a "new analytical tool, border inspections, to the current metaphor of 'border crossings.'"[39] Lugo adds that "border inspections are more pervasive among failed border crossings of the working classes, who too often experience border exclusions; whereas successful border crossings are more characteristic of relatively privileged sectors."[40] Does this theorization hold for Mexican migrants who travel deeper into the space of the United States? Indeed, how this articulates with an understanding of borders, identity, race-making, and race-ordering processes is the border riddle I seek to explain here.

In the United States context, I argue that inspections do not disappear as Mexicans travel north; these processes acquire an intense colorism which a border theory framework helps to uncover. In the context of Latin America, we know that much of the nationalisms that emerged after the battles of independence as nation-states were defining their borders were critical of the colonial caste system, and part of the need for an independence movement focused on attempting to erase those color differences. While different nationalisms in Latin America did produce desired results (in that they created those imagined communities that Benedict Anderson helps us to understand), they practiced a flagrant erasure of colorism. For example, Tanya Katerí Hernández points on her analysis of customary versus formal law in the United States and Latin American suggested recently that in fact, we have never left color behind, and that is also what my theorization of colorism as experience among Mexican migrants attempts to illuminate through my ethnographic study of working-class experiences of my interlocutors in the Mexican Midwest.[41]

Once at the US-Mexican border, documented and undocumented migrants continuously cross class, gender, race, color, and other borders, redefining their relation to others and society. While in my theorization of transborder Chicago, border inspections lose descriptive analytical accuracy in the process of migration, Mexicans in Chicago experience an intensification of inspections based on color, enhanced by a transborder sensibility and an organizational structure that oscillates between Mexico and the United States in an elastic and malleable connective tissue connecting Zacatecanos/as to transborder Chicago. Thus, the term *color inspections* becomes a critical ethnographic tool to document the lives of Latinx communities in Chicago, at times within ingroup relations and later in relational terms vis-à-vis other racial and ethnic groups (i.e. African Americans, Asian Americans, and other Latinos/as). Indeed, the diagnostic, practical, and theoretical tool of "color inspections" can be mobilized to better understand how Mexican yarderos experience racism through class, labor, and color hierarchies in Chicago. Their color imaginings are rooted in colonial origins south of the current US-Mexico border much in the ways that Tanya Katerí Hernández has described a type of "racial innocence" in which Latinx individuals engage with these logics of colorism as they interact with other Latinx groups.[42] Indeed, the color inspections theorized and found among yarderos in South Chicago are produced through the uneven interaction of US-based ethnic, racial, and skin-color hierarchies in Chicago. These skin-color orders are neither static nor rigid—we know that by now—but their enactment and mobilization produce drastic effects on the subjective understanding of their world from my collaborators' points of view and what it means to be Mexican beyond Mexico's borders. Thus, the problem of skin color found among populations of Mexican origin within the United States, as already mentioned, is an issue that requires further analytical and ethnographic investigation to capture the complexity of how racism works within and beyond a Black-and-white dichotomy.[43]

Embodied Colorism in *el Norte*

As experienced by Mexican landscapers or yarderos in Chicago, when examined carefully, the term *color inspections,* allows us to view the multiple ways in which colorism is not just about racialized beliefs regarding skin color but is anchored in this cultural formation by encompassing other areas of the human experience. For example, the use of a baseball cap requires a "thick [color] description" as explored by anthropologist Gilberto Rosas as explored below.[44]

By using color hierarchies as a starting point and returning to colorism in the social analysis, for example, critical race study scholars have pointed out that racism is about more than color; it is about comportment, attitudes, behaviors. In their analysis, the body is the central conduit for the productions and reproduction of culture.[45] For example, the US-Mexico border offers a glimpse of how Mexican encounters with racism in Chicago may be experienced later in the migratory trajectory. At Nogales, Sonora, and Nogales, Arizona, anthropologist Gilberto Rosas offers a cultural analysis of the *chuntaro*, who is described as follows, "His weathered skin, clothing, and indigenous accent, if he speaks Spanish at all, betray his unsuccessful efforts to fit in at a place designed to reveal nations,' biologized as racial, differences officially."[46] The ethnographic details provide us with specific clothing items; for example, the baseball cap (*una gorra*) serves as a marker of class and racialized status in Rosas's example.

While performing lawn service, my collaborators and yardero friends also wore baseball caps as part of the job. First, because it is necessary to protect their faces from the sun while mowing, and second because of the cultural meaning attached to this item. For example, concomitant with Rosas's description of skin color is the "weathered skin" of the *chuntaro*. Another way to speak about the color inspections that I now investigate is by examining how yarderos in Chicago dress at work. Usually, yarderos do not wear a uniform to work, but from my observations, dress depicts aspects of cultural and personal preferences and environmental necessities. In the last months of my fieldwork, I began to see lawncare service crews wearing either a dark-green or dark-blue uniform. I rarely saw lawncare service women wearing any type of uniform to work. However, in more established companies, which are usually not owned by Mexicans but by a corporation, a uniform is a standard feature. The cultural weight that baseball caps have for working-class Latinx migrants has been under analyzed from a critical approach. For example, we find similar analyses of scholars describing how working-class folks dress. For example, in Seth Holmes's study of farmworkers in California, he observes that dressing with soft cloth pants, buttoned cowboy-style shirts, and a baseball cap, at least for males, is a typical way of class distinction.[47]

Indeed, among my yardero interlocutors, wearing a baseball cap was a practical necessity during the hot, grueling summer months in Chicago, and the issue of skin color appears within this context. For instance, early in April 2013, José Flores's son, Guillermo, discussed his experience as a yardero in Chicago. He was born in Mexico but came to the United States at an early age. Even with a thin figure and "white" (*blanco*) skin tone, he does not cover his head while mowing grass. During the summer of 2013, I only once saw him wearing a fisherman's hat that covered his face, and that was because it was boiling that day. Guillermo came to work with Don Antonio just before the Fourth of July. We started mowing near 89th Street and Yates Avenue. Guillermo was not wearing a hat, so I asked whether he wanted an extra baseball cap from the cargo van. He said that he did not want it. I asked why. Guillermo said, "What for? Either way, I always get dark during the summer and change to whiter in the winter." I took his refusal to wear a hat as adequate, but it puzzled me that Guillermo had such a malleable understanding of skin tonality as being able to change with time. Upon further reflection on using a baseball cap, I recalled that when I worked with Cesar Hernandez from September to November 2012, he told me that he did not wear a baseball cap when he started working in las yardas. He believed that when people saw him working while wearing a baseball cap, they would imagine that he did not know English or would look down on him.

Indeed, the baseball cap has become a marker of working-class identity for many Mexicans in Chicago, especially those who mow grass. This marker of identity is similar to what Juan Thomas Ordóñez noticed among the jornaleros in Berkeley, California, who dress to embody a working-class identity as migrant workers.[48] Yarderos wear baseball caps in various styles, but many have the White Sox logo, New York Yankees, or any other baseball or football team logo. For example, Don Antonio would hardly leave his house without a baseball cap on, and he would rarely wear any other type of hat on his head. Despite always covering his head to alleviate the effects of being out in the sun all day, Don Antonio still has profound, wrinkled lines from age and working outside all his life. I recall seeing him in early 2013, when he first arrived from vacationing in Mexico for the start of the landscaping season, and his skin tone was like mine, which is a light brown. Still, by the time we had both worked at the peak of the landscaping season, we both had a darker, brown complexion. Despite this temporary darkening, some yardero peers often joked after work that I was also getting darker from working. They would say, "That is fine, you will get whiter during the winter season."

The covering of hands is also tied to ideas of colorism and gender. Among yarderos/as in South Chicago, given that the work involves using their hands all the time, they need to grip the lawn mower, blower, or weed whacker. Toward the start and end of the landscaping season, gloves are common because of the cold temperatures in early March or late November. However, there are times that yarderos wear gloves during the scorching summer months too. While working for Don Antonio, we always encountered a lawncare crew of Mexican migrants from the state of Zacatecas near 92nd Street and Crandon Avenue on Tuesdays. I did not talk with them, but I would raise my hand to say hello, just as other yarderos would. I noticed that the chalanes, who help the lawncare company owner with work, would wear gloves while mowing.

In my journal, I recorded a discussion with my boss, Don Antonio, on this issue sometime in late July. I asked him why the lawncare workers we always encountered on Tuesdays would wear gloves while mowing. Don Antonio smiled and said, "Well, they do not want to get their hands dirty. They want to keep their hands soft and *blanquitas* [whiter]." In Don Antonio's view, not wanting to get one's hands "dirty" while working as a yardero meant a different work ethic, which he associated with the new generation of younger yarderos that had just begun to do this kind of work. Don Antonio would often say that if you do not want to get your hands dirty, then do not work as a yardero, since you always dirty your hands while mowing, handling garbage, grass clippings, or just being outside. The other element that was revealed in our discussion of the use of gloves while mowing was a feminizing component. As described above, Don Antonio said that the chalanes who wore gloves wanted to keep their hands soft (*suavecitas* in Spanish), which is why they wore gloves. In other words, using words such as "dirty," which meant masculine, and "soft," in this case meaning feminine, was a way for Don Antonio to express a work-ethic differentiation in gender terms and, at the same time, to construct his work activity as masculine and respectable.

On the other hand, wearing gloves while mowing can also be tied to beliefs of color and beauty. Given that light or bleached skin is preferred and often associated with beauty, it is fascinating that chalanes take care of their hands and cover them with gloves during the summer. During the many months with my collaborators, especially when I helped Don Antonio during the season in 2013, I noticed that my hands and arms would gradually get darker in tone, resembling a dark, cinnamon-like color. This often happens during July and August, when the sun hits the hardest and sunset does not occur until eight o'clock in the evening. However, I did not put any special lotion on my hands or cover them with gloves. Don Antonio would laugh if I did. On one occasion after work, I spent time with Cesar Sanchez near his home, and Andres showed up to hang out for a couple of minutes. Given that Andres's skin tonality is darker than either mine or Cesar's, I raised the subject of the wearing of gloves by the yarderos I would often see on Tuesdays while working with Don Antonio. I asked Andres directly what he thought about it, and without any hesitations, this was the exchange that followed:

SERGIO: What do you think about wearing gloves while mowing?
ANDRES: They want to be *mujercitas,* if they want to wear gloves, they should stay home washing the dishes."
SERGIO: Well, it is not so much that they want to be women, but they do not want to get darker.
ANDRES: No . . . they want to be different; they do not want to be yarderos.
SERGIO: Or they do not want to be looked at differently because of the color of their skin.
ANDRES: Look, I will tell you. Yes, maybe they do not want to be *moreno* like me, but wherever they go, they will always have *el nopal en la frente* [the cactus on their forehead].

While I did push the issue of color on Andres, his use of the statement "*el nopal en la frente*" captures the struggles that Mexican migrants face as they interact with other ethnic and racial groups in Chicago and in the United States. The *nopal* is a relevant metaphor or figure of speech that suggests cultural markers that unavoidably place Mexicans in a racial hierarchy among other Mexicans. In other words, these are cultural scripts that are not often spoken. Despite Andres's refusal to address the issue of color, which I pushed further in our interaction, he suggests that color marks you as a Mexican when working as a yardero.

Women Experience Color Hierarchies

Women who perform lawncare services and the partners of yarderos have a significantly different experience marked by gender and other forms of color inspections. En las yardas, it was obvious that Mexican women form a vital part of the yardero labor force, even when they are not the people behind the lawn mowers or driving the pickup trucks. My ethnographic observations of younger women's experiences are from the dialogue and discussions I had with yarderos, women who work alongside their husbands, family members, and less frequently with other women who were small company owners.[49]

Feliciano and Martina

Aware that gender is another window that qualitatively provides and sometimes challenges theories about identity and nationhood, I used these everyday moments to engage with questions of colorism, Mexican identity, and perceptions of how the family was affected by these sociocultural processes by documenting the moments where color appeared as an important category or subject of discussion.

Feliciano Garcia is a migrant from the state of Zacatecas. I met him while working for Cesar Sanchez, the owner of the first lawncare service company I worked for. Cesar would recall and categorize Feliciano's crew as one of the fastest to mow yardas in the South Side of Chicago, if not the entire city. His crew can mow close to eighty to one hundred houses daily. After getting married, Feliciano's wife, Martina Garcia, a migrant from Zacatecas, came to the United States and lived for three years in Los Angeles. They told me that, in the early 1990s, Feliciano worked various construction jobs with family members who lived in California in the San Bernardino Valley. However, despite living with and having the help of Feliciano's branch of the family, Martina could not adjust to life in the United States. Martina recalled that she missed her mother and sisters. In 1998, upon visiting Chicago on a trip to see Martina's father, the couple decided to migrate to the Mexican Midwest. Since that year, Feliciano has worked mowing lawns for a living in South Chicago and the surrounding neighborhoods. Martina is in her late forties, with a broad smile and a sharp sense of humor that disregards her unpleasant experience in the Southwest, a quality admired by her family. She and Feliciano have three boys and a girl, all born in Chicago except the oldest, who was born in Ontario, California.

After the Fourth of July in 2012, I saw Feliciano near 88th Street and Anthony Avenue, and I asked him if he would be willing to talk to me about how he began to work as a landscaper. Later that day, I arrived at his home in the Hegewisch neighborhood near 141st Street and Avenue A. Feliciano and Martina began recalling when they first migrated to Los Angeles and then to Chicago:

> FELICIANO: Well, I arrived just like everyone else, with nothing. I was already working in Ontario, close to Riverside, California. I worked with my relatives in construction or whatever job was available. I had

just married Martina in December of '88, and as soon as January came, off to the north.

SERGIO: And how did you end up in Chicago?

FELICIANO: Well, because of my father-in-law. He invited us to spend a few days, and my wife liked it. She already had plans.

SERGIO: What plans did you have, Mrs. Martina?

MARTINA: Well, imagine being alone in Ontario, and here in Chicago, my mom and siblings were here. It didn't take long for me to decide and insist to Feliciano that we needed to move here.

SERGIO: And what did you think, Feliciano, when Martina mentioned that?

FELICIANO: Well, the lady's the boss. I told my father-in-law if we could go pick up my stuff from California, and we spent almost five days going back and forth. Honestly, I don't regret it. I arrived, and the next day, bam, straight to work, cutting grass almost twelve hours every day. Even on Sundays when it was urgent, or work was behind.

Following this conversation, Martina discussed their struggles at the beginning of their marriage, especially with her mother-in-law. With a sad look and breaking voice, Martina told me that her mother-in-law did not like her from the beginning when she and Feliciano began to date. The main reason was that she was darker—in her words, "*muy morena*"—and she was seen as not worthy of Feliciano. Following her statement, I asked whether this had changed over the years, given that Feliciano and Martina had been married for over twenty years. Martina quickly responded that nothing had changed. For example, since Feliciano and Martina had become better off, economically, they were able to travel to Mexico at least once a year to visit Feliciano's family in their hometown of Zacatecas. When they went back during the annual fiestas in December, they always stayed in the home of Martina's mother and only visited Feliciano's mother during the day. Martina recalled that, when they returned, she was still not treated like Feliciano's brothers' wives, who have lighter skin tones.

Rodrigo and Julia

Color preferences and color inspections among couples continue to take place in Chicago. For example, Rodrigo migrated to Chicago with his immediate family in 2001 and eventually married Julia from his hometown in Zacatecas. When we spoke Rodrigo was in his mid-twenties, tall, and had a broad back and a round face. He always cuts his hair in a short military style and has a brown to deep brown skin tone. He had worked as a lawncare service worker since he arrived in Chicago in 2001, and at the time of our conversation, had been driving sixteen-wheel trailers carrying materials around the Chicagoland area for the preceding two years, from 2012 to 2014. Julia, who is also in her mid-twenties but shorter than Rodrigo, has curly black hair and a light-brown skin tone. When I saw them during the summer months, they both looked mildly brownish, and both looked pale white during the winter months. Julia worked as a receptionist at a public hospital back in Zacatecas before migrating to Chicago in 2010; they have a four-year-old daughter.

Rodrigo and Julia invited me to their house for dinner on December 27, 2013. They live in a one-story brick house in the East Side neighborhood. They bought the house through Rodrigo's brother, Jorge. These informal economic practices are more common than we tend to imagine. In other words, Rodrigo did not have to apply for a bank loan to buy the house from Jorge. They simply sat down, discussed the deal, and made it happen by the power of a spoken agreement. They both knew that if one of them did not keep their word, it would damage their reputations and shake the foundations of their manhood and the family honor on which trust, loyalty, and family bond are cemented. We ate *tacos de cabeza* (head tacos) and *tacos de cecina* (meat tacos). As our conversation turned toward some of the recent events back in the state of Zacatecas, I began directing the conversation toward their experiences with color, given that their only child has light, white skinned (*guera*), fair haired, and blue eyed. They began to tell me two recent stories about people around them who made their child's color an issue.

The first event occurred when Julia drove down Avenue O in the East Side neighborhood. She recalled that it was just after she had arrived in Chicago with her daughter. As she retold the story, her voice followed a rhythm, as if the event had just happened yesterday. Julia recalled that a police officer stopped her for driving above the speed limit. Julia did not have a valid Illinois driver's license then, but she had her Mexico license and her green card. When the officer approached the driver's window, he at once asked for her license, registration, and car insurance. Julia was driving a 2010 Toyota minivan. Julia recalled that before even checking the registration and driver's license, the police officer asked her whether the minivan was hers. Julia recalled that the officer slowly looked at the seat behind her and saw her child in the back. Upon seeing the child, Julia recalled that the officer looked at her and then looked at the child again, and in a confused way, asked Julia if she was the babysitter of the child she had in the back. By that time, recalled Julia, she felt angry with the officer because he thought Julia had stolen the vehicle and her child. Of course, Julia specified, the police officer was white (*pinche guero*). She was let go after fifteen minutes, as the police officer did not find anything wrong with her record history.

The other event occurred at a major grocery store in the East Side neighborhood. Julia recalled that earlier in November, she had to go to the grocery store because, at that time, her husband Rodrigo was working full time as a commercial driver and had little time to take care of household tasks. Julia told me that she took her daughter with her, and as she approached the cash register, the cashier looked at her daughter, turned to Julia and said, "Is she your daughter? She does not look like you." Julia recalled that she did not know what to think at first. Julia said she did not want to be rude to the middle-aged Latina woman but simply said, "Yes, she is my daughter." However, as Julia described the cashier as not being happy with the answer Julia had given, the Latina woman further said, "She [the daughter] is *guerita,* and you are not. Is your husband also like you, or is he *blanquito* [white skin looking] like your daughter?" Julia recalled feeling angry with the lady. Not knowing how to respond anymore, Julia took her daughter and left the grocery store without further response to the lady's inquiries.

Conclusion

In the everyday life of Mexican working-class yarderos in transborder Chicago, I have examined the meanings produced through the discursive and material elements of skin-color references and lived experiences captured through color hierarchies, which may at times have deeper historical presence and carry within the mobilization of these hierarchies what Ann Stoler has termed "imperial debri."[50] Simultaneously, color hierarchies capture the prevailing ways subjects are designated through skin-color markers that navigate Mexican-based ethnic and racial classification and US-based racial order in complex ways and actively utilize culture as an expression of colorism/o of a Latin American or US imperial debri.[51]

Among the yarderos I spoke with, color hierarchies are practical categories used to make sense of the world, even if they do not specifically understand their colonial, national or postcolonial origin. These categories also reinforce other class, gender, and ethnic classifications within ethnic Mexicans in Chicago. We now know that Mexican-origin skin-color hierarchies are not easily mapped on the so-called mestizo population's bodies in places such as South Chicago, where colorism has a more profound racial history. But the term *mestizaje* is used to claim a kind of postnational identity in many transborder contexts such as Chicago. For example, as I mentioned earlier Katerí Hernández work on race and racism has helped us think through this complexity of color meanings as experienced by Latinos in the United States. In my own reading of *colorismo*, I am bringing border theorizing closer to the ways in which W. E. B. Du Bois framed the color-line debate in the United States but am keenly aware of the racial innocence we quickly fall prey to in our disregard for anti-Blackness permeating Latinx folks.[52]

Within the context of the United States, Mexican immigrants do not leave behind their skin-color categories of Spanish and later Mexican origin, but instead carry them all the way north to the Midwest. As ethnic Mexicans arrive in the Midwest, they channel specific work activities and are placed into other colored social structures depending on the necessities of capital. For example, at the turn of the twentieth century, production owners—those that hire migrants—attempted to fit them within the prevailing color dichotomy. Therefore, in South Chicago, Mexicans were placed in the "less-than-white" category to make sense of their class relation to whites and African Americans in Chicago.

Mexicans in the United States discriminate against one another based on color. There are two reasons for this behavior. First, in transborder Chicago skin color and *colorismo* are fundamental to processes of identity formation. Second, the intensification of discussions about skin color within the context of the United States' long history of racial oppression seems to subjectively influence and trigger a sense of Mexican identity based on color that recaptures skin-color meaning to make sense of and produce a postnational Mexican ness. The cultural device Mexicans in South Chicago use, aware or unaware of this practice, to make sense of racial differences is what we can call *color inspections*.

What's new about the color meanings and cultural practices we are documenting here in this chapter is that, in the context of South Chicago, skin color continues to be inspected to extract value from labor based on its hierarchical organization, significantly and obviously, among working-class Mexicans. Indeed, we can conclude that, in its most simple terms, producing and reproducing those uneven color hierarchies is the labor of the few who have the means to produce surplus value in contrast to the vast majority of migrants who continue to be dominated by color structures, sometimes not of their own making.

In transborder Chicago, Mexican yarderos interact with other ethnic and racial groups, such as African Americans. Exploring Mexican, working-class folks' range of color experiences and their encounters with Blackness and anti-Black sentiment is a vital lateral relation we need to engage with further to expand simple notions of colorism/*colorismo* transborder dyads among and beyond the Mexican community in South Chicago. The next chapter should in fact help us untangle and better understand the Mexican-*Moreno* relations found en las yardas.

CHAPTER 5

Los Morenos y Los Mejicanos

On Colorism, Mugging, and Lateral Race-Making in South Chicago

> The function, the very serious function of racism is distraction. It keeps you from doing your work. It keeps you explaining, over and over again, your reason for being. Somebody says you have no language, so you spend twenty years proving that you do. Somebody says your head isn't shaped properly, so you have scientists working on the fact that it is. Someone says you have no art, so you dredge that up. Somebody says you have no kingdoms, so you dredge that up. None of that is necessary. There will always be one more thing.
>
> —Toni Morrison, "Black Studies Center Public Dialogue"

Ernesto Morales is a twenty-eight-year-old Mexican yardero living in Chicago's East Side neighborhood near 112th Street and Avenue O. Ernesto has a medium-size figure and light-brown eyes. A thin shaded line forms his mustache. The mustache recaptures the 1950s look of Mexican cinema singers such as Jorge Negrete, comedian Tin Tan (German Valdez de Castillo, 1915–73), and even Marco Antonio Campos (1919–96) from the famous popular culture television film series of *Viruta y Capulina*. Ernesto prefers to wear green pants and button-down shirts when working as a gardener. Quick-tempered, he boasts of having the best landscaping company in South Chicago. Born in the United States, he hesitates to make conversation as he encounters other yarderos while traveling through the neighborhoods.

During the summer weekends, many yarderos I got to know would travel to a flea market called La 47 (at 41st and Ashland Avenue) to replace their worn-out work clothes with secondhand shirts and pants. Ernesto mentioned this practice a few times. I also replenished my clothing stock twice during the 2013 landscaping season. Swap-O-Rama-style flea markets first opened their doors in the Midwest in 1969, thanks to the efforts of founder Rex Meadows. These openair markets are an important cultural and economic engine for Latino-owned businesses. If you need a pair of cowboy boots or a *tejana* (Texas-style cowboy hat), *chiles rojos* (red peppers) or a shirt from your favorite Mexican soccer team, this is the place to go. For many single, working-class yarderos, this is also one of the only public spaces to seek a potential partner.

Ernesto comes from a family of well-known landscapers in South Chicago; people often identify his family as "Los Morales." He lives in a three-story house located at 103rd and Torrence Avenue. His father, Don Ramon Morales, came to the United States in the early 1980s, after a few good years of his company's economic growth as landscapers in Chicago, he established himself as a company owner. Ernesto lives in an apartment on the third floor with his wife, Maricela, and three children. Maricela migrated to Chicago from Jalisco, Mexico, in the mid-1990s and went to James H. Bowen High School, the oldest school in the South Chicago area. Established in 1889, Bowen initially had only four rooms allotted to high school students.[1] The school is named for Colonel James Harvey Bowen, who became the Calumet and Chicago Canal and Dock Company president in 1869. Bowen is commonly known as the "father of South Chicago," as his company played a formative role in the area's economic development.

Ernesto is three years older than I am. He is sarcastic in his conversations, and he would often ask me, "*¿Y que vas a hacer con lo que escribes? Vas a sacar dinero o qué?*" (And what are you going to do with what you write? Are you going to make money from it or what?). I would reply that I expected to be a professor sometime soon. I could see from his glance that Ernesto doubted this would happen. I was with him in that sentiment, but I tried to hide it. When I visited his home one Sunday afternoon in early April after the landscaping season began, Ernesto wanted to sell me one of his used lawn mowers to start my landscaping company. "*Pa que hagas dinero*" (to make money), he explained.

Ernesto saw me mowing near 91st Street and Phillips Avenue a few months later. The following discussion is an excerpt from our short talk in late November while I was helping Don Antonio finalize the work for the season:

ERNESTO: Hey, I have not seen you. What is up with you?
SERGIO: Here, working.
ERNESTO: How is your work in las yardas coming along?
SERGIO: Good, I guess. I have been helping mow grass, but you know it is hard to get money from clients.

ERNESTO: Why is that? What is going on?
SERGIO: The clients do not want to pay. You know, as always.
ERNESTO: Make them pay! Fuckin' [*pinches*] Black asses.
SERGIO: [Nervous laugh] What can I do? Nothing! Just come again to mow the grass and knock on their door to see if they open and pay every week.
ERNESTO: Motherfuckers. We need to make them pay; we need them to sign a contract! Fuckin' Black folks. They spend their money on nice cars and do not want to pay us.
SERGIO: What else could be done? Nothing.

Documenting the presence and emergence of racism within and against Mexicans characterizes a substantial amount of my interactions with my collaborators. While I strongly disagree with the derogatory ways many of the yarderos viewed and talked about African Americans, I resisted my urge to correct them on the spot. Instead, in later conversations with my interlocutors, I inquired about their anti-Black attitudes, hoping they would come to see that labeling others because of their socially and culturally perceived skin color is incorrect. I hoped I would change how they viewed Black folks and practices of Blackness through deep conversations. I also wanted our dialogues to help me understand and capture the ruthless and insidious character of race-making and race-disordering processes en las yardas as a type of racial capitalism embedded among Mexican, working-class folks. Indeed, specifically on this topic, law scholar Tanya Katerí Hernández emphatically argues that there is a latent (and virulent at times) discrimination from fair-skin Latinos against darker-skin Latinos—and African Americans as well. As such, the analysis of anti-Black sentiments is one area of social life that scholars of law—judges, for example—have not been able to take a closer look. As the previous chapter on color inspections has ethnographically documented, race relations or racialization processes take the white-and-Black dichotomy as a given to inquire into forms of discrimination, and anything that falls outside that color line falls from being considered as racial discrimination.[2]

A closer look at my conversation with Ernesto reveals the way he understands his relation vis-à-vis African Americans in South Chicago becomes less so as he discusses his own work experience en las yardas. At first, the discussion revolves around class. However, as soon as Ernesto critiques how clients take advantage of this class relation—by not paying for the lawn service—racism emerges as an explanatory framework to make sense of uneven capitalist relations. As I have mentioned before, in the city of Chicago, lawn service, as performed by the folks I talked to, is usually organized so that lawncare companies mow each residence weekly. At the end of the month, the company places a bill in the customer's mailbox. Often, the bill is a simple printed statement of the services done with a return envelope included. The idea is that the next time a yardero arrives to mow the lawn, the invoice will be paid in full in person. More seasoned landscapers allow clients to pay by sending a check to a PO Box at a local post office. Most clients pay in cash or write personal checks when they see the company owners—yarderos—mowing the grass for the week.

However, many clients also postpone payment for two weeks or even a month or two. It was common to hear about yarderos who had clients who did not pay for up to three months. A season's worth of service ranges from $500 to $600. If a client decides not to pay that amount, they could do so; there are no formal mechanisms other than the client's goodwill. You may wonder why yarderos do not just terminate the service. This is not an easy decision to make. Many yarderos' clients have hired them for one year, and the contract will renew each year based on whether the company owner needs their yard cut. At times, my collaborators would tell me that they felt compelled to give a break to clients experiencing financial difficulty. At other moments, Ernesto would mow the lawn of three or four consecutive houses within a block and briefly mention the lack of payment to the unpaying client's neighbor. The following week the client would come outside and pay him. We can theorize this as neighborhood shaming and yarderos actively use this strategy when they think it might work.

In Ernesto's comments about African Americans, his words and emotions are the key cultural areas that make racism legible and felt. For example, the discursive reference produced through Ernesto's plural adjective *pinches* (fucking) creates an emotional element generated by the yardero's interaction with the racially defined Black client. In this instance, upon experiencing and remembering that customers often lag in payment, Ernesto raises his voice in disgust. He responds emotionally toward a behavior (not paying for lawn service) in which gender and class become racially marked in the context of labor and capital demands.[3] As a transborder raciality emerges, Ernesto shifted his use of the general word *moreno* (to describe the general population of African American folks). Here, Ernesto also emphasized their color marking in Spanish, meaning Black, to speak about the perceived labor injustice through a color logic that recaptures race as an explanatory framework.[4] Ernesto secondly described African American clients as *culeros,* which in Spanish means "big asses." My interpretation suggests that racism is produced not just by saying a word or calling someone a general color name but by generalizing and biologizing perceived cultural characteristics. In other words, in this context where class matters, racism finds its nesting ground; it is birthed and evolves through adjectives, the tone of voice, and the emotional weight of the social interaction.

In the context of Chicago, interactions between Mexicans and African Americans form the bulk of the lived experiences of Mexican yarderos. Today, we know more about Mexican and Black interactions, but few studies examine these cross-racial interactions from emancipatory Black and Brown solidarity models.[5] From a spatial view, it makes sense that there would be strong connections, relations, and intercultural exchanges between Mexicans and Mexican Americans and their Black neighbors. At times, ethnic Mexicans and African Americans do inhabit the same American neighborhoods. Still, the scholarship on Mexican and Black relations has slowly documented this apparent blind spot in both Latino Studies and African American Studies in the United States.[6]

The literature on racial formation describes racism as a social phenomenon operating through theoretical frameworks such as structural racism and racialized social systems.[7] Often, racism is defined as symbolic in nature.[8] At other times, race is associated with material power linked to economic structures or ideological, racial differences that reinforce structural inequalities.[9] Racism has been described as an embodied experience.[10] Scholars have also documented how race and racism are created within Latin American populations before immigrants migrate to the United States and within those populations settled when the United States annexed the Southwest region after 1848.[11]

Thus, this chapter explores how race-centered experiences are constructed between Mexican working-class people vis-à-vis Black residents in the city of Chicago. As mentioned above, relational studies posit that racialization happens dynamically. Group-based racial constructions are formed in relation to whiteness and to devalued, marginalized groups (e.g., African Americans, Native Americans, Latinos, Asian Americans, and Pacific Islanders) whose own racialization is continuously in play. By studying race relationally, scholars can examine the logic that underpins the particular forms of inclusion and subordination a group may face when the gravitational force of whiteness is "absent" physically but not discursively. Here, I also demonstrate that, despite historically produced racial differences, as groups interact, culture does develop potentially cosustainable, but not positive, aspects within these unequal networks of work and life. This is a call to elaborate a racial analysis that captures the mutual and inseparable bonds, momentarily cosustainable but not emancipatory, that people construct through racism. For example, without African Americans' desire to have a nice lawn throughout the summer season in Chicago, Mexican landscapers would not exist in their current form. These are the details discussed in this chapter to offer a larger transborder vision of how internal racial borders are produced and reproduced through, for example, stories of muggings and color imaginations of both US-based and Mexican-based ethnic and racial classificatory schemes from the perspective of Mexican migrants only. Indeed, mobilizing what we can term "transborder raciality"—that is, the logic that underpins our understanding of racism beyond the nation-state—is relevant to better understanding border conceptions of subjecthood beyond the US-Mexico border with local bordered spaces in transborder Chicago.

Los Morenos

Within the city of Chicago, yarderos usually mow the lawns of middle- to upper-class African Americans and those of the white populations in the neighborhoods of Calumet Heights, Avalon Park, Beverly, Hyde Park, and Stony Island Park. At times, yarderos mow lawns farther west by Kedzie Avenue and farther south at the city limits around 127th Street and beyond. In these interactions, Mexican yarderos encounter other groups throughout the areas of the city in which they work.

Scholars of group-based identity have clearly identified racism in American society by framing the problem through the expression or theorization of the "color-line." While in this chapter I use the color-line metaphor to suggest that even though Mexican or Mexican American identity tends to be associated with ethnic identification, in the context of an intense racialized interaction such as the ones that occur within Chicago, color subjectivity takes center stage for ethnic Mexicans as in the previous chapter. In other words, there are many "racial" systems at play. In telling the story of Mexicans and their sense of color subjectivity, I am alluding to the problem of the color-line as it applies to ethnic Mexicans and African Americans—that is, the color line between Blackness and Brownness.[12] Of course, we need to be careful, and I am not directly mapping these color identifications as equivalent experiences. However, I identify particular (often circular) discourses associated with these identities and interpreted by Mexican yarderos.

To ground my discussion on color, I discuss the multiple ways I encountered racialization in Mexican terms early in my fieldwork. When I mowed for Sanchez Lawn Care on Tuesdays in October and November of 2012, I would work in the neighborhood of Roseland, located near Cottage Grove Avenue and 115th Street. Today, like South Chicago and much of the city's southern areas, the Roseland neighborhood suffers from many social, economic, and political ills associated with extreme poverty rates. In the mid-1980s, this neighborhood was a training ground for the then-social justice activist just out of college Barack

Obama. He harnessed the existing network of Black religious organizations to alleviate some of the issues affecting housing and social work in the area.[13] Indeed, few residents had the economic means to hire a landscaper or a lawn-care company in Roseland. Compared to Calumet Heights or Avalon Park, Roseland has fewer Mexicans performing lawn-service work. Still, there was a constant stream of available apartment buildings we were directed to mow.

Regardless of which neighborhood I traveled to while mowing grass, the constant interaction of Mexicans with other groups in the streets of Chicago brought us closer to socialize with African Americans.[14] There were specific color references found, especially against African Americans. I learned that my interlocutors actively mobilized a transborder raciality in engaging with Blackness. Indeed, it was Gloria Anzaldúa who first suggested that the border experiences ethnic Mexicans encountered once they cross into the United States and the problems that undocumented migrants face are embodied in—and even found in—northern cities such as Chicago. My sensibility as an ethnographer makes me theorize that, given how culture works, ethnic Mexicans do not leave three hundred years of Spanish colonialism or Mexican nationalism behind; the cultural legacies are brought on as they cross the bifurcated border and are experienced by working places farther north. Further, as I argued in the last chapter, one way to understand how ethnic Mexicans shift from a national identity based on *mestizaje* to one based on the white-and-Black dichotomy is through what I called "color inspections," which are also expressed in different assemblages in the Mexican and African American interactions that are discussed in this chapter. But more specifically, to capture the complexity of the anti-Black discourse found within Mexican yarderos, I follow the insights from law scholar Tanya Katerí Hernández in her analysis of anti-Black sentiments that Latinos have when dealing with anti-Blackness within the larger Latino category. Often, this relation is one where lighter skin Latinos tend to discriminate darken skin African Americans and other Latinos as well.[15]

In my own ethnographic study, there in a Zacatecan's racial innocence discourse that connects with the erasure of Black presence in Mexican nationalism as well. For example, in Zacatecas, the state from which many of my interlocutors migrated, the term *moreno* is not equated with "black" skin. For example, when I would ask yarderos/as what they thought a moreno person looked like, they would often say it was someone with deep-brown skin. They also tended to associate references to this specific skin color with "Indianness." I would push my questions further and ask them about the difference between morenos from Mexico and morenos from the United States. In those instances, the moreno identity acquired a different color identification that pointed to skin color and Blackness. Thus, what we see with the example of the *moreno* identifier is a creative way of mobilizing color hierarchies from Mexico and the United States to make sense of the new space and place that Mexicans came to experience after they migrated to Chicago.

The change in skin tonality that the term *moreno* acquires in the context of the United States emerges given that, to make sense of Blackness, many Mexicans use the actual color domain around the term *moreno*. Depending on the context, the word can encompass a double meaning in Spanish. For instance, *moreno* can mean "brownness" but a slight change can also denote the color purple, or *morado*. Moreover, in everyday experience, whenever a Spanish-speaking person hits himself or herself against a harder material than the body, they get a bruise—that is, a *morete*. A *morete* is understood to have the color proximity to that of "black" skin; thus, here we also find a common everyday experience and linguistic domain that is readily available among my interlocutors to understand skin tonality and the naming of difference through color inspections. For example, and to be more concrete, when yarderos are edging there is always the risk that the line trimmer would pick up rocks that are on the ground, and with an intense velocity these would travel to anyone standing within ten to fifteen feet. If one of these rocks hits someone, it would hurt a lot, and by consequence, that person would get a *morete* that would last for a couple of days, until the swelling would go down and their "blackened" skin would return to its "normal" tonality.

These linguistic domains are where I believe the association between Blackness and the terms *moreno* and *morete* acquire the metaphoric association that, when mobilized culturally in Chicago, is re-signified by Mexican migrants. When describing African Americans, Mexicans tend to say "moreno/a" in reference to a perceived purplish skin tonality. Thus, the available discursive domain of color suggests that Mexicans use the color purple in Spanish—*morado or morete*—to, by close metonymic association, from moreno as it is understood in Mexico to moreno as it is understood in the United States, and thus intensify it as a racial label to denote a "Black" individual. Thus, the term *moreno* becomes a traveling color metaphor with a creative way to be exploited in a transborder context.

But let us return to the context of Chicago. Indeed, the acknowledgment that many of these processes are culturally mediated is critical to understanding how labels or color hierarchies denote racialized or biologized features. Making generalizations at the population level (as in the case of morenos hanging out on their front porches in the Roseland neighborhood) is the role that emotions play in producing racial categories. In anthropology, the need to provide a structure for cultural processes was the chief concern for most of the twentieth century; later, a chorus of voices challenged this form of anthropological practice and enabled poststructuralist revisions of culture. For Mexican migrants, once in the context of Chicago, and following anthropologist Laura Lewis's suggestion from the Costa Chica region in relation to her analyses of blackness in Mexico, the term *moreno* seems to be also a "polite" form of referring to the generalized population of African Americans. For instance, during weekends or at social gatherings with yarderos during the summer months, I noticed Mexican yarderos would say "los morenos" in its generalized plural version when they talked about the relations between Mexicans and African Americans. Thus, the cultural malleability of the term *moreno* is corroborated through several observations and conversations with my interlocutors. Still, when Mexican yarderos want to emphasize US-based racial classification in conversation, the Spanish version of the N-word is, sadly, often utilized as well.

As we mowed around the Roseland neighborhood, I documented the yarderos' often gendered discourses on color and laziness. As we worked, we often saw African American youth (usually males, though not all the time) sitting on the front steps of their homes, walking in groups, or standing near the house where we were mowing the lawn. After we finished and returned to the pickup truck, Cesar often expressed his view that African American males were lazy (*huevones*). He added the skin color reference through the linguistic expression *pinches n——s huevones*. This phrase in Spanish is composed of an adjective, a noun, and a qualifier. In this case, the adjective is *pinche* (fuck or fucking). When Cesar would mobilize discriminatory remarks based on color, he would describe young African American males with the N-word instead of the word *morenos* (Black people in the context of Chicago). In Spanish, the word for the color black does not have the same history or emotional significance as the English N-word. Thus, my argument is that when Mexican immigrants want to utilize a similar semantic and linguistic expression as the N-word, they always use an adjectival expletive before the skin color description (e.g., adjective plus skin color reference). Like Ernesto, Cesar injected an emotional force into his tone when using the phrase *pinches n——s huevones*, disparaging the observed behavior and contrasting it indirectly with yarderos. Cesar's comment was meant to identify yarderos as real working-class people relationally—that is, the opposite of lazy—and by definition, *lazy* then becomes a racially marked word.

CHAPTER 5

Pero es Lo Mismo (It is the same thing)

Among Mexican yarderos, I often encountered stories during social and family gatherings about the experience of being robbed. One story came from Ruben Valadez, a Mexican yardero who arrived in Chicago in the early 2000s. Ruben is tall, robust in posture, and has narrow eyes and thick eyebrows. In Mexico he was studying to become an elementary-school teacher. Ruben was able to study for a year at the Autonomous University of Aguascalientes. While studying in the state's capital of the Aguascalientes territory, he saw that staying in Mexico may not have been the best option if he wanted a successful life. Ruben decided to go to Chicago on a tourist visa and started working as a yardero in the summer of 2000. Ruben started his lawncare company faster than many other Mexican migrants. I met Ruben in the summer of 2012, when he needed extra help to install sod. My boss, Cesar, took me to the worksite to *echarle una mano* (offer a hand) with the task. During our lunch break around noon, the following conversation happened:

SERGIO: That blower we have today looks new. Is it new?
RUBEN: Yes, it is. I just bought it. It cost me around $600.
SERGIO: $600! Wow, it is expensive!
RUBEN: Yes, so if you use it, make sure you always keep an eye on it. They are ready to steal it.
SERGIO: Who? I do not see anybody.
RUBEN: *Los morenos* [Black individuals]. *Pinches* n——s (Ruben shifted to use the term "Black" in Spanish), they are always ready to steal our blowers, wiros, or hedge trimmers. They do not take our lawn mowers because they are not able to carry them on their backs.
SERGIO: And how? Do they just grab it and start running? Is it not heavy?
RUBEN: They do not care. Often, there is someone with a car nearby, and they throw it inside and run away. Later, you find a *paisano* [fellow countryman] selling it at *la garra* [the flea market].

Like Ernesto when he discussed not receiving monthly payments for lawn work, Ruben talks in a generalized way about African Americans (*los morenos*) as thieves since "they" are the people he assumes may steal his equipment. It is pertinent to open a parenthesis here and emphasize that the tropes of criminality immediately materialized in these lawncare workers' minds are not accurate objectively. As an ethnographer, it has been troubling to write about these acts of theft because by doing so, I am reifying racial stereotypes of African American males and their relation to criminality. Still, the social fact that I constantly encountered these stories merited a serious discussion; they are important sociocultural constructions requiring further cultural inspection.

The relational racial elements within African American and Mexican communities have acquired additional layered marked color or coloring tropes. We can consider their interactions en las yardas beyond the client-yardero relation. For example, when speaking about their interactions with the African American population in South Chicago, Mexicans referred to them in color terms by using the plural noun morenos. However, they added the adjective *pinche* when they made a generalization or stereotype about the behavior of African Americans.

Indeed, mugging stories kept appearing in my everyday interactions with Mexican yarderos. In late August, I visited the home of Don Carlos and Doña Josefa. Theirs is a mixed-status family in which only some members are documented. They live in a constant state of legal limbo from which it is hard to escape.[16] In Don Carlos's words, *a mi no me gusta el lujo cuando trabajo* (I do not like to be fancy when I work). He rarely buys new blowers or weedwackers but makes sure that even his old equipment is well maintained. On this occasion, I was invited for *a comida* (formal lunch) to celebrate his son's birthday. Recalling the discussion I had the previous week with Ruben, I asked Don Carlos whether he usually buys new equipment during peak lawncare season in June and July. His quick answer was, "*¿Pa' qué Luego, me lo roban los morenitos*" (What for? Soon after, the "little" Black folks steal it from me). Wanting to explore this experience in detail, I asked, "*¿A poco, sí lo han robado?*" (Really, have they stolen from you?). Don Carlos started telling the following story:

> DON CARLOS: I recall that when we start the gardening every season, you have people that come where you are mowing and ask you for estimates. I remember that we were mowing a house near 83rd Street and Kingston Avenue when a moreno approached me, and he wanted me to go about half a block away to estimate how much I would charge him to mow his lawn. My brother Manuel was mowing the backyard of the house we were at, and I decided to go with el moreno to his house and do the estimate. I did not tell Manuel about it. As soon as we went to his house about a block away, I saw that he turned his head back as if looking for someone else and told me to see the backyard. I went in first, and he was behind me. I got to the backyard, and we started talking about what his lawn needed to make it grow well at the beginning of the season. [Leaning closer toward me] Sergio, look, I knew something was wrong. El moreno began to act like he was looking for

someone else. I had the blower on my back, and I immediately thought if he pulled a knife or gun, I would immediately turn my back and hit him with the blower.

SERGIO: And, what happened? Did he do something to you?

DON CARLOS: No, he did not. El moreno put his hand inside his pockets, looking for something. I began to worry, and I just said, "Look, you let me know if you want service; I have to go now." I hurried back from the backyard to the front of the house and immediately yelled at my brother. "Hey, I am here, come this way" (*Vente pa ca cabrón*). I turned toward where el moreno was in the backyard, and he started running toward the back fence and jumped over it. I got really scared; who knows what they are up to? That is why, if they approach you, just tell them that yes, soon, or give them your business card. If you think about it, homeowners are not following you seeking service. They just ask you once, and that is it.

SERGIO: Well, I am glad nothing happened to you or your brother.

This ethnographic vignette explores a few of the tensions and racial dynamics that *Mexicanos* in South Chicago experience in relation to Blackness. The first tension is spatial. The geographic space in South Chicago is demarcated by race and class. For example, Mexican gardeners carry out their daily work in working-class to middleclass neighborhoods composed of primarily African American populations. While Mexicans are not driving around performing yard work for much of the year, as soon as the season begins in mid-March, Mexicans and African Americans are on the street, procuring their daily means for the neighborhood's scarce resources to offer. In simple terms, in March every year, we find the Mexican gardener doing yard work for a wage; in other words, they sell their labor to the African American homeowner. Both engage in a mode of production that reproduces the other, involving a circular form of dispossession (see chapter 2) juxtaposed at the level of the racial mode of production.

The second relational tension is that of color and, by consequence, of potential inclination toward racism. As the ethnographic vignettes demonstrate, when the discussion turns to talk about the social interaction between Mexican gardeners and their clients, a color differentiation is developed between the Mexican and the term *moreno* (Black). As I mentioned, the term *moreno* has the linguistic capacity to encompass either Brownness or Blackness depending on the particular social circumstances. To put it another way, a Mexican may be mobilizing the term *moreno* when referring to someone of Brown skin or Black skin tonality. The term *moreno* and other linguistic expressions enable a racialized interaction through language combined with articles and adjectives. This rhetorical and cultural difference acquires meaning through the article *el/la* (the) in singular form and *los/las* (the) in plural form. This linguistic differentiation produces a cultural distance or space between "us" (Mexicans) and "them" (los morenos). Thus, the possibility of attaching the descriptive color designation as Black emerges in this context.

The third tension is how racialized discourse is present in everyday life. Several explanations help highlight why Don Carlos, for example, refers to African Americans as morenos or *morenitos*, the diminutive Spanish form. First, the Mexican working-class folks I spoke with believe that only *los Mexicanos*—not African Americans—mow grass. This first cultural idea emerges because, in practice, those who do the mowing in South Chicago tend to be Mexican immigrants, and those who hire lawncare workers tend to be Black homeowners. Thus, sadly, the association between Blackness and criminality forms an integral part of how Mexican gardeners envision themselves as workers in South Chicago. More importantly, this historical association is transmitted over time, reproducing the logic perpetuating relational racism. Of course, and let us be clear here, nothing natural or social connects Black individuals to innate forms of criminality. It is also the case that Mexicans have stolen from other Mexicans. However, many yarderos believe that African American youths do all the stealing. During my fieldwork, these theft stories were so pervasive and insidious that I even heard them from older yarderos such as Don Antonio. The following story that I recorded while being a *chalan* documents additional instances in which stories of theft become the present of yarderos everyday life.

> March 21, 2013
>
> We started power raking on 89th Street and Luella Avenue. As we started the day, we began to get slower in the rhythm of the work. However, we were a bit too trusting, and a few times early in the morning, we left one of our blowers on the side of the house, out of eyesight. When we got to the second house, I left it right in front of the doorsteps. I then went back to the backyard to help Don Antonio finish power raking the yard. No more than three minutes had passed when Don Antonio stopped at once what he was doing and asked me, "Where is the other blower?" I said, "I think it is by the front stairs." Don Antonio screamed, "*Córrele y ve por él!*" [Run and get it!]. I ran as fast as I could. To my relief, the blower was there. I received a disapproving glance when I got to the backyard. Don Antonio told me, "Do not leave the blower or any equipment from your sight; *pinches morenos* [fucking Black folks], they are always ready to take it and sell it at *la garra*."

Indeed, to my surprise, Don Antonio did not refer to African Americans with the N-word in Spanish. However, we both knew he suggested that an African American, not a Brown Mexican, may be after the blower. After this experience, I rarely let the blower out of my sight.

While driving the route to another house the week after this exchange over the leaf blower, Don Antonio talked about how he had two blowers stolen the year before. The first time, he did not see who it was. It was taken from the side of the house while he was not looking. The second time, he did see who it was. Don Antonio recalled the following anecdote of that experience:

> We were mowing by 88th Street and Phillips, and we had a few houses to mow. I had just left it by the stairs of the third house on the corner and went for about two minutes to pick up a payment for the house next door. As I collected the payment, I suddenly saw a shadow move from the corner of my eye. "*Un pinche moreno se lleva el soplador*" [a fucking black person was stealing the blower]. I could not chase him, but my son José was nearby, and he started chasing the moreno. José chased the Black man for about two blocks and saw him enter an alley. He approached the alley, and the moreno disappeared along with the blower. José looked in about ten trash cans until he found the blower. We did not see the moreno again.
>
> And let me tell you of another time . . .
>
> About a year ago, around the fourth of July, we were mowing 79th Street and Kingston Ave on a Saturday afternoon. We were about to end the week. They knew that we had money because it was the time when many clients paid us. So it happened that Pablo [a current temporary worker] was mowing the backyard, and I was cutting the grass in the front yard. I saw two Black males talking to each other near the corner. Then, I saw one of them looking toward where we were. I sensed that they were up to something. I shouted to Pablo, "*Wachale! Ay andan unos morenos; nos quieren chingar!*" [Watch out, some Blacks want to fucking us over!]. [At this point, his voice and tone hint at suspense while talking.] I placed the mower in the trailer and started the blower to clear the debris as we usually do. I blew the front sidewalks and was going to the backyard when I heard a loud "Hey!" I turned around, and there he was, pointing the gun at my face. Look, everything passes through your mind. I was thinking that was it, I would be killed. My hands got very stiff, and I was just looking at the gun; I was not even looking at the face of the moreno. The Black male asked me for my money and told me to give him my wallet. It all happened very fast. Can you imagine that I still finished blowing the sidewalk, and it was when I drove off for half a mile, I began to shake. Believe me; my hands could not stop shaking until I stopped the truck and rested for five to ten minutes. I did not call the police officers and continued mowing the rest of the day. What else could I do?

The experience of being mugged or robbed while going about an everyday work routine is an emotionally intense one. For many yarderos, these moments and the stories surrounding them define who they are and how they perceive the people they fear will steal their power equipment.

Toni Morrison reminds us that racism's serious function is distraction—it distracts us from our work. This is true for African Americans and, I argue, within Mexican communities. Stealing a yardero's equipment is a complete disruption of his work schedule. Most yarderos do not have the reserves to buy a new blower or edge trimmer at a moment's notice. If we recall, they receive their payment for their services at the end of each month. *Chalanes* are paid at the end of each month or weekly. While this disruption from doing their work creates an emotional rage as the yardero attempts to make sense of the incident, the initial response attempts to justify why morenos take their equipment—to justify it racially rather than structurally. But as soon as these incidents happen, the yarderos start associating an individual act with the tendencies of the group. In other words, metonymically, yarderos relationally associate Blackness or skin color differences with criminality. Of course, we know that the connection between criminality and Blackness has a long historical trajectory in US racial relations and originates in privileged whites' minds. Despite my attempts to decouple this link in conversations with my collaborators, at the end of the day, every time a yardero had equipment stolen from his pickup truck, the experience was again explained in color terms, which is to say, in terms of race-making and race-ordering processes. As a promoter of social justice ideals, I failed to change the minds of my yardero friends. Despite my insistence on the structural constraints in which both they and morenos find themselves situated; they continue to hide their equipment from *los morenos* daily at work.

Conclusion

This chapter showed that racialization happens dynamically. While we know that whiteness is always present in the construction of racism, when suspended momentarily at the analytical level, this exercise allows us to see the relational, lateral networks that develop between racialized groups. Suppose we force ourselves to distance or decenter the dominant modes of understanding racism, this helps shed light into how brownness is also articulated in the United States. In that case, we may better decipher how race-making and race-doing processes occur in everyday life and how other forms of racism are expressed within minority ethnic groups. In this context, the foregrounded analysis allows us to see the malleability of the term *moreno* to denote Brownness and Blackness situationally.

Further, as we theorize and ethnographically explore the diverse ways Mexican migrants in transborder Chicago interact with African Americans, we have seen the production of apparent coproducing racial networks, but we cannot be positive if these are based on racism. These relational processes teach us that race and racism are not givens; they are made, require cultural work to maintain, and become a distraction from living our lives as decent human beings.

Toward the end of my fieldwork period in 2013, an intricate discourse on immigration began affecting Mexican working-class migrants in other areas of social life. In some states, stricter immigration laws subjected undocumented populations to new, post-9/11 regimes of control. In many ways, this was a response to the *longue durée* of the Obama administration's ineffective policies toward immigration, which are also legacies of past federal administrations. We also encountered a shift in how communities in the United States actively policed undocumented migrants and other brown skin looking Latinos/as.

The previous chapters have offered the bulk of the ethnographic material. In contrast, the concluding chapter focuses our lens on a broader, national view of anti-immigrant discourse and policies that inflicted pain on many families and directly affected the ability of working-class folks to travel across the US-Mexico border. By the end of the formal fieldwork, many small company owners, in fact, began complaining about the lack of workers because of stricter enforcement at the southern border.

Thus, the next chapter argues for this moment's exceptionality as it focused on the negative and nativist discourse against immigrants, especially Mexicans in the United States, at the end of the second decade of the twentieth century, which led to the harsher treatment of migrant men, women, and children as they attempted to cross to el Norte after 2016.

CHAPTER 6

On Mexican *Sacer*

Anti-Immigrant Discourse, Deportability, and Working-Class Criminalization

> When we leave in the morning, we know we are going to work . . . but we don't know if we will be coming home.
>
> —Elena Garcia, forty-seven-year-old resident of Waukegan, Illinois

> I know everything about Waukegan; it's my town. . . . I know the high school, the first Mexican restaurant. I should feel free to go in and out whenever I want to. But it's not the same freedom anymore.
>
> —Anonymous woman from Waukegan, Illinois

By 2013 Chicago and its suburbs had become the center of Mexican migration to the Midwest. The influx of Mexican migrants to areas where white populations dominated political and public life has generated responses ranging from acceptance to outright disapproval.[1] Acceptance may mean a generalized tolerance of the Mexican presence or political integration of Latinx residents into a community's daily workings and special events. Disapproval of Latinx residents has taken the form of discriminatory practices such as denying them rental property—as happened early in the 1900s in Chicago—or reporting people to immigration services. The increasingly punitive nature of how specific communities respond to documented and undocumented populations has birthed a new surveillance. In many ways, this hypervigilance intensified after the events of 9/11.

The tragic incidents of September 11, 2001, in the United States generated an increased mobilization of the state apparatus to fight terrorism worldwide.[2] This intensification of surveillance by the United States' punitive and security state agencies concentrated on curtailing the travel and immigration of foreign-born populations, especially those from the Middle East.[3] As the United States attempted to secure all of its borders, a direct consequence of the new policy was an increased focus on the US-Mexico border region and the intensification of surveillance methods to control the bodies of Mexican men, women, and children. If we remember, this intensification was already in the works a decade earlier, in the mid-1990s. However, the heightened scrutiny of Mexican immigrants as they attempted to cross the border took an even greater necropolitical turn in more recent decades, that is, engaging in a politics where those deemed sovereign subjects attain the benefits of the state. These processes occurred in urban areas and beyond them, where merciless deserts served as nonhuman agents carrying out the effects intended by policies that some scholars have termed Prevention Through Deterrence (PTD).[4]

While talking to yarderos in South Chicago, a place 1,400 miles from the nearest major port of entry from the Southern border, I would ask about the US-Mexico border and how the process of crossing at the border had shifted over time. Many told me how difficult crossing the US-Mexico border became after 9/11. These similar stories of border crossings were readily expressed by the interlocutors of anthropologist Ruth Gomberg-Muñoz, whose research had also taken place in the context of Chicago.[5] In comparison, in my study, yarderos explained that it had become standard practice for undocumented yarderos not to travel to Mexico under post-9/11 conditions because crossing back to the United States was too difficult. As Jason De León explains, the idea behind this PTD policy was to make it so hard for migrants to cross through official entry points into the United States that, in order to avoid them, they would have to travel through some of the most inhospitable and treacherous terrain.[6] Can you imagine what it would be like to cross to the United States through mountainous and desert regions filled with cacti, mesquites, and uneven terrain? Writing about PTD as a part of a hybrid collectif, De León allows us to see that undocumented folks have become critical gears of the American empire and capital expansion.[7]

This chapter documents the ways in which the Homeland Security State—that is, the punitive and security structures of the American state—operate in the capillaries of society.[8] I analyze how everyday discourse on immigration acts as an *actants*, in De León's terms, and how other sovereign subjects, such as US citizens, also participate in the securitization and policing of the undocumented

Mexican subject. Thus, I argue that from the end of the 2000s to the end of the 2010s, sovereign subjects actively transformed their local communities to stop, police, and expel undocumented ethnic Mexicans through discriminatory practices. Their aim, in a Foucauldian sense, was to defend American society. This was fueled by an anti-immigrant discourse incubating within a revival of American nationalism by the early 2010s, birthed again through neoliberal punitive measures.[9]

Indeed, to understand the continuous and insidious insistence on policing Mexican bodies, first we must know that the American state continually excludes them, paradoxically, by including them in the state apparatus. In other words, by discursively marking ethnic Mexicans as outsiders, they are—in practice—included in society through an act of exclusion. It may seem that we can now speak of a Mexican *homo sacer* as a fundamental figure of American society and of the workings of the state. The Mexican *homo sacer* needs to exist for American capitalism to structurally maintain a constant labor supply within and across the transborder space or the transborder hybrid collectif of Mexico and the United States. To excavate the Mexican *sacer*, we need first to cover a few general genealogical pathways.

Homo Sacer Genealogy

In *The History of Sexuality* (1980), Michel Foucault describes how modern states exercise biopower over populations. Foucault argues that, beginning in the seventeenth century, power over life evolved into two primary forms: "The first to be formed, it seems—centered on the body as a machine . . . [the second] focused on the species as body, the body imbued with the mechanism of life and serving as the basis of the biological processes."[10] For Foucault, the second mechanism of power could be in the emergence of the modern nation-state throughout Europe at the end of the seventeenth century. In this era, a different state logic directed toward the population's wellbeing emerged. States, according to Foucault, began to exercise and promote regulatory controls—biopolitics of the population. The power to decide who should live or die—for Foucault, this means sovereign power—was, at the end of the seventeenth century, "carefully supplanted by the administration of bodies and the calculated management of life. . . . Hence there was an explosion of numerous and diverse techniques for achieving the subjugation of bodies and the control of populations, marking the beginning of an era of 'biopower.'"[11]

Further, under this paradigm, Foucault tells us that in the classical theory of sovereignty, "the lives and deaths of subjects become rights only as a result of the will of the sovereign. . . . The sovereign can grant life in the same way that he can inflict death."[12] However, Foucault does not want to pursue discussion only at the level of political theory. Instead, he sets out to investigate sovereignty at the level of "the mechanism, techniques, and technologies of power."[13] In less complex terms, Foucault suggests that the analysis of the modern state should examine what the actors of the state are doing, not just what they are saying or implying. This requires, for example, that within the context of Mexican working-class folks in Chicago and beyond, we focus on the level of the application of techniques of control, whether at the point of entering the United States or beyond, among American communities. I take the latter approach to focus on how the local response to immigration polices allows the Mexican *sacer* to be included through its exclusion.

Suppose we use Foucault's claims to consider the Mexican immigrant in the United States. In that case, we see that, historically, ethnic Mexicans do not necessarily experience the productive end of the biopolitical spectrum. Instead, it is a punitive biopolitical regime ethnic Mexicans encounter if or when they deviate from their roles within the market's social structure and capitalist necessities. In other words, Mexican immigrants are allowed a certain sovereign status only if their behaviors align with the available roles within the capitalist system. These roles tend to be structured around low-level, low-skill jobs such as landscaping, food service, construction, and domestic work, despite requiring a high level of expertise and endurance.

Giorgio Agamben elaborates on this assertion by expanding on Foucault's concept of biopolitics to investigate its underside, the dark side of biopower, in contemporary biopolitical state formation.[14] In his work, Agamben uses the paradox of modernity to explain the historical intersection of state formation and its power over human life. Following a different trajectory than Foucault's analysis of power, Agamben's theory of the "state of exception" becomes helpful in discussing how the Homeland Security State currently (de)politicizes immigrants in the United States. Agamben suggests that natural life is excluded from the polis strictly in the classical world, remaining confined as reproductive life—the sphere of the *eikos* (home). Agamben sees *Zoë* (life or the simple fact of living common to all beings) slowly entering the realm of "the *polis*—the politicization of bare life as such—constitut[ing] the decisive event of modernity and signal[ing] a radical transformation of the political-philosophical categories of classical thought."[15] By criticizing Foucault for his imprecise theoretical formulation, which failed to point to "the zone of indistinction" where the modern Western state integrated techniques of subjective individualization with procedures of objective totalization, Agamben sets out to analyze precisely "the hidden point of intersection between juridico-institutional and the biopolitical models of power."[16] The protagonist in this work is the concept of bare life, "that is, the life of *homo sacer* (sacred man), who may be killed and yet not sacrificed, and whose essential function in modern politics we intend to assert."[17]

Agamben situates biopolitics within his paradigm of the exception. Agamben contends that Foucault's biopolitics concept does not address how totalitarian states have excluded specific populations from the *polis*. Agamben's notion of bare life is generally placed in the foundation of modern democracy. For Agamben, bare life is produced through an act of sovereignty, or by the sovereign exercising the right to live or let die. In other words, when *Zoë* is excluded from the *polis* by the sovereign, abandoned as *homo sacer*, bare life is produced by the act of inclusion. Here, we can juxtapose Agamben's *homo sacer* to the socially structured positionality of the ethnic Mexican in the United States, allowing the figure of the Mexican *sacer* to emerge. This is an analytical proxy to explain the American state apparatus's inner workings vis-à-vis Mexican immigrant populations. Thus, documenting the emergence of the Mexican *sacer* becomes a theoretical and practical necessity. In other words, speaking about the concrete is how one speaks about the theoretical through specific historical circumstances and shocking interactions between Mexican migrants and the American state.

Exclusion by Inclusion

During the Great Depression (1929–39) in the United States, Mexican immigrants experienced a significant shift in the US deportation strategy. Even some US citizens of Mexican descent were included in the deportations. The US state apparatus carried out a "mass deportation of at least 415,000 Mexican migrants and many of their US-citizen children, and the 'voluntary' repatriation of 85,000. Then, from 1954 to 1955, Operation Wetback was a major effort by the US government that culminated in expelling at least 2.9 million "illegal" Mexican migrant workers."[18] Nicholas De Genova argues the Homeland Security State traditionally has engaged in policies against specific populations, including Mexicans, in times of economic crisis or extreme nationalist rhetoric. Since the start of the twentieth century, ethnic Mexicans have been the main target.[19] In short, the productivity of immigration law is not so much the deportation itself, which creates an environment of legal vulnerability, but "rather deportability that qualifies undocumented migrant labor as a commodity of choice."[20] As De Genova continues, "This is only possible when migrant 'illegality' is produced and deployed on a mass scale."[21] Indeed, as Ruth Gomberg-Muñoz puts it simply in her analysis of busboys in Chicago, "Border policies do not stop labor migration; rather, they generate inequality by assigning illegal status to a segment of the global labor force."[22]

Another change in the discourse around immigration took place early in 2000 as Mexico's newly elected president, Vicente Fox, ended the seventy-one-year rule of the Partido Revolucionario Institucional (Institutional Revolutionary Party). As a Partido de Accion Nacional (PAN) candidate, President Fox became the first political alternative in Mexico's presidential elections since the early 1920s. News media described Vicente Fox as a "successful businessman and natural campaigner, who [had] gained popularity in the polls."[23] Early in his presidential campaign, Fox claimed that immigration policy would be of central concern to his administration. Once elected, Fox engaged in discussions with George W. Bush to find a viable alternative for deportation for the millions of Mexicans classified as "illegal" in the United States.

Over the next four years, conversations between the two presidents yielded initial proposals to solve the United States' "immigration problem." However, these proposals addressing economic, political, and social issues did not become actual policies. After September 11, 2001, it became evident that such an overhaul would not happen, and immigration reform took a backseat. It was not until early 2004 that President Bush urged Congress to pass his plan to give immigrant workers temporary legal status. The proposal would "let millions of illegal immigrants obtain work visas for three years, renewable for an unspecified period," provided they could prove they had jobs and that their employers couldn't find Americans to do them.[24] Since then, no major immigration reforms have developed in Congress about the issue. In 2012 President Barack Obama signed an executive order that created the Deferred Action for Childhood Arrivals (DACA). This order granted some individuals who entered the country as undocumented minors a two-year renewable period of work eligibility and deferred deportation. Through the DACA program, around two hundred thousand undocumented minors and young students have remained in the United States to attend college or graduate school and enter the workforce, despite the limited structural constraints.

9/11 and Immigration

Initial analysis of immigration after 9/11 revolved around the US State Department and Department of Homeland Security's increasing efforts to police immigrants from Arabic countries and those deemed threats to national security.

For example, in an address to the American Society of International Law, assistant secretary for Population, Refugees, and Migration, Arthur E. Dewey, discussed the effects that 9/11 had on immigration. After 9/11, Dewey argued, "a freeze on refugee admissions was put into effect for over two months while a comprehensive review of procedures was undertaken." He said, "9/11 may have given us reason to be more vigilant about those who may threaten us."[25] The discourse on banning immigrants from the Middle East was not only turned toward increasing security along the US-Mexico border, but the borderland's condition thickened, and its effects and modalities of power became increasingly implemented inside the space of the American nation-state.[26]

The War on Terrorism, or the fight against extremist groups globally, as it was often labeled in mainstream media, increased the security of borders and ports of entry and heightened specific security measures in everyday workplaces. For example, the years after 9/11 did not diminish state efforts to secure workspaces throughout the United States. In February 2008, the US Immigration and Customs Enforcement Agency released a four-page document instructing employees and employers to notify Immigration and Customs Enforcement (ICE) about fraudulent documents in the workplace. The document offers advice on "things to look for" when employees claim citizenship or immigrant status. Advice given to employers began with the following: "No one knows your work force better than you. . . . When you customarily hire aliens with authorization to work in the US, and you notice your employees claiming to be US citizens in numbers that strike you as abnormally high or atypical for your region or industry, you should consider contacting your local ICE office."[27] The document provides two case studies that indicate what "atypical" or "out of the ordinary" patterns an employer may encounter in the workplace. One of the cases details a prosecution of middle management for failing to adhere to strict ICE enforcement policies. In practice, this scenario is rare. The message contained in the second case is for "employers to use diligence in the recruitment and hiring of employees and . . . that employers should not ignore relevant information."[28]

Indeed, through its various security agencies, the state apparatus increased efforts to "crack down" on "illegality." E-Verify emerged as a newly crafted program from the US Citizenship and Immigration Services (USCIS). According to the USCIS office, E-Verify is a web-based system that electronically verifies employment eligibility. E-Verify is a partnership between the Department of Homeland Security, the Social Security Administration (SSA), and the USCIS office. The program allows "participating employers to electronically compare employee information taken from the Form I-9 [the chapter-based employment eligibility verification form used for all new hires] against more than 425 million records in SSA's database and more than 60 million records in DHS (Department of Homeland Security)' immigration databases."[29] The rationale for implementing the program was that "unauthorized employment minimizes verification-related discrimination . . . and protects civil liberties and employee privacy."[30] The goal of the program is to obtain initial verification within "3 to 5 seconds." It can be implemented at workplaces such as "food services and drinking places, administrative and support services, professional and technical services, other information services, and clothing and accessories stores."[31] In short, the places where we find an increasing demand for immigrant labor tend to have the greatest surveillance and policing of their communities.

After 9/11, efforts to surveil immigrant populations, especially those coming from Mexico and Latin America, became pervasive. Frequently, the struggle for mainstream society was differentiating between those who came to the United States to make a better life (the yarderos I write about) and those nonnormative immigrants who end up having problems with the criminal system. However, we must remember that the policing of ethnic Mexicans has an extensive history. They have long been included as part of the state apparatus and society through exclusionary and violent practices, such as the horrid practice of lynching Mexicans in the Southwest in the late nineteenth and early twentieth centuries, which historian Monica Muñoz Martinez writes about. Her meticulous work has allowed us to think critically about state practices that have sometimes taken a violent turn toward Mexicans.[32] While some efforts, especially by individual states, are slowly attempting to reconcile this violent history, much needs to be done to right the wrongs inflicted on all the families, daughters, brothers, fathers, mothers, and children affected by the practices of a country that considers these populations a threat to society.

Immigration as a social discourse represents a threat to the United States and other advanced liberal nations.[33] For example, Didier Bigo illustrates how state actors mobilize discourse against immigrants to perpetuate political control and include them in the economic hybrid collectif through their exclusion as undocumented immigrants.[34] Bigo investigates why immigration is perceived as a threat to governments worldwide. His central thesis states that immigration's securitization is "a transversal political technology, used as a mode of governmentality by diverse institutions to play with the unease."[35] Further, Bigo argues that, because immigration is understood from the state's frame at the national level, it becomes challenging to speak against securitization because immigration and the protection of borders are intrinsically linked. In relying on Foucault's work on the genealogy of state technologies, Bigo also makes the excellent point that securitization works through everyday technologies and that securitization results from developing those forms.[36] In other words, we can rightly argue that the securitization against undocumented immigrants does not stop at the US-Mexico border. Beyond this major international inspection station, the nation-state space is permeated by dense webs of inspection procedures that produce in immigrants—Mexican immigrants precisely—a perpetual sense of deportability.[37]

Calls for Immigration Reform

On April 9, 2006, state policies were openly challenged when thousands of immigrants filled the streets of major metropolitan cities in the United States to protest the increasingly invasive security measures implemented after 9/11. In Dallas, Texas, protesters estimated to have been "as high as 500,000 . . . march[ed] in downtown Dallas in the largest of the protests. Some 20,000 rallied in San Diego, 7,000 in Miami, and 4,000 in Birmingham."[38] Protesters' voices were heard that day across the United States. For example, Robert Martinez, who crossed the Rio Grande in 1984 and eventually became an American citizen, commented, "For years, we never say nothing. . . . We just work hard, follow the rules, and pay taxes. And they try to make these laws. It is time people knew how we felt."[39] While one might assume the protesters were young, rebellious, or leftist, this was not entirely the case. For example, in Dallas, the protesters were diverse:

> Some [protesters] were families pushing baby strollers. Some walked with canes; others rolled along in wheelchairs. There were members of unions, churches, civil rights organizations, and business groups, but many were strangers to one another. Some spoke passionately about their desire to be Americans, to vote and to hold a job without fear.[40]

Even though immigrants carried the fight through other means, thousands again marched in cities across the nation on May 1, 2006. Immigrants who participated in that year's rallies said they feared there would be an increase in immigration raids due to their protests. It has been documented that during 2007, the United States deported 280,000 people (about half the population of Wyoming), a 44 percent increase from the previous year.[41] Los Angeles Mayor Antonio R. Villaraigosa was one of a few politicians who suggested to the Department of Homeland Security that these policies had detrimental economic effects, especially within and among immigrant communities in the United States. Villaraigosa announced the results of a study conducted by the city council, which found that "50 percent or more of workers in some local industries were in the country illegally, and it projected great harm to the region if businesses closed or moved because of the immigration sweeps."[42]

As I have suggested, the biopolitical and punitive state actors mobilized the state to combat Mexican immigration, excluding them through deportability practices and including them as state non-sovereign folks. This practice continues to be a central mechanism of subjection and subject creation. For example, Richard M. Stana, then the director of Homeland Security, stated how difficult it is to exercise control over immigration along the US-Mexico border and the interior of the United States. Stana argues, "What we've done is put a lot of people on the line of scrimmage, but when you do that, the other side can just lob a little pass and score a touchdown. . . . Trying to get a better balance between border enforcement and interior enforcement would go a long way."[43] Over the last several decades, law enforcement has looked the other way as US employers have benefitted from Mexican immigrants' cheap labor. For instance, Gordon H. Hanson commented to the *New York Times* that "employers feel very strongly about maintaining access to immigrant workers, and exert political pressure to prevent enforcement from being effective. . . . While there are lots of groups concerned about immigration on the other side . . . it's not like their livelihood depends on this."[44] North of the US-Mexico border, response to increasing immigration has manifested in more frequent workplace raids of industries traditionally occupied by immigrants.

Before the 2006 demonstrations, immigration agents arrested two managers and more than sixty employees at Illinois's industrial cleaning and meatpacking plants. One of the raids occurred around 1:30 a.m. at Cargill Meat Solutions in Beardstown, a town of six thousand people northwest of Springfield. The company reported, "Forty-nine employees were taken into custody for alleged immigration violations. In all, 54 of the 62 people arrested are from Mexico; 5 are from Guatemala; 2 from El Salvador and 1 from Argentina."[45] In December 2006, according to reporter Libby Sander, agents "raided six meat-processing plants operated by Swift and Company in six states, detaining 1,282 immigrants believed to be in the country illegally and charging 219 so far, mostly with identity theft." After two years of raids across the US interior, it became evident that the Homeland Security State was escalating a war against immigrants.[46] In April 2008, the government raided several chicken processing plants operated by Pilgrim's Pride. About 280 workers were accused of being illegal immigrants. The common charge against workers was not their undocumented status but a new criminal charge of identity theft. The arrests were part of a strategy by immigration officials to bring charges against unauthorized immigrants. According to the *New York Times*, "The identity theft charges carry a maximum penalty of five years in prison upon conviction."[47] Similar incidents have been reported across the country, and the impact on individuals is dramatic. For example, having an adverse criminal record, such as a felony charge, highly inhibits the ability to apply for any type of temporary permit or visa.

Small-Town Governing

An aspect rarely discussed in national and political discourse on immigration is that citizens themselves engage in security practices customarily exercised by the federal state.[48] We see American citizens constantly engaging in policing practices against immigrants.[49] This situation is a consequence of the shift in governmentality in this neoliberal era. In other words, from the rendering of securitization practices from the federal government to individual communities taking on these responsibilities, especially around the US-Mexico border. As Jonathan X. Inda explains, to understand this postsocial citizen under neoliberal governmentality, the "post-social domain is best conceived as a reconfigured zone of governmental thought and action. . . . It designates the broad assembly of mentalities, agencies, and technologies that make up the prototypical ways of conceptualizing and administering the targets of government in contemporary liberal democracies."[50] In plain language, the vision that the government assumes is that everyday citizens, to some degree, act as part of an immigration police force, ready to interrogate perceived noncitizens about their legal standing in the United States.

However, the picture of everyday governance on immigration gets complicated when considering how the subjects are created in countries we would not consider advanced and liberal. Postsocial subjects have, to follow the argument posed by Nikolas Rose, taken on the responsibility of managing their own lives. The ethical subject is not created vis-à-vis the state but instead "results in large part from active engagement with a diverse range of market-based, nonstate (or quasi-state) institutions and practices. . . . [The postsocial citizen] is one who fulfills his or her civic obligation to the national polity not through relations of dependency, but through seeking to realize him—or herself as a free, self-reliant subject."[51] As I have been arguing here, the outcome is that the postsocial subject is slowly taking on managing every aspect of his or her life. In the case of undocumented immigration, this area gradually becomes an assemblage connected to the postsocial subject. In many ways, citizens, by their acts of policing, become responsible subjects of the state. Indeed, the literal or metaphorical creation of the Mexican *sacer* is from which the sovereign needs to defend society and themselves.

We need to look at concrete examples to see how citizens have reacted to and actively exercised their sovereign power against undocumented subjects. The following cases demonstrate that the process described by scholars truly is happening. For example, campaigns against immigration in the post-9/11 era have encouraged small towns throughout the country to exercise greater local control over immigration policy. In 2006 a municipality in New Jersey became the first to enact legislation penalizing anyone employing an "illegal" immigrant. In Riverside, New Jersey, people did not understand the legislation's consequences. As the *New York Times* reported, with the departure of immigrants from Brazil and other Latin American countries, "the local economy suffered. Hair salons, restaurants, and corner shops that catered to immigrants saw business plummet; several closed. Once-boarded-up storefronts downtown were boarded up again."[52] Belson and Capuzo further report that more than thirty towns nationwide had enacted laws to address "illegal" immigration problems over the prior two years. Riverside residents reacted to what they saw as a genuine problem, but they dramatically underestimated just how much of their community was made up of immigrants. Indeed, some residents have suggested that even though it hurt the town's economy, "the ordinance was a success" because it drove the immigrants out of the municipality.

In February 2008, an Arizona judge ruled against a lawsuit by construction contractors who sought to halt a state law imposing penalties on employers who knowingly hired undocumented immigrants. In December 2007, "a judge in Oklahoma, James H. Payne, threw out a lawsuit against a state statute enacted [the previous] year requiring state contractors to verify new employees' immigration status. Judge Payne said the immigrants should not be able to bring their claims to court because they were living in the country in violation of the law."[53] From the number of immigration restrictions examined, it is not surprising that immigrants lose the opportunity to take their cases to court when injustices occur. This crescendo of anti-immigrant discourse I heard while in the field in the early 2010s had peaked and needed to be contained. The presidential election in 2016 was the moment to revive the Mexican *sacer* to defend the American nation. The containment of these feelings exploded after my long-term interaction with Mexican yarderos.

Anti-immigrant Discourse

On June 16, 2015, there was a significant buzz about a New York businessperson who had launched a presidential campaign. Everyone was surprised, including major television programs, public networks, and cable news outlets. The candidate was Donald J. Trump. The business mogul, who had never held public office, entered a crowded field of Republican presidential hopefuls, numbering seventeen candidates at its busiest.[54] At that time, mainstream media and the public had little faith that Trump had any chance of winning the nomination, let alone the presidency. We were all wrong.

On November 6, 2017, shock and dread swept through major metropolitan areas. In the countryside and in smalltown America, the opposite was the case. For many, especially those who supported him, the hope of a better future was present more than ever in the slogan "Make American Great Again." With the Republican nominee winning the presidential election over Democratic contender Hillary Clinton, many folks adhering to a strong nationalist sentiment felt vindicated. The age of political correctness was over.

In the June 2015 announcement of his candidacy, the way Trump spoke about Mexicans became the basis for a discourse that would later become a chant, a cry, and a call of war against the Mexican working class in the United States. For example, in Trump's announcement speech, while making celebratory remarks about his jingoistic campaign slogan, he blamed an entire group of people—Mexican immigrants—for the ills of the United States. Without citing evidence (we would learn later that evidence is not particularly present in many of his speeches), he offered his worldview on what is wrong with the country. In discussing the United States' role as a trading partner, he suggested the United States was losing the trade battle with China and Japan. Then he asked, setting the tone for what would follow, "When do we beat Mexico at the border?" He continued: "The US has become a dumping ground for everyone else's problems." After this, Trump spoke the words that were deeply felt in Mexican communities around the United States and beyond its geopolitical borders: "When Mexico sends its people; they're not sending their best. They're not sending you. They're not sending you. They're sending people that have lots of problems, and they're bringing those problems with them. They are bringing drugs. They're bringing crime. They are rapists. And some, I assume, are good people."[55]

Few assumed he had a remote chance of winning the presidential election, and many of us missed the mark in predicting what lay ahead. We were all being pushed to a threshold in many ways. We moved toward a new unexplored historical borderland—between the success of electing the first African American president and a radical shift toward a politics of fracture, uninformed dissent, and hypernationalist overtones. Mexican immigration plays a role in both political scenarios, but I am still uncertain what role we will play moving forward in this rocky terrain. This anti-immigrant stance would take striking overtones in a pandemia that would lay ahead by the end of 2019, but little did we know what the future entailed. But that is a discussion that can be taken up later. The goal of documenting the interrelation between the Mexican *sacer* and American sovereignty is that, once we see how the exclusion includes what is perceived as nonsovereign, we may *de-sacerize* the Mexican subject and better understand the power relation embedded in sustaining a deportability system for the benefit of those who hire immigrants for meager wages.

While the increasing deportation of undocumented ethnic Mexicans accelerated under President Barack Obama, his administration claimed to focus on deporting folks who had served sentences for felonies or other crimes. In practice, however, the system began to capitalize on the state apparatus's need to deport hundreds of Mexicans from the nation-state space systematically. Following the Obama administration, we have seen a radical, nationalist discourse against undocumented folks and an intensification of the desire to streamline deportation—separating families as they seek asylum in the United States, removing people at night, detaining children, and setting up for-profit detention centers. We saw the expansion of Mexican *sacer* into areas beyond the workplace, in people's homes.

The anti-undocumented-immigrant discourse has inflicted economic blows on major businesses in the United States and has contributed to a lack of a reliable workforce in agriculture and other service sectors. Under this set of conditions, the Mexican yarderos live their working-class lives in transborder Chicago. While this book offers a slide across a *long history* of Mexican migration, I hope the stories presented in the previous chapters provide some hope for a better future where deportation and deportability are now the central regimes governing Mexican migrants in the United States.

Conclusion

We now know that immigrants have not complacently accepted these impositions from the Homeland Security State. Excluded nonsovereign subjects, immigrant activist groups, NGOs, and immigrants have turned to the street to protest unjust policies. Facing overwhelming opposition to immigration policy, the state turned back some policies, leaving many undocumented immigrants with restricted and compromised civil liberties. As their voices are absent in legal proceedings, protest has given immigrant communities the hope that one day everyone will be free to travel in and out of the United States without any problem. The state is not using only one policy against immigrants; instead, it pushes incremental policy changes such as increased scrutiny in the workplace, revisions of detailed immigration procedures, and exploiting loopholes and technicalities when immigrants travel in and out of the country. The state's nativist mentality has also successfully provoked an oppressive sense of unease in immigrant populations.

The call for justice at immigrant marches and rallies is a cry to be treated the same as any other human being: with respect, access to basic services, and freedom to live decent lives. Many immigrants do not necessarily want to become full citizens; although this is the end goal for many, some simply call for respect for their human rights. Indeed, while there have been some gains through the demonstrations, there is a long road ahead. The fact remains that immigrant groups will continue to resist, finding novel ways to fight against unjust state policies that seek to maintain a labor force in a minimalist biopolitical state of exception.

To summarize what I have been arguing in this chapter, the Homeland Security State has successfully enforced worksite environments through immigration raids. Small townships have mobilized legislation against immigrant residents throughout the United States. Through efforts by the state apparatus and American citizens alike, undocumented immigrants have been slowly placed in a tough position through their relationship to the concept of the "legal" individual. Through legislation restricting access to health care, housing, and work, undocumented immigrants are placed in a state of exception for violating the law when they cross the United States border. However, immigrants have not remained silent in the face of all this.

Even when the state apparatus and its citizens argue that immigrants should be barred from the territory, the fact remains that the labor of immigrants is essential in many industries such as meatpacking, chicken processing, agriculture, manufacturing, and of course landscaping the lawns in cities and suburbs across the United States. Only those who suffer the consequences of these exploitative economic regimes can offer a sense of the changes that have occurred. Although beneficial to the American state, the Mexican *sacer* should finally be buried six feet under—*enterrado seis pies abajo*. Everyone needs to be reminded that all migrants deserve to be treated with respect and dignity. Eventually, by preventing migrants from living here in the United States, we are missing opportunities to welcome innovators, strong workers, doctors, engineers, lawyers, and successful entrepreneurs like the *yarderos* I have been writing about here. While it is hard to remain optimistic about the future of Mexican migrants in the United States, the following conclusion of the book offers a few alternative imaginings as we head into an uncertain future in American society.

Conclusion

Yardero Lives Matter

Without borders, there will only be mobility.

—Nicholas De Genova, *The Borders of "Europe"*

The capitalist mode of production . . . produces also the premature exhaustion and death of this labour-power itself. It extends the labourer's time of production during a given period by shortening his actual lifetime.

—Karl Marx, *Capital*

This book has engaged with the dynamics of working class, Mexican yarderos in transborder Chicago. Yarderos struggle through class and color hierarchies, but they still reproduce their working-class lives despite the racially based, systemic elements of living in the Windy City. It has been my hope that this book contributes to a better understanding of a group of people—yarderos/as—under specific historical, economic, and cultural conditions as they seek a better life in the north.

To examine yardero lives, I discussed how the Mexican working class in Chicago is currently experiencing racial discrimination for being located within specific class relations and color hierarchies. Class and color unevenly engender each other, and while one experience does not substitute for the other, *colorismo* is another way to talk about racism and more.

In this book, I linked the structural forces of Mexican migration to the city of Chicago after the 1980s, when the lawncare and landscaping economy accelerated under neoliberal conditions and the long history of transborder processes. I located the emergence of a working-class population—los yarderos/as—within the context of Mexican migration to the US Midwest. Today, this working-class population is commonly seen mowing the grass at residential homes in middle and upper-class African American and white neighborhoods in Chicago. Further, the book meticulously elaborates on the best tradition of a thick, transborder description of how these populations perform the mowing, blowing, edging, and power raking as they beautify Chicago's yards, lawns, and household landscapes.

Now, in the early 2020s, the capitalist structure of landscaping work continues to thrive despite discussions of economic recession in the United States. The COVID-19 pandemic did not slow down the need for lawn service; however, it makes it harder for company owners to maintain a constant supply of workers. Every year, after a grueling, cold Chicago winter, the desire for homeowners to have a green, nicely cut lawn offers the opportunity for Mexican migrants to capitalize on that desire and provide the service. The willingness of big businesses that sell landscaping equipment to landscapers across the city at that time of year also demonstrates the cyclical rhythms of the lawncare service and maintenance economy. Indeed, large department stores such as Menards, Home Depot, Sam's Club, and Lowe's stock their stores with lawncare and landscaping-related products.

In addition, the book dealt with three other significant themes that became central while talking with my collaborators. First, the yardero labor structure allows us to see how work, class, and culture are intimately performed by those who manage the workers and by the workers themselves. As often occurs, en las yardas freedom can become unfreedom, often unbeknownst to workers, as the capitalist logic dominates their cultural understanding of who they are as working-class folks. As we are reminded by Michel Foucault, one of the fundamental aspects of a power relation is the presence of freedom; without it, power does not exist. Second, the book's engagement with the body and capitalism highlights the intimacy of the labor process and its effect. En las Yardas, a dual process—of the worker's domination of their bodily effects to produce value adequately and rapidly in the labor process and of the governing power of a class of owners on the workers—becomes a pervasive aspect of the lawn service economy. And third, the book examined the centrality of color hierarchies and color inspections in the lives of working-class Mexican migrants in the city of Chicago and Mexican migrants' racial relations with African Americans. The last theme of the book captures the *longue durée* of nativist politics and policies against Mexican migrants and their current inclusion through a discursive exclusion in the American political space.

After Mexicans have traveled north to cities such as Chicago, color meanings still form an integral component of their worldview and allows migrants to understand who they are as Mexicans. However, this Mexican Chicago's *colorismo,* which is rematerialized through what I call "color inspections" in the Midwest, does not only operate within a Black-and-white dichotomy. Color inspections emerge within a multiplicity of color hierarchies constituted by Mexican- and US-based racial and ethnic classifications, as experienced by and within working class populations, and once these are mobilized direct the conduct of individuals. More precisely, the book argued that color hierarchies and color inspections (that unevenly fracture, and segment populations based on perceived differences in skin pigmentation) are materialized as the working-class subject acquires its working-class identity. Much can be said about color and its hierarchies, but color inspections are very real for the worker; these are lived experiences for both men and women (see especially chapters 4 and 5) that cannot easily be disregarded. The feeling that one is governed by a diffused power mechanism central to racial capitalism—or in the worker's understanding, *por el jale*—is indeed challenging for the worker, who has difficulty figuring a way out and refusing its effects (see chapters 1, 2, and 3).

The ethnographic chapters documented the period when I did anthropological research (participant observation and interviews with collaborators) in the city of Chicago in 2009, 2012, and 2013. To remind you, reader, again here, during the pilot phase in 2009, I spent three months working as a landscaper and getting to know the folks who would be my future collaborators. During the formal data collection phase, from 2012 to 2013, I focused on color hierarchies, gender relations, power, and analyses of capitalism. I worked with two lawncare service companies. They would pick me up at 8:00 a.m. and return home around 7:00 p.m. It was tough. It was hard. Luckily, I could escape; my interlocutors did not. I would often conduct interviews after work, during the weekends, or when it was raining. Yarderos do not work when it rains. Beyond these work activities, I engaged in everyday life. I would hang out in parks during the weekends, attend the local indoor soccer stadium, go to church on Sundays, visit restaurants, attend festivals, and attend yardero celebrations such as birthdays, baptisms, and other events.

For many yarderos/as, the hope for a better life lies with immigration reform. The older yarderos I spoke with benefited from the mid-1980s' IRCA (Immigration Reform and Control Act) and have made use of it by becoming documented, thus decriminalizing their work activities. The newer immigrants have had a more challenging time documenting their status, which has stifled and criminalized their lives in the United States.

Many of my participants' children are entering their adolescent years. Even at that age, the politics of color inspections are present in their day-to-day lives as they grow up in US schools, intersecting with the massive criminalization of Latina/o youth as the state actively mobilizes the figure of the Mexican *sacer* against nonsovereign subjects (chapter 6). Their political revival or renaissance under the label Latinx is a reminder of the significant role that educating the mind in higher education accomplishes. We are yet to see the term's longevity, but it works in the meantime. More recent discussion on this identity is calling not to "X-out" the history of Chicanismo and Mexican American perils suffered in the Southwest and later in the transborder Midwest. It is a productive discussion.

On Transborder Chicago

Ethnography may limit how we imagine the world; what one writes down is already an interpretation of the some evasive "real," but it is the best method to understand how people experience everyday life on their own terms. While the Mexican working-class future is still in the making, living in the United States does not easily align with the discourse of the American Dream. The children of yarderos—even if they are American citizens—are encountering an increasingly anti-immigrant and nativist rhetoric from various factions of society, especially after the election of the forty-fifth President of the United States. Again, this rhetoric is expressed and imagined in terms of borders and color. What is the future for those yarderos' children? What do the coming decades hold for the political mobilization of Mexican and Latina/o immigrants in the city of Chicago and beyond? Will the children of yarderos/as assume leadership positions as they seek a better life? More urgent than anything is the question, How will class and color inspections shift as many of these younger immigrants actively travel back and forth between Mexico and the United States? Or are they willing to engage in intra-ethnic and intra-racial mobilization, as the summer of 2020 showed us they were, at least momentarily? Time will tell, and I have to be humble and admit that I do not know these answers yet.

Indeed, one of the main goals of this book has been to offer a better understanding of the fractured Mexican, working-class identity, consciousness, and way of living that is unable to dissolve the legacies of colonial (both Spanish and American), national, class, and gender dominations expressed through yarderos' lives in the United States.

Even as Mexican working-class folks refuse to leave the dream of modernity behind, sometimes at the expense of life itself, I hope I did them justice and described their lives accurately because they are the future. And they are the best of us.

Notes

Preface

1. *See* Anzaldúa and Moraga, *This Bridge*; and Anzaldúa, *Borderlands*. See also Lugo, "Fragmented Lives."

Introduction

Epigraphs: Anzaldúa, *Borderlands, La Frontera*; and Ordóñez, *Jornalero*.

1. See Padilla, *Latino Ethnic Consciousness*; Perez, *Near Northwest Side Story*; De Genova and Ramos-Zayas, *Latino Crossings*; De Genova, *Working the Boundaries*; and Mike Amezcua, *Making Mexican Chicago* (Chicago: University of Chicago Press, 2023).

2. I use the term, *yardero* because it is an emic category mobilized by my interlocutors. Juan Thomas Ordóñez follows a similar approach when exploring the lives of Mexican migrants in the United States and labels them "jornaleros" because that is the way in which they identify in class terms.

3. Ruiz, "Nuestra América."

4. See Gramsci, *Selections from Prison Notebooks*. For an elaboration of the "war of position" and the "war of maneuver" in the context of South Texas, the work of José E. Limón is a must-read example: Limón, *Dancing with the Devil*.

5. See Anzaldúa, *Borderlands, La Frontera*; Rosaldo, *Culture and Truth*; Lugo, "Fragmented Lives, Assembled Parts"; Rosas, "Managed Violences"; Rosas, "Thickening Borderlands" 2006; Vega, *Latino Heartland*.

6. For a theorization of how the scholarship of transnationalism views the current globalized moment, examine Glick Schiller, "Theorizing Transnational Migration," 207.

7. For an excellent analysis of another destination in central Illinois, see also Acosta, "Home Making."

8. Ordóñez, *Jornalero*, 1–2.

9. For an excellent sociological study of this topic, see Gaytán, *¡Tequila!*.

10. See Vélez-Ibañez, *Border Visions*.

11. See Paredes, "*With His Pistol*," Muñoz 2018; Vélez-Ibañez, *Border Visions*; Lugo, "Fragmented Lives, Assembled Parts"; Limón, *Dancing with the Devil*; Gutierrez, *Walls and Mirrors*; and Nieto-Phillips, *Language of Blood*.

12. Alvarez, *Border Land, Border Water*, 32; and Martinez, *Injustice Never Leaves You*.

13. See Paredes, "*With His Pistol*," Limón, *Dancing with the Devil*.

14. See Gamio, *Mexican Immigration*; Sepulveda, "Colonia Del Harbor"; Louise Año Nuevo Kerr, "Chicano Settlements in Chicago"; Louise Ano Nuevo Kerr, "Mexican Chicago"; Hondagneu-Sotelo, *Gendered Transitions*; Davis, *Mexican Voices, American Dreams*; Montejano, *Anglos and Mexicans*; Garcia, *Operation Wetback*; Garcia, *Mexicans in the Midwest*; Chavez, *Shadowed Lives*; Chavez, *Covering Immigration*; 2001; Alvarez, *Mangos, Chiles, and Truckers*; De Genova, "Race, Space, and Reinvention"; De Genova, *Working the Boundaries*; Massey, Durand, and Malone, *Beyond Smoke and Mirrors*; Arredondo, *Mexican Chicago*; Acosta, "Home Making"; and Innis-Jiménez, *Steel Barrio*.

15. Vélez-Ibáñez, *Hegemonies of Language*.

16. Valerio-Jiménez, Omar S. *River of Hope: Forging Identity and Nation in the Rio Grande Borderlands* (Chapel Hill, NC: Duke University Press, 2013).

17. Garcia, *Mexicans in the Midwest*.

18. Vargas, "Armies"; and Vargas, *Proletarians of the North*.

19. Limón, "Al Norte toward Home"; see also Acosta, "Reshaping the Rural Heartland."

20.-Omar Valerio-Jiménez, "Racializing Mexican Immigrants in Iowa's Early Mexican Communities," *Annals of Iowa* 75, no. 1 (2016): 1–46.

21. See Mendoza, "Conversations Across 'Our America.'"

22. Garcia, *Mexicans in the Midwest*, 26.

23. See Acosta, "Home Making."

24. Vega, *Latino Heartland*.

25. Chávez, *Sounds of Crossing*. See particularly chapter 1 for his specific discussion of the ranchero chrono-trope.

26. Nodín Valdés, *Barrios Norteños*, 25–26.

27. Nodín Valdés, *Barrios Norteños*, 25–26.

28. Vargas, *Proletarians of the North*, 14.

29. Vargas, 14; see also Montejano, *Anglos and Mexicans*.

30. Najera, *Borderlands of Race*.

31. Vargas, *Proletarians of the North*, 15.

32. Nodín Valdés, *Barrios Nortenos*, 34–35.

33. Vargas, *Proletarians of the North*, 47; Nodín Valdés, *Barrios Norteños*, 32.

34. Garcilazo, *Traqueros*; and Innis-Jiménez, *Steel Barrio*, 32–33.

35. Gamboa, *Mexican Labor*, xix; and Loza, *Defiant Braceros*.

36.-Gomberg-Muñoz, *Labor and Legality*, 29–30.

37. Ngai, *Impossible Subjects.*

38. Zúñiga and Hernández-León "New Destinations," 30.

39. See Innis-Jiménez, *Steel Barrio*; and Fernandez, *Brown in the Windy City.*

40. Fernandez, *Brown in the Windy City*, 5.

41. Betancur and Cordova, "Economic Restructuring," 119.

42. Betancur and Cordova, 127.

43. The noun *jornalero* comes from the Spanish noun, "jornada" which means an arduous usually one-day journey across a stretch of time or space. A semantic association is found in the Spanish verb *jordar*, which means daily wage. Thus, *jornalero* means someone who works for a day or so for a wage; it does not carry the sense of a long-term commitment or contact.

44. Ordóñez, *Jornalero.*

45. See Betancur and Cordova, "Economic Restructuring," 126, tables 5.1 and 5.2.

46. Betancur and Cordova, "Economic Restructuring," 127. See recent ethnographic studies such as Ruth Gomberg-Muñoz 2012; Zlolniski, "Informal Economy," Zlolniski, *Janitors*; and Walley, *Exit Zero.*

47. US Census Bureau, *Quick Facts: Chicago City, Illinois*, 2018. https://www.census.gov/quickfacts/fact/map/IL,chicagocityillinois/SB0020217. QuickFacts: Chicago City, Illinois, 2018 (website).

48. QuickFacts (website).

49. Refer to Map 1.1, "South Chicago Borders."

50. Limón, "Al Norte toward Home."

51. In this book, I prefer to use the term *interlocutor* because, even though I ultimately decide what voices to include, the people I had conversations with do become coproducers of a better understanding of yardero lives. The term *participant* is also useful, but it denies the agency of the subject.

52. For an excellent analysis of a case study of day laborers in which family and kinship is rather absent or distant from their experience of migration, please see Ordóñez, *Jornalero.*

53. These companies will be referred to as Sanchez Lawn Care and Flores Lawn Care for the purposes of confidentiality. Using fictitious names for the companies, owners, and workers is crucial given the sensitive nature of the discussions we had.

54. On witnessing ethnography, see Behar, *Vulnerable Observer*; Lugo, *Fragmented Lives*, 10; and Rosas, *Barrio Libre*, 24. Also see Gramsci, *Selections from Prison Notebooks*, 238.

55. See Rosaldo, *Culture and Truth.*

56.-Mora, *Kuxlejal Politics.*

57. Anthropology has a long history of documenting how ethnographic enterprise produces a clear difference between "other" and "Other." Fabian, "Presence and Representation"; Spivak 1988 and Said, *Orientalism*. In the context of the production of the "Other," one can point to how the state apparatus in modernity also produces "Others." See Foucault, *History of Sexuality*; and Foucault, *Discipline and Punish*. But if one focuses on those "Others" within the Mexican community, an interesting critique of nationalism and culture can be found in Anzaldúa, *Borderlands, La Frontera.*

Chapter 1. Becoming Yarderos

1. Zlolniski, *Janitors*. See, specifically, chapter 3.

2. Ordóñez, *Jornalero*.

3. Harvey, "From Managerialism to Entrepreneurialism"; and Harvey, *Brief History*.

4. Simon Malpas and Paul Wake, *The Routledge Companion to Critical and Cultural Theory* (New York: Routledge, 2013), 88; and Derrida, "Deconstruction."

5. "Occupational Employment Statistics," US Bureau of Labor Statistics (website), 2012, http://www.bls.gov/oes/current/oes373011.htm.

6. "Occupational Employment and Wages," (2012).

7. In the discussion that follows, keep in mind that the estimate by the Department of Labor does not include self-employed workers, meaning yarderos. Still, it is very important to get a sense of the range of the landscaping and maintenance of economic activity since it is the economic space from which many yarderos operate.

8. "Occupational Employment and Wages," (2012).

9. "Occupations Employment and Wages," (2012).

10. "Occupational Employment and Wage Statistics," US Bureau of Labor Statistics (website), 2021, https://www.bls.gov/oes/current/oes370000.htm.

11. See Pisani and Yoskowitz, "Maid Trade"; Pisani and Yoskowitz, "Grass, Sweat, and Sun"; Pisani and Yoskowitz "Opportunity Knocks"; Steinberg, *American Green*; Huerta, "The Answer," Huerta, "Los Angeles Gardeners Organize," Huerta, "Looking Beyond"; Huerta "Examining" (2007); and Mahler, "Workers and Strangers."

12. See Pisani and Yoskowitz, "Grass, Sweat, and Sun," 235–36.

13. Pisani and Yoskowitz, 235–36.

14. Huerta, "Looking Beyond," 11–12.

15. Ordóñez, *Jornalero*.

16. Ramirez and Hondagneu-Sotelo, "Mexican Immigrant Gardeners," 71.

17. Seth Holmes, *Fresh Fruit, Broken Bodies*.

18. Stephen, *Transborder Lives*, 96

19. Stephen, 102.

20. Stephen, 102.

21. Upon starting the interview, I asked Andres what he wanted to be called in the interview and subsequent documents, and he said that he wanted his last name to be Mota. The word *mota*, in Spanish, means "weed," which I took as a playful maneuver on his part to relieve the anxiety of being interviewed. I asked him twice whether he wanted that last name, to which he again said yes.

22. In the book, I always navigate a difficult racial paradox. Historically, describing someone in color terms has denoted a colonialist approach toward what Carlos Vélez-Ibáñez calls "the seeing man" approach (*Hegemonies of Language*). See also chapter 2 in Alejandro Lugo's *Fragmented Lives, Assembled Parts*. In my study I make the case that these color understandings are lived realities for many working-class folks, especially as they interact within the black-white dichotomy that is highly present in the United States and from which migrants see or understand their racial subjectivity, at times, through the lens of illegality.

23. De Genova, *Working the Boundaries*, 3–5 (emphasis added). I discuss this in detail on the chapter on color inspections.

24. De Genova, *Working the Boundaries*, 4.

25. See Stephen, *Transborder Lives*.

26. De Genova, "Production of Culprits," 161.

27. De León, *Land of Open Graves*.

28. Gomberg-Muñoz, *Labor and Legality*, 52.

29. Gomberg-Muñoz, 43.

30. See De Genova, "Production of Culprits"; De Genova, *Working the Boundaries*; Nicholas P. De Genova, "Migrant 'Illegality' and Deportability in Everyday Life," *Annual Review of Anthropology* 31 (2002), http://www.jstor.org/stable/4132887.

31. See Ordóñez, *Jornalero*.

32. Gomberg-Muñoz, *Labor and Legality*, 19.

33. Michael Kearney, "Borders and Boundaries of State and Self at the End of Empire," *Journal of Historical Sociology* 4, no. 1 (1991): 52–73; Michael Kearney, "The Local and the Global: The Anthropology of Globalization and Transnationalism," *Annual Review of Anthropology* 24 (1995): 52–74.

34. See Stephen, *Transborder Lives*.

35. Gomberg-Muñoz, *Labor and Legality*, 59.

36. There is a concern that a resident may identify where the photo was taken, especially if it is someone who has lived in this area for many years. I took care to show neither the house numbers nor the descriptions from the whereabouts of the photos.

37. Zlolniski, *Janitors*, 15. See also Zlolniski, "Informal Economy."

38. Davila, *Latinos Inc*.

39. Davila, 2.

40. Limón, *Dancing with the Devil*.

41. See Geertz, "Thick Description"; Geertz, "Deep Play"; Bourdieu, *Outline of a Theory*; Rosaldo, *Culture and Truth*; Ortner, "Theory in Anthropology"; Sahlins, *Historical Metaphors*; and Sahlins, *Islands of History*.

42. Rosaldo, *Culture and Truth*, xviii.

43. Foucault, *History of Sexuality*; Rosaldo, *Culture and Truth*; and Lugo, *Fragmented Lives*.

44. Zlolniski, *Janitors*, 90.

45. Zlolniski, "Informal Economy," 174.

46. Zlolniski, *Janitors*, 91.

47. Zlolniski, *Janitors*, 104.

48. Ordóñez, *Jornalero*, 27–28.

49. Ordóñez, 28–29.

50. For an analysis of the metaphor "huevon," please see Alejandro Lugo, "Cultural Production and Reproduction in Cuidad Juarez, Mexico: Tropes at Play among Maquiladora Workers," *Cultural Anthropology* 5, no. 3 (1990): 173–96.

51. I understand that the line of questioning may not appear appropriate in this case, but I wanted to investigate how male yarderos perceive female workers and how gender

becomes a heightened category to investigate. Moreover, my insistence on asking Enrique about the female worker is because the demands of capital are not easily accommodated across gender lines.

Chapter 2. Dispossessed Masculinity

1. For instance, Alex Schlenker offers an analysis of Quintanilla's lyrics, stating that they were oftentimes central to the folklore in relation to an emerging elite military force that often ended up working for the narco economy in northeastern parts of Mexico. Schlenker, "Narcotráfico," 75–87.

2. Beasley, "Rethinking Hegemonic Masculinity."

3. Duerringer, "Be a Man," 137–52.

4. Bernal, Jaime. "La Construcción."

5. For an exemplary analysis of what the term *carne asada* means and its symbolic elements, see Limón, *Dancing with the Devil,* which is perhaps the best folkloric analysis of Mexican and Mexican American culture on this subject. See especially chapter 6.

6. See Paredes, "*With His Pistol in His Hand.*"

7. See Butler, "Performative Acts"; and Butler, "From Interiority."

8. Fourcade and Healy, "Moral Views."

9. Smith, *An Inquiry,* 15.

10. Fourcade and Healy, "Moral Views," 286.

11. Elyachar, *Markets of Dispossession,* 27.

12. More specifically, in the context of Cairo, Julia Elyachar argues that "a mode of accumulation by dispossession, a mode that speaks the language of empowering the poor, is yet another side of more familiar forms of dispossession encouraged by neoliberal economic policies such as enforced privatization and structural adjustment programs." Elyachar, *Markets of Dispossession,* 29.

13. Gálvez, *Eating NAFTA,* xiii.

14. Gálvez, 210n 27.

15. See Zlolniski, *Janitors;* Ordóñez, *Jornalero.*

16. See Sassen, "New York's Informal Economy"; see also Harvey, *Condition of Postmodernity.*

17. Portes, "Economic Sociology."

18. See Zlolniski, "Informal Economy"; Zlolniski, *Janitors;* Lopez-Garza, "A Study"; and Dohan, *Price of Poverty.*

19. See Nodín Valdés, *Barrios Norteños.*

20. See Alejandro Lugo and Bill Maurer, eds., *Gender Matters: Rereading Michelle Z. Rosaldo* (Ann Arbor: University of Michigan Press, 2000).

21. See Gutmann, *Meanings of Macho;* Lancaster, *Life Is Hard;* and Mirande, *Hombres y Machos.*

22. Chávez, *Sounds of Crossing.*

23. Sujey Vega, *Borders of Belonging* (New York: New York University Press, 2015).

24. Jose Limón, "Carne, Carnales, and the Carnivalesque: Bakhtinian Batos, Disorder, and Narrative Discourses," *American Ethnologist* 16 (1989): 475–86.

25. See James W. Messerschmidt, "The Salience of 'Hegemonic Masculinity,'" *Men and masculinities* 22, no. 1 (2019): 85–91. The literature of gender studies has pointed out this division of home versus public, while useful to theorize culture or any other social process, but given its dichotomous nature, sometimes we miss on providing a more nuance analysis. To move the analysis of masculinity forward, I prefer to concentrate on the "public" aspects of this cultural formation, in part, because the public—the workspace—is the area that I spent most of the time observing and participating with my interlocutors en las yardas.

26. See R. W. Connell, "The Men and the Boys," *Polity* (2000).

27. See Hernan Ramirez, "Masculinity in the Workplace: The Case of Mexican Immigrant Gardeners," *Men and Masculinities* 14, no 1 (2011): 97–116.

28. See Ordóñez, *Jornalero*.

29. Gomberg-Muñoz, *Labor and Legality*, 48–49.

30. Gomberg-Muñoz, 48–49.

31. Anderson, "Tagged as a criminal," 9.

32. Anderson, "Tagged as a criminal," 23. See also De Genova, *Working the Boundaries*, 166.

33. Boehm, *Intimate Migrations*.

34. Boehm, *Returned*.

35. "Celebrating 50 Years of Business and the Next 50," access date: December 2014, 2014. https://www.russopower.com/about-us.

36. Danahey, "Russo Power Equipment."

37. Danahey, "Russo Power Equipment."

38. Schiller et al., "Long-Distance Nationalism," 3. See also Schiller and Fouron, *Georges Woke Up Laughing*.

39. See Rosaldo, *Ilongot Headhunting, 1883–1974*.

40. See Vélez-Ibáñez, *Reflections*.

41. See Limón, *Dancing with the Devil*.

42. Limón, *Dancing with the Devil*.

43. While the price of the lawncare equipment may indeed be spent for utilitarian purposes, there is the other side of the coin: wanting to impress clients in order to obtain contracts and, as the informant suggested a couple of times, *pa ganarles a los demas* (to win against other landscapers).

44. The literature on Mexican laziness covers a vast array of disciplines. If we focus only on the work of major scholars from Mexico, it is wise to consult the works of Octavio Paz (*Labyrinth of Solitude*) and Samuel Ramos (*Profile of Man*). By the mid-1990s the ethnography by Matthew Gutmann, *Meanings of Macho*, helps complicate overly simplistic readings of Mexican masculinity. In the context of the US Southwest, the work of José Limón (*Dancing with the Devil*) is critical as is the work of Alejandro Lugo (*Fragmented Lives*), who explores the relationship between laziness and colonialism at the border between Ciudad Juarez and El Paso.

Chapter 3. Performing Power

1. Within a Marxist framework, there is a clear distinction between those who are working-class subjects and those who are part of the entrepreneurial class. Among immigrants in South Chicago making a living through gardening activities, these lines are blurry.

2. By analogizing between the borderlands as the term has been perceived in the context of the US-Mexico border and the borderlands of the intersections between Michel Foucault and the work of Marx, this is a theoretical exercise to bring these two bodies of scholarship together to speak directly about the case of Mexican yarderos in Chicago.

3. See Zlolniski, *Janitors*. Further, excellent examples on this anthropological work in relation to laziness is Lugo's ethnography of maquiladora workers in Ciudad Juarez, Mexico, *Fragmented Lives*.

4. See Holmes, *Fresh Fruit, Broken Bodies*; and Stuesse, *Scratching Out a Living*.

5. Marx, *Capital*, 1:256.

6. Marx, 257.

7. Foucault, *Society Must Be Defended*, 242.

8. Foucault, *Discipline and Punish*: 220–21.

9. Recent literature on immigration focuses on the how the legal status of Mexican migrants affects their behavior at work, given that there is always the possibility of deportation. While this question is very important, this book strategically distances itself from explicitly addressing the ways in which individuals strategize, mobilize, and organize their life through their undocumented social status and experience. There is the possibility that self-disciplining interacts in complex ways with being undocumented, and indeed it is a question to explore in other spaces. The demographic composition of my participants in fact included individuals who were US citizens, permanent residents, and undocumented subjects, all working in the same gardening economy in Chicago. Thus, the relation between self-discipline and yardero subjectivity still holds ethnographic validity. I write about undocumented lives in the last chapter more directly.

10. A similar process was examined by Juan Thomas Ordóñez in his study of jornaleros in Berkeley, California. See *Jornalero*.

11. Obama, *Becoming*, 24.

12. See Holmes, *Fresh Fruit, Broken Bodies*. See chapter 5 specifically.

13. Much is lost in attempting to translate the culturally significant metaphors discussed by Don Antonio. However, in most of the translations in this book, the effort has been made to come linguistically close to the expressions exposed in the original conversation.

14. This insight emerges out of a long discussion with the work of Renato Rosaldo. See *Culture and Truth*.

15. In the context of the city of Chicago, Mexican migrants are probably not the first to offer edging as a generalized practice in the landscaping economic sector. Italian migrants in the decades before the 1970s were one of the major migrant groups that actively participated in the gardening economy, especially in the formation of Highwood, Illinois.

16. I was not able to collect information on the long-term effects of performing lawn-care services while doing this activity. Don Antonio and others would always complain about their right hands and said that, usually when autumn would arrive, the pain in their right shoulders would not go away for days. This ethnographic evidence calls for medically based (and most likely long-term) anthropological research to examine the effects of work on the bodies of laborers.

17. See Holmes, *Fresh Fruit, Broken Bodies*; Ordóñez, *Jornalero*; and Sergio Lemus, "Class.."

18. See Rosaldo, *Culture and Truth*; Stephen, *Transborder Lives*; and Lugo, *Fragmented Lives*, 2008.

19. See Hernández, *Racial Innocence*.

Chapter 4. Color Inspections

1. Anderson, *Imagined Communities*.

2. Chávez, *Sounds of Crossing*.

3. Johnathan Hernandez, "Pepe Aguilar anuncia gira 'Jaripeo Sin Fronteras USA,' *La Noticia*, May 5, 2021, https://lanoticia.com/primerafila/pepeaguilar-jaripeo-sin-fronteras-usa-como-comprar-los-boletos/.

4. See Nájera-Ramírez, Olga. "Engendering nationalism: identity, discourse, and the Mexican charro." *Anthropological Quarterly* (1994): 1–14.

5. Within the context of Mexican American poetic expressions, folklorist Américo Paredes and the later José Limón have documented these genres in the lives of South Texans. Much of this folkloric analysis emerges from their insights into the relationship between culture, power, and the state. See Paredes, *"With His Pistol"*; and Limón, *Dancing with the Devil*.

6. In 1992, a popular iconic *banda*-style group named Banda Machos produced one of its greatest hits entitled, "Sangre de Indio," which is still heard in weekend ballrooms in places where Mexican families gather together to celebrate a *quinceañera* or *cumpleanos* (birthday celebrations). See Cantú, "La Quinceañera"; and Alvarez, *Once Upon a Quinceañera*.

7. Rosaldo, *Culture and Truth*.

8. For an excellent analysis of the term *moreno/a* and its connections to Blackness and indigeneity, Laura Lewis's masterful ethnography of the Costa Chica tells us how local residents of a town of San Nicolas Toledino, in the state of Guerrero, despite being constantly labeled as Afro-Mexicanos, reject this identification for a more "mixed" ancestry that offers them the opportunity to become part of the Mexican mestizo nation-state and refuse a direct engagement with a diasporic Black identification. Lewis, *Chocolate and Corn Flour*.

9. See Oscar Lewis, *The Children of Sanchez: Autobiography of a Mexican Family* (New York: Vintage, 1961) Lewis, *Chocolate and Corn Flour*; Lewis, "Blacks, Black Indians, Afromexicans"; and Lewis, "Modesty and Modernity."

10. See Lugo, *Fragmented Lives*.

11. Hernández, *Racial Innocence*.

12. On José Vaconcelos's role within the perceptions and imaginings of *mestizaje* as a discourse of the nation-state, Marylin Grace Miller notes that La Raza Cosmica "marked the inception of a full developed ideology of *mestizaje* that tied political and aesthetic self-definition and assertion to a racial discourse at both the national and regional levels." Miller, *Rise and Fall*, 27.

13. Vasconcelos, *La Raza Cosmica*, 9.

14. See Anthony Russell Jerry, *Blackness in Mexico: Afro-Mexican Recognition and the Production of Citizenship in the Costa Chica.* Gainsville: University Press of Florida, 2023); Jerry, "Chasing Blackness."

15. Batalla and Dennis, *México Profundo*.

16. Horscasitas, La Modernidad Desbordada, 19–20.

17. See Vélez-Ibañez, *Hegemonies of Language*.

18. Hernández, "Colorism and the Law," 683–84.

19. See Jerry, *Blackness in Mexico*.

20. See Bennett, *Colonial Blackness*; Vaugh, "Race and Nation"; Sue and Golash-Boza, "More Than"; Lewis, "Blacks, Black Indians, Afromexicans"; and Jerry "Chasing Blackness."

21. See, for example, Lewis, *Chocolate and Corn Flour*; Jerry, *Blackness in Mexico*; Hernández, "Colorism and the Law"; and Hernández, *Racial innocence*.

22. In the context of yarderos in the city of Chicago, very little class mobilization has taken place. I argue that this is a consequence of the very nature of the structure of the work itself, which is rapid and intense. In other words, there is very little room or time left for workers to organize. However, in other contexts, immigrants have been successful in organizing, given the structure of their informal work.

23. While theorizations of the relation between race and color refocus our attention to the level of skin color and perception, critical race theory scholars have reminded us that race is much more than color. For example, Junaid Rana discusses how race and migration are lived on Muslim bodies as these circulate in the global economy through concepts, media, popular culture, and narratives of migration (Rana, *Terrifying Muslims*). Leo Chavez has explored the production of race and racism by analyzing magazine images and how fertility and Latina sexuality become markers used to racialize entire immigrant populations (Chavez, *Covering Immigration*; and Chavez, *Latino Threat, 2013*).

24. See Morrison, "Black Studies Center."

25. As discussed by Katerí Hernández, one of the successes of "white supremacy" is the idea that makes us think that the term *white* is not a racial category but a natural one. In the US racial order, for example, the focus is on producing an "anti-Black" sentiment not only within the racialized "white" population but even within "racialized" groups themselves. In the context of Latinos in the United States, Hernández has called thin the "Latino innocence cloak" or the ways in which, within the law profession, for example, judges and lawyers are unable to see Latinx folks as perpetrators of clear anti-Black racists or having the intention of engaging racism. See Hernández, *Racial Innocence*, 14

26. Arredondo, *Mexican Chicago*, 3.

27. See Omar S. Valerio-Jiménez, *River of Hope: Forging Identity and Nation in the Rio Grande Borderlands* (Chapel Hill, NC: Duke University Press, 2013).

28. For example, anthropologist Gilberto Rosas notes that Anzaldúa's work critiques Chicano scholars because of anthropology's "structural functionalist residues and its search for autonomously developed, deep, coherent patterns of a uniformly shared culture that are unaffected by hierarchical division and quotidian patterns." Rosas, *Barrio Libre*, 18–19.

29. Anzaldúa, *Borderlands, La Frontera*, 18.

30. Anzaldúa, 3.

31. On this particular line of questioning a central theoretical answer has been provided by anthropologist Gilberto Rosas as he has explored the expansion of what he calls the "borderlands condition" or "coupling of 'exceptionality' with political imaginaries. The former term represents an iteration of the diffused governance of race." Rosas, "Thickening Borderlands," 2006: 335.

32. See Aparicio, *Dominican-Americans*; Vega, *Latino Heartland*; and Rosas, *Barrio Libre*.

33. Anzaldúa, *Borderlands, La Frontera*, 34. In the context of the US-Mexico border, "checkpoints" are usually placed along or near the border where travelers are stopped for inspection. During these checkpoints, or revisions, immigration officers check people's visas and other pertinent documents—whether or not there is a motive—and even their vehicles. For elaborations of what Anzaldúa means by 150 years of racism, the studies of Américo Paredes (*"With His Pistol"*) and Monica Muñoz Martinez (*Injustice Never Leaves You*) are useful reminders.

34. See Innis-Jiménez, *Steel Barrio*.

35. Rosaldo, *Culture and Truth*, 28. Further, Renato Rosaldo comments on the "classical period," roughly between 1921 and 1971, as a time when "the discipline's dominant objectivist view held that social life was fixed and constraining" (332). Rosaldo further notes how anthropologist Sally Falk Moore writes with clarity about this period as a time when "society was a system. Culture had a pattern. The postulation of a coherent whole discoverable bit by bit served to expand the significance of each observed particularity." Rosaldo, *Culture and Truth*, 32.

36. Rosaldo, *Culture and Truth*, 28.

37. Rosaldo, *Culture and Truth*, 28.

38. Rosaldo, *Culture and Truth*, 208.

39. Lugo, *Fragmented Lives*, 117.

40. Lugo, 117. Emphasis in original.

41. Anderson, *Imagined Communities*; and Hernández, "Colorism and the Law."

42. See Hernández, *Racial Innocence*.

43. Addressing the problem of color has been more productive from scholars working with the Black population in Mexico. See Lewis, "Of Ships and Saints"; Lewis, *Chocolate and Corn Flour*; Lewis, "Blacks, Black Indians"; Lewis, "Modesty and modernity"; Jerry, Blackness in Mexico: Afro-Mexican Recognition and the Production of Citizenship in the Costa Chica; and Jerry, *Chasing Blackness*.

44. See Geertz, "Thick Description."

45. See Richard Delgado and Jean Steafanic Delgado, *Critical Race Theory: An Introduction* (New York: University of New York Press, 2023); Hernández, "Colorism and the Law"; Hernández, "Multiracial Discourse"; Ann Laura Stoler, *Race and the Education of Desire: Foucault's History of Sexuality and the Colonia Order of Things* (Durham, NC: Duke University Press, 1995); Leith Mullings, "Interrogating Racism: Toward and Antiracist Anthropology," *Annual Review of Anthropology* 34 (2005); Bonilla-Silva, *Racism without Racists*; Bonilla-Silva, *White Logic, White Methods*; and Lee D. Baker, "The Racist Anti-Racism of American Anthropology," *Transforming Anthropology* 29, no. 2 (2021).

46. Rosas, *Barrio Libre*, 75–76.

47. See Holmes, *Fresh Fruit, Broken Bodies*; Bourdieu, Pierre. "Distinction." In *Social Theory Re-Wired*, pp. 177–192. Routledge, 2023. Bourdieu, Pierre. "Masculine domination revisited." *Berkeley Journal of Sociology* 41 (1996): 189–203.

48. Ordóñez, Jornalero.

49. Without falling into ethnographic "thinness," as anthropologist Sherry Ortner advises us, I hope I made justice to portray their arguments in a culturally dense fashion. See Ortner *Anthropology and Social Theory*, 43–46.

50. Ann Laura Stoler, "Imperial Debris: Reflections on Ruins and Ruination," *Cultural anthropology* 23, no. 2 (2008): 201.

51. See Stoler, "Imperial Debris"; Hernández, *Racial Innocence*; Hernández, "Colorism and the Law"; Hernández, "Multiracial Discourse."

52. See W. E. B. Du Bois, *Black Reconstruction in America, 1860–1880* (New York: Harcourt, Brace, 2017 [1935]); Hernández, *Racial Innocence*; and Hernández, "Colorism and the Law." In regard to border theorizing, this analysis is situated within the insights of works such as Paredes, *"With His Pistol"*; Limon, *Dancing with the Devil*; Menchaca, *Recovering History*; Rosaldo, *Culture and Truth*; Anzaldúa, *Borderlands, La Frontera*; Lugo, *Fragmented Lives*; Vega, *Latino Heartland*; De Genova, "Race, Space"; De Genova and Ramos-Zayas, *Latino Crossings*; De Genova, *Working the Boundaries*.

Chapter 5. *Los Morenos y Los Mejicanos*

1. For additional information, visit: https://www.bowenhighschool.com/apps/pages/index.jsp?uREC_ID=1626322&type=d&pREC_ID=1766101

2. See Hernández, *Racial Innocence*.

3. An intersectional understanding of identity suggests that race, class, and gender are a triad of great importance for philosophers, sociologists, and anthropologists. In societies such as the contemporary United States, which actively promotes the cultural and political ideology of a colorblind, classless, and gender-equal society, this understanding is central to the question of how these identity-formation processes operate. See Omi and Winant, *Racial Formation*, 53–69.

4. For an in-depth discussion of how Blackness has been imagined in the context of Latin America, anthropologists Norman E. Whitten and Arlene Torres offer a theorization

of the legacies of Africaness in the American continent. Whitten and Torres, *Blackness in Latin America*, 5–13.

5. See Márquez, *Black-Brown Solidarity*.

6. For exceptions, see Greenbaum, *More Than Black*, 2002; and Márquez, *Black-Brown Solidarity*.

7. Bonilla-Silva, *Racism without Racists*; and Bonilla-Silva, *White Logic, White Methods*.

8. Henry and Sears, "Symbolic Racism."; Schuman et al., *Racial Attitudes*.

9. Goldberg and Essed, *Race Critical Theories*; and McGibbon, Etowa, and McPherson, "Healthcare access."

10. Hook, "'Real' of Racializing."

11. See Paredes, *"With His Pistol"*; Almaguer, *Racial Fault Lines*; Menchaca, *Recovering History*; and Reséndez, "National Identity."

12. For additional readings, see classical studies such as Bois, WEB Du. *The problem of the color line at the turn of the Twentieth Century: the essential early essays*. Fordham University Press, 2020; and Du Bois, *Souls of Black Folk*.

13. See Obama, *Dreams*.

14. Of course, this is not the first time that I interacted with African Americans. While growing up in the city of Chicago myself, I had African American friends in middle school and later in high school. However, I do not recall ever visiting them at their homes. While performing work as a landscaper, I did visit the homes of African Americans but only to mow grass.

15. See Gloria Anzaldúa, *Borderlands, La Frontera*. Roberto Delgadillo Hernandez, *Coloniality and Border (ed) Violence: San Diego, San Ysidro and the US///Mexico Border* (Berkeley: University of California Press, 2010); Hernández, "Colorism and the Law"; Hernández, *Racial Innocence*.

16. See Miranda, "Living in Legal Limbo."

Chapter 6. On Mexican *Sacer*

1. See Vega, *Latino Heartland*.

2. Rana and Rosas, "Managing Crisis."

3. Rana, *Terrifying Muslims*.

4. See De León, *Land of Open Graves*. For argumentative purposes here, I am specifically analyzing the period and transformations after 9/11; however, the necropolitical or punitive end of the American state apparatus had been in operation even earlier in the late nineteenth and early twentieth centuries, as expressed through the lynching of ethnic Mexicans, especially in the state of Texas. See Martinez, *Injustice Never Leaves You*; Carrigan and Webb, *Forgotten Dead*; and Villanueva, *Lynching of Mexicans*.

5. Gomberg-Muñoz, *Labor and Legality*; see specifically her introduction to "the Lions" in reference to the city from which this network of undocumented worked migrated—that is, Leon, Guanajuato.

6. Gomberg-Muñoz, *Labor and Legality*, 35–36.

7. De León, *Land of Open Graves.*

8. De Genova, "Production of Culprits."

9. See Vega, *Latino Heartland.* In this ethnography, Vega further makes this case by examining the anti-immigrant discourse in West Lafayette, Indiana. See also Foucault's take on this metaphor of defending society most analytically expressed in *Society Must Be Defended*

10. Foucault, *History of Sexuality,* 1:139.

11. Foucault, *History of Sexuality,* 1:140.

12. Foucault, *Society Must Be Defended,* 240.

13. Foucault, *Society Must Be Defended,* 241.

14. See Agamben, *Home Sacer.*

15. Agamben, 3–4.

16. Agamben, 6.

17. Agamben, 8.

18. See Garcia, *Operation Wetback.*

19. See De Genova, "Production of Culprits"; Martinez, *Injustice Never Leaves You*; and Paredes, *"With His Pistol."*

20. De Genova, "Production of Culprits," 427.

21. De Genova, "427–29.

22. Gomberg-Muñoz, *Labor and Legality,* 34–35.

23. BBC News, "End of an era for Mexico," July 3, 2000. http://news.bbc.co.uk/2/hi/americas/816533.stm

24. Richard W. Stevenson and Steven & Greenhouse Stevemson, "Bush on Immigration: The President: Plan for Illegal Immigrant Workers Draws Fire From Two Sides," *New York Times, January 8* (New York), January 8, 2004. 2004, Electronic, Americas.

25. Dewey, "Immigration after 9/11."

26. See Correa "After 9/11"; Correa and Thomas, "Rebirth"; and Rosas, *Barrio Libre.*

27. U. S. Immigration and Customs Enforcement. "Worksite Enforcement Advisory." February 2008, 2. https://www.fosterglobal.com/govt_websites/ICEWorksiteAdvisoryForFebruary2007.pdf.

28. U. S. Immigration and Customs Enforcement. "Worksite Enforcement Advisory." February 2008, 2. https://www.fosterglobal.com/govt_websites/ICEWorksiteAdvisoryForFebruary2007.pdf.

29. U. S. Immigration and Customs Enforcement. "Worksite Enforcement Advisory." February 2008, 2. https://www.fosterglobal.com/govt_websites/ICEWorksiteAdvisoryForFebruary2007.pdf.

30. E-Verify. "What is E-Verify." https://www.e-verify.gov

31. E-Verify. "What is E-Verify." https://www.e-verify.gov

32. See Martinez, *Injustice Never Leaves You.*

33. See Chavez, *Covering Immigration.*

34. See Bigo, "Security and Immigration."

35. Bigo, 65.

36. Bigo, 73.

37. See Lugo, *Fragmented Lives, Assembled Parts*; and Rosas, Barrio Libre.

38. McFadden, Robert D. "Across the U.S., Growing Rallies for Immigration." *New York Times, April 10* (New York) http://www.nytimes.com/

39. McFadden, Robert D. "Across the U.S., Growing Rallies for Immigration." *New York Times, April 10* (New York) http://www.nytimes.com/

40. McFadden, Robert D. "Across the U.S., Growing Rallies for Immigration." *New York Times, April 10* (New York) http://www.nytimes.com/

41. Archibold, Randal C. "Crowds Are Smaller at Protests by Immigrants," *New York Times, May 2* (New York), 2008.

42. Archibold, Randal C. "Crowds Are Smaller at Protests by Immigrants," *New York Times, May 2* (New York), 2008.

43. Porter, Eduardo. "The Search for Illegal Immigrants Stops at the Workplace," *New York Times,* March 5 (New York), 2006.

44. Porter, Eduardo. "The Search for Illegal Immigrants Stops at the Workplace," *New York Times,* March 5 (New York), 2006.

45. Sander, Libby. "Immigration Raid Yields 62 Arrests in Illinois," *New York Times,* April 5 (New York), April 5, 2007.

46. The formation of the Homeland Security State can be traced to George W. Bush's two terms in office. A concept already advanced by Nicholas De Genova explains that the Homeland Security State stands in contradistinction to the Cold War era when the United States was unchallenged globally. This new formation is "routinely acknowledged by persistently affiliating it rhetorically with the ever-elusive figure of 'totalitarianism' as a unifying frame of antagonistic reference . . . [which] nonetheless signals a momentous and qualitative improvisation, historical specificity of which therefore commands intense critical scrutiny." De Genova, "Production of Culprits," 422–23.

Mexican immigrants in particular have been rendered as "targets" as well as the primordial "illegal" subject. See De Genova. "Production of Culprits"; Inda, *Targeting Immigrants*; and Chavez, *Covering Immigration*. Immediately after the events of September 11, 2001, there was an increased securitization of the global tactics and strategies of the government.

47. Preston, Julia. "Immigration Sweep Ends in 280 Arrests at 5 Plants," *New York Times,* April 17 (New York), 2008.

48. For an example, please see: "Q&A: Trump Administration's 'Zero-Tolerance' Immigration Policy." Human Rights Watch (website), August 16, 2018. https://www.hrw.org/news/2018/08/16/qa-trump-administrations-zero-tolerance-immigration-policy.

49. Martinez, *Injustice Never Leaves You.*

50. Inda, *Targeting Immigrants,* 17.

51. Inda, 32.

52. Belson, Ken and Capuzzo, Jill P. "Towns Rethink Laws against Illegal Immigrants," *New York Times,* September 26 (New York), 2007. http://query.nytimes.com/gst/fullpage.html?

53. Julia Preston. "In Reversal, Courts Uphold Local Immigration Laws," *New York Times*, February 11 (New York), 2008. http://www.nytimes.com/2008/02/10/us/10immig.html?/.

54. Time Staff. "Here's Donald Trump's Presidential Announcement Speech" *Time Magazine*, June 16, 2015.

55. Time Staff. "Here's Donald Trump's Presidential Announcement Speech" *Time Magazine*, June 16, 2015.

References

"About Us: Celebrating 50 Years of Business & the Next 50." Russo Power Equipment (website). Accessed May 1, 2020, 2020. https://www.russopower.com/about-us.

Acosta, Aide. "Home Making in Small-Town America: Mexican and Latina/O Diasporas and Citizenship Practices in the Midwest." PhD, University of Illinois at Urbana-Champaign, 2010. http://hdl.handle.net/2142/17029.

———. "Reshaping the Rural Heartland" *In Latina/o Midwest Reader*, edited by Valerio-Jimenez, Omar, and Santiago Vaquera-Vasquez. Urbana: University of Illinois Press, 2017.

Agamben, Giorgio. *Home Sacer: Sovereign Power and Bare Life.* Stanford, CA: Stanford University Press, 1998.

———. *Means without End: Notes on Politics.* Minneapolis: University of Minnesota Press, 2000.

Almaguer, Thomas. *Racial Fault Lines: The Historical Origins of White Supremacy in California.* Berkeley: University of California Press, 1994.

Alvarez, C. J. *Border Land, Border Water: A History of Construction on the US-Mexico Divide.* Austin: University of Texas Press, 2019.

Alvarez, Julia. *Once Upon a Quinceañera: Coming of Age in the USA.* New York: Penguin, 2007.

Alvarez, Robert R. *Mangos, Chiles, and Truckers: The Business of Transnationalism.* Minneapolis: University of Minnesota Press, 2005.

Amezcua, Mike. *Making Mexican Chicago: From Postwar Settlement to the Age of Gentrification.* Chicago: University of Chicago Press, 2022.

Anderson, Benedict. *Imagined Communities: Reflections on the Origin and Spread of Nationalism.* New York: Verso, 2006.

Anderson, Jill. "Academic Advocacy with 'Dreamers' in Mexico: From US American High Schools to Mexican Higher Education." *AERA Online Paper Repository,* April 12 (2016).

———. "Bilingual, Bicultural, Not Yet, Binational: Undocumented Immigrant Youth in Mexico and the United States." Wilson Center, Mexico Institute (2016).

———. "Tagged as a Criminal: Narratives of Deportation and Return Migration in a Mexico City Call Center." *Latino Studies* 13, no. 1 (2015): 8–27.

Año Nuevo Kerr, Louise. "Chicano Settlements in Chicago: A Brief History." *Journal of Ethnic Studies* 2, no. 4 (1975): 22–32.

———. "Mexican Chicago: Chicano Assimilation Aborted, 1939–1954." In *Ethnic Chicago,* edited by Melvin G. Holli and Peter d'A Jones, 269–98. Grand Rapids, MI: William B. Eerdmans, 1977.

Anzaldúa, Gloria. *Borderlands, La Frontera: The New Mestiza.* San Francisco: Aunt Lute Books, 1987.

Anzaldúa, Gloria, and Cherrie Moraga, eds. *This Bridge Called My Back: Writings by Radical Women of Color.* Watertown, MA: Persephone Press, 1981.

Aparicio, Ana. *Dominican-Americans and the Politics of Empowerment.* Gainsville: University Press of Florida, 2005.

Archibold, Randal C. "Crowds Are Smaller at Protests by Immigrants " *New York Times,* May 2 (New York), 2008.

Arredondo, Gabriela F. *Mexican Chicago: Race, Identity, and Nation, 1916–39.* Urbana: University of Illinois Press, 2008.

Baker, Lee D. "The Racist Anti-racism of American Anthropology." *Transforming Anthropology* 29, no. 2 (2021): 127–42.

Batalla, Guillermo Bonfil, and Philip A. Dennis. *México Profundo: Reclaiming a Civilization.* Austin: University of Texas Press, 1996.

Beasley, Christine. "Rethinking Hegemonic Masculinity in a Globalizing World." *Men and Masculinities* 11, no. 1 (2008): 86–103.

Behar, Ruth. *The Vulnerable Observer: Anthropology That Breaks Your Heart.* Boston: Beacon Press, 1996.

Belson, Ken and Jill P. Capuzzo, "Towns Rethink Laws against Illegal Immigrants," *New York Times,* September 26 (New York), 2007. http://query.nytimes.com/gst/fullpage.html/.

Bennett, Herman L. *Colonial Blackness: A History of Afro-Mexico.* Bloomington: Indiana University Press, 2009.

Bernal, Jaime. "La Construcción de la figura del narcotraficante: Desde el romance español hasta el narcocorrido." PhD, University of Calgary, 2018.

Betancur, John J., and Teresa Cordova. "Economic Restructuring and the Process of Incorporation of Latinos into the Chicago Economy." In *Latinos in a Changing U. S. Economy: Comparative Perspectives on Growing Inequality,* edited by Rebecca Bonilla Morales and Frank Bonilla Morales. Newbury Park, CA: Sage, 1993.

Bigo, Difier. "Security and Immigration: Toward a Critique of the Governmentality of Unease." *Alternatives* 27 (2002): 63–92.

Boehm, Deborah A. *Intimate Migrations: Gender, Family, and Illegality among Transnational Mexicans.* New York: New York University Press, 2012.

———. *Returned: Going and Coming in an Age of Deportation.* Series in Public Anthropology 39. Berkeley: University of California Press, 2016.

Bonilla-Silva, Eduardo. *Racism without Racists: Color-Blind Racism and the Persistence of Racial Inequality in the United States.* Lanham. MD: Rowman and Littlefield, 2006.

———. *White Logic, White Methods: Racism and Methodology.* Lanham, MD: Rowman and Littlefield, 2008.

Bourdieu, Pierre. "Distinction." In *Social Theory Re-Wired,* 177–92. New York: Routledge.

———. "Masculine Domination Revisited." *Berkeley Journal of Sociology* 41 (1996): 189–203.

———. *Outline of a Theory of Practice.* Cambridge: Cambridge University Press, 1977.

Butler, Judith. "From Interiority to Gender Performatives." *Camp: Queer Aesthetics and the Performing Subject: A Reader* (1999): 361–68.

———. "Performative Acts and Gender Constitution: An Essay in Phenomenology and Feminist Theory." *Theatre Journal* 40, no. 4 (1988): 519–31.

Cantú, Norma. "La Quinceañera: Towards an Ethnographic Analysis of a Life-Cycle Ritual." *Southern Folklore* 56, no. 1 (1999): 73.

Carrigan, William D., and Clive Webb. *Forgotten Dead: Mob Violence against Mexicans in the United States, 1848–1928.* Oxford: Oxford University Press, 2013.

Chávez, Alex E. *Sounds of Crossing: Music, Migration, and the Aural Poetics of Huapango Arribeño.* Durham, NC: Duke University Press, 2017.

Chavéz, Alex E., and Gina M. Pérez, eds. *Ethnographic Refusals, Unruly Latinidades.* Albuquerque: University of New Mexico Press, 2022.

Chavez, Leo R. *Covering Immigration: Popular Images and the Politics of the Nation.* Berkeley: University of California Press, 2001.

———. *The Latino Threat: Constructing Immigrants, Citizens, and the Nation.* Stanford: Stanford University Press, 2013.

———. *Shadowed Lives: Undocumented Immigrants in American Society and Experiences of Incorporation.* New York: Harcourt Brace Jovanovich, 1992.

Connell, R. W., and James W. Messerchmidt. "Hegemonic Masculinity." *Gender and Society* 19, no. 6 (2005): 829–59.

Correa, Jennifer G. "'After 9/11 Everything Changed': Re-Formations of State Violence in Everyday Life on the US-Mexico Border." *Cultural Dynamics,* no. 25 (2013): 99–119.

Correa, Jennifer G., and James M. Thomas. "The Rebirth of the US-Mexico Border: Latina/O Enforcement Agents and the Changing Politics of Racial Power." *Sociology of Race and Ethnicity* 1, no. 2 (2015): 239–54.

"Covid-19 United States Cases by County." Johns Hopkins University and Medicine (website), https://coronavirus.jhu.edu/us-map.

Danahey, Mike. "Russo Power Equipment Plans to Open in Elgin Spot That Was a Wal-Mart." *Chicago Tribune*, June 23, 2015.

Davila, Arlene. *Latinos Inc.: The Marketing and Making of a People.* Berkeley: University of California Press, 2001.

Davis, Marilyn P. *Mexican Voices, American Dreams: An Oral History of Mexican Immigration to the United States.* New York: Henry Holt, 1990.

De Genova, Nicholas, ed. *The Borders of "Europe": Autonomy of Migration, Tactics of Bordering.* Durham, NC: Duke University Press, 2017.

———. "Migrant 'Illegality' and Deportability in Everyday Life." *Annual Review of Anthropology* 31, no. 1 (2002): 419–47.

———. "The Production of Culprits: From Deportability to Detainability in the Aftermath of 'Homeland Security.'" *Citizenship Studies* 11, no. 5 (2007): 421–48.

———. "Race, Space, and Reinvention of Latin America in Mexican Chicago." *Latin American Perspectives* 25, no. 102. (1998): 91–120.

———. *Working the Boundaries: Race, Space, and "Illegality" in Mexican Chicago.* Ethnography. Durham, NC: Duke University Press, 2005.

De Genova, Nicholas, and Ana Y. Ramos-Zayas, eds. *Latino Crossings: Mexicans, Puerto Ricans, and the Politics of Race and Citizenship.* New York: Routledge, 2003.

De Leon, Jason. *The Land of Open Graves: Living and Dying on the Migrant Trail.* Berkeley: University of California Press, 2015.

Delgado, Richard, and Jean Stefancic. *Critical Race Theory: An Introduction.* Vol. 87. New York: New York University Press, 2023.

Derrida, Jacques. "Deconstruction." *A Dictionary of Literary Terms and Literary Theory* (2010): 217–18.

Dewey, Arthur. E. "Immigration after 9/11: The View from the United States." US Department of State, May 4, 2008, 2003. Delivery Address. Available at: https://2001-2009.state.gov/g/prm/rls/2003/37906.htm.

Dohan, Daniel. *The Price of Poverty: Money, and Culture in the Mexican American Barrio.* Berkeley, CA: Berkeley University Press, 2003.

Du Bois, W. E. B. *Black Reconstruction in America: Toward a History of the Part which Black Folk Played in the Attempt to Reconstruct Democracy in America, 1860–1880.* New York: Routledge, 2017 [1935].

———. *The Problem of the Color Line at the Turn of the Twentieth Century: The Essential Early Essays.* New York: Fordham University Press, 2020.

———. "The Souls of Black Folk." pdf. (1903).

Du Bois, W. E. B., and Manning Marable. *Souls of Black Folk.* New York: Routledge, 2015.

Duerringer, Christopher. "Be a Man—Buy a Car! Articulating Masculinity with Consumerism in Man's Last Stand." *Southern Communication Journal* 80, no. 2 (2015): 137–52.

Elyachar, Julia. *Markets of Dispossession: NGOs, Economic Development, and the State in Cairo.* Durham, NC: Duke University Press, 2005.

Emerson, Robert M., Rachel I. Fretz, and Linda L. Shaw, eds. *Writing Ethnographic Fieldnotes.* Chicago: University of Chicago Press, 1995.

Essed, Philomena, and David Theo Goldberg. *Race Critical Theories: Text and Context.* Hoboken, NJ: Blackwell Publishing, 2001.

Fabian, Johannes. "Presence and Representation: The Other and Anthropological Writing." *Critical Inquiry* 16, no. 4 (1990): 753–72.

Fernandez, Lilia. *Brown in the Windy City: Mexicans and Puerto Ricans in Postwar Chicago.* Chicago: University of Chicago Press, 2012.

Flores, John H. *The Mexican Revolution in Chicago: Immigration Politics from the Early Twentieth Century to the Cold War.* Urbana: University of Illinois Press, 2018.

Foucault, Michel. *The Birth of Biopolitics: Lectures at the Collège de France, 1978–1979.* New York: Palgrave Macmillan, 2008.

———. *Discipline and Punish: The Birth of the Prison.* Translated by Alan Sheridan. New York: Vintage, 1979.

———. *The History of Sexuality.* Translated by M. Hurley. Vol. 1. New York: Pantheon, 1978.

———, ed. *Power/Knowledge: Selected Interviews and Other Writings, 1972–1977.* Edited by Colin Gordon. New York: Pantheon, 1990.

———. *"Society Must Be Defended": Lectures at the College De France 1975–1976.* Edited by Arnold I. Davidson. Translated by David Macey. New York: Picador, 2003.

Fourcade, Marion, and Kieran Healy. "Moral Views of Market Society." *Annual Review of Sociology* 33, no. 2 (2007): 285–311.

Gálvez, Alyshia. *Eating NAFTA: Trade, Food Policies, and the Destruction of Mexico.* Berkeley: University of California Press, 2018.

Gamboa, Erasmo. *Mexican Labor and World War II; Braceros in the Pacific Northwest, 1942–1947.* Seattle: University of Washington Press, 2000.

Gamio, Manuel. *Mexican Immigration to the United States: A Study of Human Migration and Adjustment.* New York: Dover, 1971.

Garcia, Juan. *Mexicans in the Midwest, 1900–1932.* Tucson: University of Arizona Press, 1996.

———. *Operation Wetback: The Mass Deportation of Mexican Undocumented Workers in 1954.* Westport, CT: Greenwood, 1982.

García, Lorena, and Mérida Rúa. "Processing Latinidad: Mapping Latino Urban Landscapes through Chicago Ethnic Festivals." *Latino Studies* 5 (2007): 317–39.

Garcilazo, Jeffrey Marcos. *Traqueros: Mexican Railroad Workers in the United States, 1870 to 1930.* Denton: University of North Texas, 2012.

Gaytán, Marie S. *¡Tequila!: Distilling the Spirit of Mexico.* Palo Alto, CA: Stanford University Press, 2014.

Geertz, Clifford. "Deep Play: Notes of Balinese Cockfight." In *The Interpretation of Cultures.* New York: Basic, 1973.

———. "Thick Description: Toward an Interpretive Theory of Culture." In *The Cultural Geography Reader,* 41–51. New York: Routledge, 2008.

Gomberg-Muñoz, Ruth. *Labor and Legality: An Ethnography of a Mexican Immigrant Network.* Oxford: Oxford University Press, 2011.

———. "Inequality in a 'Postracial' Era: Race, Immigration, and Criminalization of Low-wage Labor." *Du Bois Review: Social Science Research on Race* 9, no. 2 (2012): 339–53.

Gramsci, Antonio. *Selections from Prison Notebooks by Antonio Gramsci*. Translated by Quintin Hoare and Geoffrey Nowell Smith. 2nd ed. London: Lawrence and Wishart, 1971.

Greenbaum, Susan. *More Than Black: Afro-Cubans in Tampa*. Gainsville: University Press of Florida, 2002.

Gutierrez, David G. *Walls and Mirrors: Mexican Americans, Mexican Immigrants, and the Politics of Ethnicity*. Berkeley: University of California Press, 1995.

Gutmann, Matthew C. *The Meanings of Macho: Being a Man in Mexico City*. Berkeley: University of California Press, 2006.

Harvey, David. *A Brief History of Neoliberalism*. Oxford University Press, 2007.

———. *The Condition of Postmodernity: An Enquiry into the Origins of Cultural Change*. New York: Wiley-Blackwell, 1989.

———. "From Managerialism to Entrepreneurialism: The Transformation in Urban Governance in Late Capitalism." *Geografiska Annaler. Series B, Human Geography* 71, no. 1 (1989): 3–17. http://www.jstor.org/stable/490503.

Henry, Patrick J., and David O. Sears. "The Symbolic Racism 2000 Scale." *Political Psychology* 23, no. 2 (2002): 253–83.

Hernandez, Roberto Delgadillo. *Coloniality and Border (ed) Violence: San Diego, San Ysidro and the US-Mexico Border*. University of California, Berkeley, 2010.

Hernández, Tanya Katerí. "Colorism and the Law in Latin America-Global Perspectives on Colorism Conference Remarks." *Washington University Global Studies Law Review* 14 (2015): 683–93.

———. "Multiracial Discourse: Racial Classifications in an Era of Color-Blind Jurisprudence." *Maryland Law Review* 57 (1998): 97–173.

———. *Racial Innocence: Unmasking Latino Anti-Black Bias and the Struggle for Equality*. Boston, MA: Beacon, 2022.

Holmes, Seth. *Fresh Fruit, Broken Bodies: Migrant Farmworkers in the United States*. Berkeley: University of California Press, 2013.

Hondagneu-Sotelo, Pierrette. *Gendered Transitions: Mexican Experiences of Immigration*. Berkeley: University of California Press, 1994.

Hook, Derek. "The 'Real' of Racializing Embodiment." *Journal of Community and Applied Social Psychology* 18, no. 2 (2008): 140–52.

Horcasitas, Ricardo Pozas. "La Modernidad Desbordada." *Revista Mexicana de Sociologia*, no. 1 (1999): 149–75. http://www.jstor.org/stable/3541218.

———. *Los Nudos Del Tiempo: La Modernidad Desbordada*. Mexico City: UNAM, 2006.

Hubbell, F. Allan. "Looking Beyond 'Mow, Blow and Go': A Case Study of Mexican Immigrant Gardeners in Los Angeles." *Berkeley Planning Journal* 20 (2007): 1–23.

Huerta, Alvaro. "The Answer Is Blowin' in the Wind: A Case Study of Latino Gardeners Organizing in Los Angeles." PhD diss., University of California, Los Angeles, 2006.

———. "Los Angeles Gardeners Organize for Jobs and the Environment." *Progressive Planning* 167, no. 31 (2006).

Inda, Jonathan X. *Targeting Immigrants: Government, Technology, and Ethics.* Malden, MA: Blackwell, 2006.

Innis-Jiménez, Michael. *Steel Barrio: The Great Mexican Migration to South Chicago, 1915–1940.* New York: New York University Press, 2013.

Jerry, Anthony Russell. *Blackness in Mexico: Afro-Mexican Recognition and the Production of Citizenship in the Costa Chica.* Gainsville: University Press of Florida, 2023.

———. "Chasing Blackness: Re-Investing Value and Mexico's Changing Racial Economy." PhD diss., University of Illinois at Urbana-Champaign, 2014.

Kanter, Deborah E. *Chicago Católico: Making Catholic Parishes Mexican.* Latinos in Chicago and the Midwest. Urbana: University of Illinois Press, 2020.

Kearney, Michael. "Borders and Boundaries of State and Self at the End of Empire." *Journal of Historical Sociology* 4, no. 1 (1991): 52–74.

———. "The Local and the Global: The Anthropology of Globalization and Transnationalism." *Annual Review of Anthropology* 24, no. 1 (1995): 547–65.

Kelley, Sam. "Pill Hill, Chicago, 1973–1983." Chicago: Play Yale Repertory Theater, 1990.

Lancaster, Roger N. *Life Is Hard: Machismo, Danger, and the Intimacy of Power in Nicaragua.* Berkeley: University of California Press, 1992.

Lemus, Sergio. "Class, Labor, and Color Hierarchies: An Ethnographic Study of Mexican Yarderos/as in South Chicago." PhD diss., University of Illinois at Urbana-Champaign, 2015.

———. "Performing Power En Las Yardas (at the Yards): The Body, Capitalist Discipline, and the Making of Mexican Yardero Lives in South Chicago." *Anthropology of Work Review* 38, no. 2 (2017): 104–12.

Lewis, Laura. "Blacks, Black Indians, Afromexicans: The Dynamics of Race, Nation, and Identity in a Mexican Moreno Community (Guerrero)." *American Ethnologist* 27, no. 4 (2000): 898–926.

———. *Chocolate and Corn Flour: History, Race and Place in the Making of "Black" Mexico.* Durham, NC: Duke University Press, 2012.

———. "Modesty and Modernity: Photography, Race, and Representation on Mexico's Costa Chica (Guerrero)." *Identities: Global Studies in Culture and Power* 11, no. 4 (2004): 471–99.

———. "Of Ships and Saints: History, Memory, and Place in the Making of Moreno Mexican Identity." *Cultural Anthropology* 16, no. 1 (2001): 62–82.

Lewis, Oscar. *The Children of Sanchez: Autobiography of a Mexican Family.* Vintage, 2011 [1961].

Limón, José E. "Al Norte toward Home: Texas, the Midwest, and Mexican American Critical Regionalism." *The Latina/o Midwest Reader* (2017): 40–56.

———. *Dancing with the Devil: Society and Cultural Poetics in Mexican-American South Texas.* Madison: University of Wisconsin Press, 1994.

Lindisfarne, Nancy, and Jonathan Neale. "What Gender Does." *International Socialism* 139 (2013): 123–53.

Lomnitz, Claudio. *Deep Mexico, Silent Mexico: An Anthropology of Nationalism.* Minneapolis: University of Minnesota Press, 2001.

Lopez-Garza, Marta. "A Study of the Informal Economy and Latina/O Immigrants in Greater Los Angeles." In *Asian and Latino Immigrants in a Restructuring Economy: The Metamorphosis of Southern California,* edited by David R. Díaz and Marta Christina López-Garza, 141–68. Stanford, CA: Stanford University Press, 2001.

Loza, Mireya. *Defiant Braceros: How Migrant Workers Fought for Racial, Sexual, and Political Freedom.* Chapel Hill: University of North Carolina Press, 2016.

Lugo, Alejandro. "Cultural Production and Reproduction in Ciudad Juárez, México: Tropes at Play among Maquiladora Workers." *Cultural Anthropology* (1990): 173–96.

———. *Fragmented Lives, Assembled Parts: Culture, Capitalism, and Conquest at the U.S.-Mexico Border.* Austin: University of Texas Press, 2008.

Mahler, Kristen Hill. "Workers and Strangers: The Household and the Landscape of Suburban Fear." *Urban Affairs Review* 38, no. 6 (2003): 751–86.

Márquez, John D. *Black-Brown Solidarity: Racial Politics in the New Gulf South.* Austin: University of Texas Press, 2014.

Martinez, Monica Muñoz. *The Injustice Never Leaves You: Anti-Mexican Violence in Texas.* Cambridge: Harvard University Press, 2018.

Marx, Karl. *Capital.* New York: Everyman's Library, 1867.

Massey, Douglas S., Jorge Durand, and Nolan J. Malone. *Beyond Smoke and Mirrors: Mexican Immigration in an Era of Economic Integration.* New York: Russell Sage Foundation, 2002.

McFadden, Robert D. "Across the U.S., Growing Rallies for Immigration." *The New York Times, April 10* (New York) http://www.nytimes.com/2006/04/10/us/10protest.html?_r=1&oref=slogin.

McGibbon, Elizabeth, Josephine Etowa, and Charmaine McPherson. "Healthcare Access as a Social Determinant of Health." *Canadian Nurse* 104, no. 7 (2008): 23–27.

Mead, Margaret. *Letters from the Field, 1925–1975.* New York: Harper and Row, 1977.

Menchaca, Martha. *Recovering History, Constructing Race: The Indian, Black, and White Roots of Mexican Americans.* Austin: University of Texas Press, 2001.

Miller, G. Marylin. *Rise and Fall of the Cosmic Race: The Cult of Mestizaje in Latin America.* Austin: University of Texas Press, 2009.

Minian, Ana Raquel. *Undocumented Lives: The Untold Story of Mexican Migration.* Cambridge: Harvard University Press, 2018.

Miranda, Almita. "Living in Legal Limbo: Migration, Citizenship, and Mexican Mixed-Status Families in the Neoliberal Era." PhD diss., Northwestern University, 2017.

Mirande, Alfredo. *Hombres y machos: Masculinity and Latino Culture.* Boulder, CO.: Westview, 1997.

Montejano, David. *Anglos and Mexicans in the Making of Texas, 1836–1986.* Austin: University of Texas Press, 1987.

Moore, Frank Sally. *Social Facts and Fabrications: "Customary" Law on Kilimanjaro, 1880–1980.* New York: Cambridge University Press, 1986.

Mora, Mariana. *Kuxlejal Politics: Indigenous Autonomy, Race, and Decolonizing Research in Zapatista Communities.* Austin: University of Texas Press, 2017.

Morrison, Toni. "Black Studies Center Public Dialogue, Part 2." Discussion presented by the Portland State Black Studies Center as part of the Public Dialogue on the American Dream Theme, Portland State University, Portland, OR. May 30, 1975. Available in the Oregon Public Speakers Collection, Portland State University, Special Collections and University Archives. https://soundcloud.com/portland-state-library/portland-state-black-studies-1?in=portland-state-library/sets/oregon-public-speakers-audio/s-Bb26P.

Myers, Quinn. "How the Covid-19 Surge Is Impacting Chicago's Latino Communities." WTTW News, November 7. 2020, https://news.wttw.com/2020/11/07/how-covid-19-surge-impacting-chicagos-latino-communities.

Najera, Jennifer. *The Borderlands of Race: Mexican Segregation in a South Texas Town.* Austin: University of Texas Press, 2015.

Nájera-Ramírez, Olga. "Engendering Nationalism: Identity, Discourse, and the Mexican Charro." *Anthropological Quarterly* (1994): 1–14.

Nayaran, Kirin. "How Native Is a 'Native' Anthropologist?" *American Anthropologist* 95, no. 3 (1993): 671–86.

Ngai, Mae M. *Impossible Subjects: Illegal Aliens and the Making of Modern America-Updated Edition.* Princeton: Princeton University Press, 2014.

Nieto-Phillips, John M. *The Language of Blood: The Making of Spanish-American Identity in New Mexico, 1880s-1930s.* Albuquerque: University of New Mexico Press, 2008.

Nodín Valdés, Dionicio. *Barrios Norteños: St. Paul and Midwestern Mexican Communities in the Twentieth Century.* Austin: University of Texas Press, 2000.

Obama, Barack. *Dreams from My Father: A Story of Race and Inheritance.* Edinburgh: Canongate Books, 2009.

Obama, Michele. *Becoming.* New York: Crown, 2018.

Omi, Michael, and Howard Winant. *Racial Formation in the United States.* New York: Routledge, 1994.

Ordóñez, Juan Thomas. *Jornalero: Being a Day Laborer in the USA.* California Series in Public Anthropology 34. Berkeley: University of California Press, 2015.

Ortner, Sherry B. *Anthropology and Social Theory: Culture, Power, and the Acting Subject.* Durham, NC: Duke University Press, 2006.

———. "Is Female to Male as Nature Is to Culture?" In *Woman, Culture, and Society,* edited by John McGee and Richard Worms, 402–13. CA: Mayfield Publishing Company, 1974. Reprint, Anthropological Theory.

———. "Theory in Anthropology since the Sixties." *Comparative Studies in Society and History* 26 (1984): 126–66.

Padilla, Felix M. *Latino Ethnic Consciousness: The Case of Mexican Americans and Puerto Ricans in Chicago.* South Bend, IN: University of Notre Dame, 1985.

Paredes, Américo *"With His Pistol in His Hand": A Border Ballad and Its Hero.* Austin: University of Texas Press, 2006.

Paz, Octavio. *The Labyrinth of Solitude: Life and Thought in Mexico.* Translated by Lysander Kemp. New York: Grove, 1961.

Pérez, Gina. *The Near Northwest Side Story: Migration, Displacement and Puerto Rican Families.* Berkeley: University of California Press, 2004.

Pisani, Michael J., and David W. Yoskowitz. "Grass, Sweat, and Sun: An Exploratory Study of the Labor Market for Gardeners in South Texas." *Social Science Quarterly* 86, nos. 229–51 (2005).

———. "The Maid Trade: Cross-Border Work in South Texas." *Social Science Quarterly* 52, no. 2 (2002): 568–79.

———. "Opportunity Knocks: Entrepreneurship, Informality and Home Gardening in South Texas." *Journal of Borderlands Studies* 21, no. 2 (2006): 59–76.

Portes, Alejandro. "Economic Sociology and the Sociology of Immigration: A Conceptual Overview." *The Economic Sociology of Immigration* (1995): 1–41.

Preston, Julia. "Immigration Sweep Ends in 280 Arrests at 5 Plants," *New York Times,* April 17 (New York), 2008.

———. "In Reversal, Courts Uphold Local Immigration Laws," *New York Times,* February 11, (New York), 2008. http://www.nytimes.com/2008/02/10/us/10immig.html.

"Race/Ethnicity of College Faculty." National Center for Education Statistics (website). Accessed July 23, 2024. https://nces.ed.gov/fastfacts/display.asp?id=61.

Ramirez, Hernan. "Masculinity in the Workplace: The Case of Mexican Immigrant Gardeners." *Men and Masculinities* 14, no. 1 (2011): 97–116.

Ramirez, Hernan, and Pierrette Hondagneu-Sotelo. "Mexican Immigrant Gardeners: Entrepreneurs or Exploited Workers?" *Social Problems* 56, no. 1 (2009): 70–88.

Ramos, Samuel. *Profile of Man and Culture in Mexico.* Translated by Peter G. Earle. Austin: University of Texas Press, 1962.

Rana, Junaid. *Terrifying Muslims: Race and Labor in the South Asian Diaspora.* Durham, NC: Duke University Press, 2011.

Rana, Junaid, and Gilberto Rosas. "Managing Crisis: Post-9/11 Policing and Empire." *Cultural Dynamics* 18, no. 3 (2006): 219–34.

Reséndez, Andrés. "National Identity on a Shifting Border: Texas and New Mexico in the Age of Transition." *Journal of American History* 86, no. 2 (1999): 668–88.

Rios, Alfredo. "Soy De Rancho." Mexico: La Disco Music, 2014.

Rosaldo, Renato. *Culture and Truth: The Remaking the Social Analysis.* Boston: Beacon, 1993.

———. *Ilongot Headhunting, 1883–1974: A Study in Society and History.* Palo Alto, CA: Stanford University Press, 1980.

———. "Notes of Poetry and Ethnography." In *The Day of Shelly's Death: The Poetry and Ethnography of Grief,* 101–14. Duke University Press, 2013.

Rosas, Gilberto. *Barrio Libre: Criminalizing States and Delinquent Refusals of the New Frontier.* Durham, NC: Duke University Press, 2012.

———. "The Fragile Ends of War: Forging the US-Mexico Border and Borderlands Consciousness." *Social Text* 25, no. 2 (2007): 81–102.

———. "The Managed Violences of the Borderlands: Treacherous Geographies, Policeability, and the Politics of Race." *Latino Studies* 4, no. 4 (2006): 401–18.

———. "The Thickening Borderlands: Diffused Exceptionality and 'Immigrant' Social Struggles During the 'War on Terror.'" *Cultural Dynamics* 18, no. 3 (2006): 335–49.

Ruiz, Vicki L. "Nuestra América: Latino History as United States History." *Journal of American History* 93, no. 3 (2006): 655–72.

Sahlins, Marshall. *Historical Metaphors and Mythical Realities: Structure in the Early History of the Sandwich Islands Kingdom*. Ann Arbor: University of Michigan Press, 1981.

———. *Islands of History*. Chicago: University of Chicago Press, 1985.

Said, Edward. *Orientalism*. New York: Vintage, 2014.

Sassen, Saskia. "The Informal Economy: Between New Developments and Old Regulations." *Yale Law Review* 103 (1994): 2289–304.

———. "New York's Informal Economy." In *The Informal Economy: Studies in Advanced and Less Developed Countries*, edited by Manuel Castells Alejandro Portes and Laura Benton. Baltimore, MD: John Hopkins University Press, 1989.

Schiller, Nina Glick. "Theorizing Transnational Migration in Our Times: A Multiscalar Temporal Perspective." *Nordic Journal of Migration Research* 8, no. 4 (2018): 201–12.

Schiller, Nina Glick, Melvin Ember, Carol R. Ember, and Ian Skoggard. "Long-Distance Nationalism," *Diaspora* 1, no. 1 (2005): 3–7.

Schiller, Nina Glick, and Georges Eugene Fouron. *Georges Woke Up Laughing: Long-Distance Nationalism and the Search for Home*. Durham, NC: Duke University Press, 2001.

Schlenker, Alex. "Narcotráfico, Narcocorridos Y Narconovelas: La Economía Política Del Sicariato Y Su Respresentación Sonora-Visual." *Revista Latinoamerica de Seguridad Ciudadana* 8, no. (September 2009): 75–87.

Schuman, Howard, Charlotte Steeh, Lawrence Bobo, and Maria Krysan. *Racial Attitudes in America: Trends and Interpretations*. Cambridge: Harvard University Press, 1997.

Sepulveda, Ciro. "La Colonia Del Harbor: A History of Mexicanos in East Chicago, Indiana, 1919–1932." PhD diss., University of Notre Dame, 1976.

Smith, Adam. *An Inquiry into the Nature and Causes of the Wealth of Nations*. 1776. New York: Modern Library, 1994.

Spivak, Gayatri Chakravorty. "Can the Subaltern Speak?" In *Marxism and the Interpretation of Culture*, edited by Cary Grossberg Nelson and Lawrence Grossberg Nelson, 171–219. Urbana: University of Illinois Press, 1988.

Steinberg, Ted. *American Green: The Obsessive Quest for the Perfect Lawn*. New York: W. W. Norton, 2006.

Stephen, Lynn. *Transborder Lives: Indigenous Oaxacans in Mexico, California, and Oregon*. Durham, NC: Duke University Press, 2007.

Stoler, Ann Laura. "Imperial Debris: Reflections on Ruins and Ruination." *Cultural Anthropology* 23, no. 2 (2008): 191–219.

Stuesse, Angela. *Stuesse, Angela. Scratching out a Living: Latinos, Race, and Work in the Deep South*. Berkeley: University of California Press, 2016.

Sue, Christina A., and Tanya Golash-Boza. "More Than 'a Hidden Race': The Complexities of Blackness in Mexico and Peru." *Latin American and Caribbean Ethnic Studies* 8, no. 1 (2013): 76–82.

Thompson, Edward Palmer. *The Making of the English Working Class*. New York: Open Road Media, 2016 [1963].

US Census Bureau. *Quick Facts: Chicago City, Illinois*, 2018.

Valerio-Jiménez, Omar S. *Forging Identity and Nation in the Rio Grande Borderlands*. Durham, NC: Duke University Press, 2013.

———. "Racializing Mexican Immigrants in Iowa's Early Mexican Communities," *Annals of Iowa* 75, no. 1 (2016): 1–46.

Vargas, Zaragosa. "Armies in the Fields and Factories: The Mexican Working Classes in the Midwest in the 1920s." *Mexican Studies / Estudios Mexicanos* 7, no. 1 (1991): 47–71. http://www.jstor.org/stable/1052027.

———. *Proletarians of the North: A History of Mexican Industrial Workers in Detroit and the Midwest, 1917–1933*. Berkeley: University of California Press, 1993.

Vasconcelos, José. *La Raza Cosmica*. 1925. 4th ed. Mexico City: Porrua, 2007.

Vaugh, Bobby Eugene. "Race and Nation: A Study of Blackness in Mexico." PhD diss., Stanford University, 2002.

Vega, Sujey. *Latino Heartland: Of Border and Belonging in the Midwest*. New York: New York University Press, 2015.

Vélez-Ibañez, Carlos G. *Border Visions: Mexican Cultures of the Southwest United States*. Tucson: University of Arizona Press, 1996.

———. *Hegemonies of Language and Their Discontents: The Southwest North American Region since 1540*. Tucson: University of Arizona Press, 2018.

———. *Reflections of a Transborder Anthropologist*. Tucson: University of Arizona Press, 2020.

———. *The US-Mexico Transborder Region: Cultural Dynamics and Historical Interactions*. Tucson: University of Arizona Press, 2017.

Villanueva, Nicholas. *The Lynching of Mexicans in the Texas Borderlands*. Albuquerque: University of New Mexico Press, 2017.

Walley, Christine J. *Exit Zero: Family and Class in Postindustrial Chicago*. Chicago: University of Chicago Press, 2013.

Whitten, Norman E., and Arlene Torres, eds. *Blackness in Latin America and the Caribbean: Central America and Northern and Western South America*. Bloomington: Indiana University Press, 1988.

Zavella, Patricia. *I'm Neither Here nor There: Mexicans' Quotidian Struggles with Migration and Poverty*. Durham, NC: Duke University Press, 2011.

Zlolniski, Christian. "The Informal Economy in an Advanced Industrialized Society: Mexican Immigrant Labor in Silicon Valley." *Yale Law Review* 103, no. 8 (1994): 2305–35.

———. *Janitors, Street Vendors, and Activist: The Lives of Mexican Immigrants in Silicon Valley*. Berkeley: University of California Press, 2006.

Zúñiga, Víctor, and Rubén Hernández-León, eds. *New Destinations: Mexican Immigration in the United States*. New York: Russell Sage Foundation, 2006.

Index

SERGIO LEMUS is an assistant professor of anthropology at Texas A&M University.

The University of Illinois Press
is a founding member of the
Association of University Presses.

Composed in 10.75/13 Arno Pro
with Adrianna Extended Pro display
by Lisa Connery
at the University of Illinois Press

University of Illinois Press
1325 South Oak Street
Champaign, IL 61820-6903
www.press.uillinois.edu

FSC
www.fsc.org
MIX
Papier | Fördert
gute Waldnutzung
FSC® C083411

Zeitfracht Medien GmbH
Ferdinand-Jühlke-Straße 7
99095 Erfurt, Deutschland
produktsicherheit@kolibri360.de